MW00636549

Gospel Sermons

Johann Christoph Blumhardt (1805–1880)

The Blumhardt Source Series

Christian T. Collins Winn and Charles E. Moore, editors

Gospel Sermons

On Faith, the Holy Spirit,
and the Coming Kingdom

By
JOHANN CHRISTOPH BLUMHARDT

Foreword by
WILLIAM A. WILLIMON

Translated by
JÖRG & RENATA BARTH

Edited by
CHRISTIAN T. COLLINS WINN
& CHARLES E. MOORE

PLOUGH PUBLISHING HOUSE

Published by Plough Publishing House
Walden, New York
Robertsbridge, England
Elsmore, Australia
www.plough.com

Copyright © 2017 by Plough Publishing House. All rights reserved.

Translated from Johann Christoph Blumhardt, *Die Verkündigung* (Zürich: Gotthelf-Verlag, 1948).

ISBN: 978-0-87486-245-4
23 22 21 20 19   1 2 3 4 5 6 7 8

A catalog record for this book is available from the British Library.
Library of Congress Cataloging-in-Publication Data

Names: Blumhardt, Johann Christoph, 1805-1880, author. | Collins Winn,
    Christian T., editor. | Moore, Charles E., 1956- editor.
Title: Gospel sermons : on faith, the Holy Spirit, and the coming kingdom /
    by Johann Christoph Blumhardt ; foreword by William A. Willimon ;
    translated by Jörg & Renata Barth ; edited by Christian T. Collins Winn
    & Charles E. Moore.
Other titles: Sermons. Selections. English
Description: Walden NY : Plough Publishing House, 2019. | Series: Blumhardt
    series | Originally published: Eugene, OR : Cascade Books, 2017.
Identifiers: LCCN 2019019178 | ISBN 9780874862454 (pbk.)
Subjects: LCSH: Bible--Sermons.
Classification: LCC BX8080.B615 A5 2019 | DDC 252/.041--dc23
LC record available at https://lccn.loc.gov/2019019178

Dedicated to Johann Christoph Arnold
Faithful shepherd and minister of God's peace
John 14:27

Contents

Contents

Contents

Series Foreword

The Blumhardt Source Series seeks to make available for the first time in English the extensive oeuvre of Johann Christoph Blumhardt (1805–1880) and his son Christoph Friedrich Blumhardt (1842–1919), two influential religious figures of the latter half of the nineteenth century who are not well known outside their native Germany. Their influence can be detected in a number of important developments in nineteenth- and twentieth-century Protestantism: the recovery of the eschatological dimension of Christianity and the kingdom of God; the recovery of an emphasis on holistic notions of spirituality and salvation; the rise of faith healing and later, Pentecostalism; the convergence of socialism and the Christian faith; and the development of personalist models of pastoral counseling.

Their collected works make available their vast body of work to scholars, pastors, and laypeople alike with the aim of giving the Blumhardts a full hearing in the English language for the first time. Given the extent of their influence during the theological and religious ferment of the late nineteenth and early twentieth centuries, we believe that these sources will be of great interest to scholars of that period across various disciplines. It is also true, however, that there is much spiritual and theological value in the witness of the Blumhardts. We hope that by making their witness more widely known in the English-speaking world the church at large will benefit.

The project outline is flexible, allowing for volumes that aim either in a scholarly direction or towards the thoughtful lay reader. The emphasis will be to reproduce, with only slight modifications, the various German editions of the Blumhardts' works that have appeared since the late nineteenth century. A modest scholarly apparatus will provide contextual and theologically helpful comments and commentary through introductions, footnotes, and appendices.

During their long ministries, the elder and younger Blumhardt found themselves called to serve as pastors, counselors, biblical interpreters, theologians, and even politicians. No matter the vocational context, however, both understood themselves as witnesses to the kingdom of God that was both already present in the world, and also breaking into the current structures of the world. Together they represent one of the most powerful instances of the convergence of spirituality and social witness in the history of the Christian church. As series editors, it is our conviction that their witness continues to be relevant for the church and society today. We hope that the current series will give the Blumhardts a broader hearing in the English-speaking world.

Christian T. Collins Winn and Charles E. Moore

Foreword

Karl Barth ends his magisterial *Protestant Theology in the Nineteenth Century,* his survey of Germany's greatest theologians of the age, with, surprisingly, a concluding chapter on Johann Christoph Blumhardt.* While he admits that Blumhardt had little interest in theologizing, Barth credits Blumhardt with demolishing nineteenth-century theology's specious reasoning and intellectual dead ends, much like Blumhardt's contemporary, Schweitzer.

Barth reports the miraculous healing of a young woman as the intellectual "breakthrough" whereby Blumhardt moved from pietism's contest between "Jesus and the unconverted heart of man" to that war "between Jesus and the real power of darkness, in which man finds himself." That firsthand experience of the miraculous led Blumhardt to be an eschatologically-driven "theologian of hope," who fully expected the immanent triumph of Christ. "On the basis of Scripture he [Blumhardt] expects above all a new *outpouring of the Holy Spirit*" and "a *new time of grace* on the earth." With an unapologetic restoration of the miraculous, and without explicitly trying, Blumhardt, according to Barth, devastated an accommodated, urbane, bourgeois "academic theology" that had "made things too easy for itself."

Barth (my theological hero) quoted Johann Christoph Blumhardt's last words, "*Veni, creator Spiritus*" [Come, Creator Spirit], in order to explain his own nascent theology. "You have been introduced to my theology if you have heard this sigh."** Reading these sermons by Blumhardt, one can

* Karl Barth, Ch. 28, "Blumhardt," in *Protestant Theology in the Nineteenth Century: Its Background and History*, trans. Brian Cozens and John Bowden, (Grand Rapids: Eerdmans, 2002), 629–39.

** Quoted in Eberhard Busch, *The Great Passion: An Introduction to Karl Barth's Theology*, trans. Geoffrey W. Bromiley, eds., Darrell L. Guder and Judith J. Guder (Grand

easily see the connection between what Karl Barth learned from the Blumhardts and Barth's explosive *Romans*. Barth acknowledged his indebtedness
by exclaiming, "Blumhardt always begins right away with God's presence,
might, and purpose: he starts out from God; he does not begin by climbing
upwards to him by means of contemplation and deliberation."

These Barthian accolades for Johann Christoph Blumhardt are well
deserved. But one of Barth's statements about Blumhardt is challenged by
this volume of sermons: "He was more a pastor than a preacher."

I've read many of Barth's sermons, and I can say that the homiletics of
my theological hero could have profited from a reading of this remarkable
collection of *Gospel Sermons*.

Encounter with these sermons can be an invigorating but also con-
victing and humbling experience for a contemporary preacher like me. For
a church languishing in the mire of moralistic, therapeutic deism, Blumhardt's sermons render an active, dynamic, present God.

Especially when one considers the sorts of flowery, academically tur-
gid sermons that were being preached in established churches in his day,
Blumhardt's sermons are disarmingly simple and direct. He expends no
energy attempting to analyze the surrounding culture or speculate on the
interiority of his listeners. He wastes no time attempting to reconstruct the
original historical context of the Scripture, shows no detailed exegesis and
makes no belabored, patronizing hermeneutical moves. Blumhardt never
explains. He assumes that every text, whether from Old or New Testament,
speaks for itself and requires no homiletical explanation or apologetic
pleading. The Word of God makes its own way without argument or external support from either the culture or human experience.

Illustrations are few, indicating that this preacher believes that the
Christian life does not require support from the experience of others; the
people listening to him have, by the power of the Holy Spirit, direct access
to God. Blumhardt displays a deep, pervasive faith that God really means to
speak through a biblical text. It's up to the Holy Spirit to make a text "work"
in the hearts and minds of hearers, and this preacher has tremendous confidence that the Holy Spirit is resourceful, present, and determined to win
a hearing. All of this confirms the son Christoph's claim that, "It was this
very watchword, 'Jesus lives!' that eventually drew countless people to him."

Blumhardt displays little effort to impress or flatter his congregation,
yet every sermon is a palpable demonstration of a pastor caring for his

Rapids: Eerdmans, 2004), 38.

people, believing that what the people most needed is direct confrontation with the biblical word that inevitably brings the presence of the living Christ.

Some of the sermons are disarmingly candid, particularly those under the heading, "The Poverty of the Church." Christ is not only our comfort but also our judge. Christ not only heals us but also loves us enough to tell us the truth; Christ is not only the way and the life but also the truth. It's as if every sermon ends in the radical Blumhardt cry, "Thy kingdom come!"

The world to which we preach doesn't simply need improvement; it needs radical, sweeping, eschatological transformation that only God can bring about. Christianity demands its own distinctive speech, which alone can adequately characterize that world, speech that is given by Scripture. It calls us to talk like the Bible and to speak of matters that the Bible talks about.

Knowing, deeply knowing, that the kingdom of God has come among us from beyond all our means of saving ourselves by ourselves is the liberating word that contemporary preachers need to hear.

In his introduction to his father's sermons, Christoph Friedrich Blumhardt notes that, "These sermons and reflections are as plain and unvarnished as they were spoken." Preached without artifice or cant, devoid of cliché, the sermons produced in me an uncanny sense of being spoken to directly by a preacher who not only believes what he says but also is intent on ministering to my deepest need. The years between me and Blumhardt disappeared.

Serious matters are engaged with a simplicity and directness that is captivating, mysteriously intense, and inescapable. Though Blumhardt's spirit is too charitable to mock fellow preachers, I found these sermons to be a judgment upon the humbug and blather, the bathos and triviality that characterizes much contemporary preaching, which is more concerned with congregational reception than the truth of Jesus Christ.

Blumhardt's sermons confirm in me the conviction that faithful preaching begins with God, with a relentlessly revealing, determined-to-have-his-way-in-the-world living God. Preaching ought not trade on pious yearning or human experience or human needs but on the strong, resourceful, active presence of God. We begin not with suppositions about the human condition but rather with prayerful questions: Who is this God we've got? Or better, Who is the God who has us? Followed by, What is God doing in our world? Preaching flows not from alleged human religious experience—the infatuation of nineteenth-century theology—but from God's actual work in the world.

I'm confident that you too will enjoy, receive sustenance, and be convicted by these sermons by one of the church's great preachers.

Will Willimon
April 2016

Acknowledgements

The editors are indebted to the Bruderhof Historical Archive, Walden, New York, USA, for providing original translated material, and to Miriam Mathis for her painstaking work in copyediting and her ongoing commitment to keeping the witness of the Blumhardts alive. We would also like to thank Hilary Ritchie, Sara Misgen, and Rolando Rodriguez for their assistance at different stages of the editorial process.

1887 Introduction
to the Gospel Sermons

By Christoph Friedrich Blumhardt

A s we make these sermons from my father available to the general public, we offer a caution. My father would never have published these sermons in their present form. Although he did edit and publish several sermons, he did so only after revising them extensively so as to protect himself against all possible objections. The sermons here are not so polished. Because his sermons were transcribed, he regarded them of insufficient literary quality and therefore not worth printing. To publish them would have made him feel quite embarrassed.

For this reason, I also feel somewhat embarrassed. Yet I am glad that this volume can now be published, for it presents my father just as he was and is characteristic of him as a preacher of God's Word. He would not mind if people got to know him by reading his sermons, because he always found tremendous satisfaction when one of his sermons was a help to someone.

These sermons and reflections are as plain and unvarnished as they were spoken. In several cases, they possess an unusual form. They differ from other sermons by a remarkable freedom in both form and content. What set my father's preaching apart was that he was often the one most deeply affected. Thus, when a sermon turned out particularly well, he would share the elation he felt with those around him as though he had been a listener. He had childlike joy whenever God's Word was directly imparted to him and when he was then able to proclaim it from the pulpit. As a result, thousands of people from many different places—including the unconverted—came away with moved hearts and uplifted spirits after hearing my father speak.

These sermons in printed form cannot do justice to my father or the way in which he delivered the gospel. Nothing can replace actually seeing and hearing the one who proclaims God's message. But we hope that the discourses presented here will at least to a certain extent create an impression akin to the one they made when they were delivered. The advantage of having his sermons in print, however, is that we can read and reread what he said, which allows us to get not only a general impression of his message but a deeper grasp of what he actually expressed.

My father was loath to create quick impressions without any real thoughts. Every word he spoke came from his profound recognition of Jesus—indeed his personal knowledge of him. Some of his thoughts are thus apt to surprise us. I am prepared to hear from readers who may have certain theological misgivings. My father was a thinking preacher, but *not* a theologian. His sermons never failed to grip the listeners' hearts and minds, and experience has shown that where at his urging listeners began to reflect on their faith in a new way, any theological problems awakened in them never created a desire to deviate from the ground of the apostles and prophets. Instead, more often than not they evoked in his listeners a craving for the original gospel itself.

Those who listened to my father often became liberated, especially from Christian words and understandings that they had learned by rote. That freeing was occasioned by the ethical character of my father's sermons. He saw with a prophet's eye the many shortcomings exhibited in the behavior of his fellow Christians. Yet, no matter how precise or even harsh his words might often have sounded, his listeners still came away with the following impression: this truly is the way to live! The gospel came alive for them. This was partially due to the fact that my father lived according to Jesus' words and was firmly committed to what was right before God. He was not just a "preacher." People could recognize in his words the voice of the chief Shepherd who calls us by name.

What was it, though, that enabled my father to become the preacher he was? Already as a small boy he would "preach" to his brothers and sisters—not as one just imitating a pastor, but in earnest and with a sense of the Savior's very presence. When barely able to read, he would pore over the Bible and, as he would often tell later on, in holy simplicity hear God and the Savior speak to him directly from it. He felt that his world was no different from that of the people of Israel, when God by means of signs and miracles endeavored to form his people into one nation, making them a light unto the nations. As a child, my father believed that the Savior was as alive today as he was at the time of the apostles, when people not only had the Scriptures but also experienced direct manifestations of his power.

Only in later years did he sadly become aware that others knew nothing of what he had sensed. His heart pulsated with the Savior; his thoughts were full of what Jesus could and did do. This is the real reason for his joyful temperament, and wherever he went people naturally responded to him. However, when he "preached," in the sense of speaking about the Savior, he noticed how many people did not understand his feelings. This pained him deeply. Even as a seminarian he often found himself in opposition to others. Unlike so many in his day, the voice of his conscience would always ask: does this or that action jibe with what the Savior means to us? He could not help but visualize Jesus as always close by and active, and so he felt duty bound to heed him come what may. This also gave his personality a kind of excellence, both as regards the fear of God (which firmly grounded him) and the freedom of a good conscience (which enabled him to face so many of life's situations with childlike nonchalance).

This is probably why as a young pastor he would inadvertently cause offense by what he said. Truthfulness had become a personal trait of his, and so he was not overly anxious or fussy about how he expressed himself. This once earned him, for example, a reprimand in Basel at the Mission School where he was teaching. He spoke about the Savior in such a way that some pious individuals felt he made Jesus too human—an accusation my father could not understand at the time because he freely regarded the Savior as his brother and as the brother of us all. On the other hand, my father was disturbed by how much nonsense was expressed by others. He often regretted having been in a company of Christians where nothing at all was said about the Savior. Witnessing to Jesus had become second nature to him; "Jesus lives!" was his personal watchword.

It was this very watchword, "Jesus lives!" that eventually drew countless people to him, despite the fact that as a preacher there was nothing special about him. At his first church in Iptingen, where he was the assistant pastor for an extended time, he left a remarkable impression. Under the impact of his preaching, people became free: hearts were deeply struck, sinners turned around, and even the separatists in the village with all their Christian principles gave way and came under his tutelage.

It was only in Möttlingen, however, that my father gained his decisive voice. At the beginning of his ministry there, his preaching proved ineffective: parishioners would simply go to church and come out again, always remaining the same. Möttlingen almost seemed like a haunted place. My father's generally cheerful nature began to turn mournful when after several years no essential changes occurred in the congregation. Despite being a very industrious minister who diligently sought personal contact with every parishioner, he became increasingly dissatisfied. The life that surrounded him refused to become truly Christian.

The story of the spiritual fight and the awakening that followed is well known. I will not recount it here.*** Yet, as if lit up by a stroke of lightning, the whole need of his congregation was suddenly revealed to him. He became aware of satanic fetters that had been forged by superstitious, magical practices stemming from idolatry—chains that held souls in bondage. The Christianity around him was but a formal one, a lifeless caricature of the true gospel. Once he realized the source of the darkness, he was compelled to go on the offensive and cry out, "Jesus is victor!" At this battle cry, uttered by a person wholly grounded in Christ, the forces of hell gave way. Like never before, he witnessed the power of Jesus Christ and how it alone was able to free people oppressed by sin and evil. Though the dragon kept writhing in a thousand convolutions, he finally decamped. Through prayer and Christ's direct intervention, the spell of spiritual darkness was broken.

It was a long struggle, stretching over almost two years and replete with instances of anxious faith, of temptations, of inner and outer need, but in the end it made my father into the preacher he later became. There is a difference between knowing who Jesus is and actually experiencing what he can do. Once the hellish powers had given way, my father's heart broke forth with a fresh word—a proclamation that poured forth from a newborn proclaimer of God's Word. A new tongue was given to my father that enabled him to lead his congregation to repentance and renewal. It seemed that shrouds, which had up till then prevented people from turning away from sin, were now stripped off their souls. From then on my father's sermons had something that gripped and shook people; many weighed down by sin and suffering became inwardly freed.

*** See Friedrich Zündel, *Pastor Johann Christoph Blumhardt: An Account of His Life*, edited by Christian T. Collins Winn and Charles E. Moore (Eugene, OR: Cascade Books, 2010), 117–245. For the same story in smaller format, see Friedrich Zündel, *The Awakening: One Man's Battle with Darkness*, (Walden, NY: Plough Publishing House, 2015).

In later years my father's preaching did not have such a striking effect. There were times when it even became somewhat quiet around him. Yet something of Christ, the one who came to destroy the works of the devil, could always be felt. It was not natural skill, rhetoric, or eloquence that made my father an effective preacher—it was a strength that came to him from the Savior himself. He did not rely on anything but a simple faith in the Savior. His preaching was steeped in the longing that whatever bound his listeners would be loosened, even if only in a few.

Though his preaching helped countless listeners, there were still many who took offense at some things my father said. This was especially so with regards to his repeated request for a new outpouring of the Holy Spirit. Most people just assumed that the Holy Spirit was in their midst. They simply couldn't comprehend the yearning my father possessed, especially since it appeared to them that he himself exuded the Spirit's very presence. At times this criticism actually intimidated my father, so much so that he suffered severe pangs of conscience because, as he put it, here and there cowardice had made him refrain from explicitly voicing the hope that the Lord might once again pour out the Holy Spirit.

This hope of a great outpouring of the Spirit is what ultimately marked my father's preaching. Although his expectation of another Pentecost raised all sorts of objections, anyone who knew my father and what he had experienced in Möttlingen had to concede that the kingdom of God can and needs to break in more fully. My father feared that unless additional gifts of the Holy Spirit were bestowed, the renewal that had begun in the Möttlingen congregation would be just a passing phenomenon. It would also never extend beyond to larger circles.

So in a very childlike way, my father asked again and again for more of the Holy Spirit. He knew full well how many souls were still bound by demonic powers and how unable he was to set them free. He saw firsthand how even though many streams of sinners, warped characters, would accept the gospel, they remained unchanged. He saw too how many sinister illnesses continued to oppress good Christian people, despite the fact that in the church this sort of thing should be done away with. He saw the dissensions between churches and sects—what an unending misery unless the Holy Spirit were to open up a way to reconciliation. All this created in him a deep longing, an almost unquenchable thirst for a new outpouring of the Spirit, who alone could illuminate the Word of God for those bound by sin and the confines of tradition. Again and again one would hear from his lips,

"We need the Holy Spirit," even as the evidence of this or that need would pile up higher and higher.

Despite the need around him, my father was a man of hope. Along with his sighing and yearning, he simply took it at face value that what we pray for can and will come to be. He felt that if we are in dead earnest, the Holy Spirit will come. His hope would at times break forth with such unusual power that his listeners were struck to the core. This was especially so in the last decade of his life. He almost took it for granted that a new time was in store for Christianity, a time illumined by the glory of God's rulership here on earth. Confidence streamed forth from his heart with such force that you would think he was already experiencing a foretaste of God's reign.

In the end, was all my father's praying and waiting in vain? No! We believe that this present volume will bring readers to the conviction that what my father proclaimed was truly the gospel of the kingdom. My father's fervent prayer for a direct manifestation of the Lord Jesus not only kept him away from false paths others have been lured into by various trends, it also kept him free of anything unreal, fleeting, and transient. His yearning and believing did in fact hasten the kingdom. We know, as many others have known, how much of an extra measure of Christ's power was given to him. The concrete work of Christ's Spirit, of healing and new life, constituted the very heart of his preaching. People who heard him couldn't help but see the evils around and in them and in response were led to repentance and a new faith. They caught a glimpse of the living God and in turn confidently began to look forward to the Savior's return, seeking anew the kingdom of God and its righteousness.

As a preacher my father must be accepted for who he was. Moreover, we mustn't sever him from what he experienced. And although he never thought of himself as a particularly gifted orator, the reader will discover for himself that his words still have power to speak to the heart. With this hope and expectancy, it is our prayer that the Lord would graciously preside over and bless the reading of these gospel sermons.

PART I
Jesus Christ

SECTION 1
THE REDEEMER

Sonship with God

You are all sons of God through faith in Christ Jesus.

—GALATIANS 3:26 (NKJV)

It is striking how often Paul refers to all people when it comes to the matter of faith, when we might think that it might not fit all people. There were all sorts of believers among the Galatians, including those to whom he had to say, "Are you so foolish? After beginning with the Spirit, are you now trying to attain your goal by human effort?" (Gal 3:3). He also found it necessary to admonish the Galatians not to gratify the desires of their sinful nature but instead to live by the Spirit (Gal 5:16).

God won't let himself be mocked. And although we might shake our heads and think that not everyone is an innocent child of God, Paul yet declares, "You are all sons of God through faith in Christ Jesus." Why does he say this? To encourage the children of God to repent and to set right what is wrong, guarding against failing in the future. For true faith has real power and significance. Genuine faith is a heartfelt trust in Christ Jesus—in Christ, the Lord who came from God and who, as a man, was anointed by God's Spirit. Jesus, the Savior, has come to save us from all sin. This faith has enormous power, and it is this and this alone that guarantees that we belong to God.

Many so-called Christians actually promote something other than faith in Christ Jesus. They focus their attention exclusively on personal improvement, on becoming free from unholy and impure thoughts and feelings, on some kind of holiness that they think they have to achieve. Yet, they never become free of their sins, and so they never dare to believe that they can become children of God. How much better it would be if they really saw who Christ Jesus is! Jesus needs only to be understood with childlike trust: he can change weak sinners into children of God. He already accepts and treats us as his children and, as with the Galatians, he will not let our fellowship with him be destroyed even if we sin.

Let us hold firmly, therefore, to our Savior, who is here for all us sinners—for such weak, frail people as we are. As long as we don't turn faith into a "cushion," he will, in the end, free us from all our shortcomings. For his life contains too much power for anyone who possesses genuine faith—for anyone who is gripped by real trust and peace of heart. Such a person will not go on sinning. Faith is not an intellectual recognition. No, it comes from knowing that Jesus is with us. Understand this! May we clearly see and accept in faith God's great compassion through Christ Jesus toward each one who commits himself to this completely, surrendering to him wholly.

Forgiveness of Sins

When Jesus saw their faith, he said to the paralytic, "Take heart, my son; your sins are forgiven."

—MATTHEW 9:2 (NRSV)

Those who brought the paralytic to the feet of Jesus went through a great deal of trouble. They couldn't even get near to Jesus because of the many people around him, not only in the house, but outside as well. So the four men carrying the pallet got up on the balcony of the house, removed part of the roof, and let down the sick man at Jesus' feet. These men had great faith and Jesus was glad about this. But the paralytic probably felt very uncomfortable. He had a bad conscience and was alarmed to be laid before this pure man. Maybe he even trembled and looked toward the opening in the roof, anxiously wishing to be pulled up again as quickly as possible. Jesus noticed this and was aware that here was a man burdened by a bad conscience and ridden with fear. His whole demeanor was that of a contrite man, ready to confess his sins before everyone.

Jesus, however, knew how the people faithfully trusted him, recognizing him as the One who came from God, doing great wonders. He wished above all to reassure the paralytic, and therefore he called to him, "Take heart, my son; your sins are forgiven." This poured balm on the wounded heart of the sick man so that he felt better in the presence of Jesus.

What a comforting word to all who were there, the great throng of people who had come to hear the Lord and who certainly felt many pangs of conscience! They may have also felt that it was to them that the Lord expressed this word of comfort and the certainty of forgiveness of sins!

Editors' Note: This sermon is dated 1876.

They could easily think this, for they saw for themselves how freely Jesus forgave people. They now saw how Jesus looked upon the paralyzed man, the anxious, trembling man, who nevertheless showed faith in him in his innermost heart. Suddenly the Lord spoke the lovely word, "Take heart, my son; your sins are forgiven."

I can just picture how those who saw the miracle would have tried to press Jesus' hand upon leaving, looking into his eyes with a glance of intense longing, quietly accepting for themselves the words, "Take heart, my son; your sins are forgiven." Whoever did this would certainly have felt forgiven, especially after the Lord had, with a word, demonstrated his authority to forgive sins by liberating the paralytic from all his sickness and pain. Would such a miracle have happened if the curse of sin had still lain upon the paralytic? No! The curse was removed! At Jesus' word the limbs of this sick man could rejoice.

If only we all made it our aim to obtain forgiveness of sins! How easily we would receive it! All we need is faith, a contrite, humble spirit—and Jesus will free us, beyond all our prayers and understanding. Oh, that this may be given to all people, everywhere! Amen.

Concerning the Spirit of Sickness

One Sabbath Jesus was teaching in a synagogue. A woman there had an evil spirit that had kept her sick for eighteen years; she was bent over and could not straighten up at all. When Jesus saw her, he called out to her, "Woman, you are free from your sickness!" He placed his hands on her, and at once she straightened herself up and praised God.

The official of the synagogue was angry that Jesus had healed on the Sabbath, so he spoke up and said to the people, "There are six days in which we should work; so come during those days and be healed, but not on the Sabbath!"

The Lord answered him, "You hypocrites! Any one of you would untie your ox or your donkey from the stall and take it out to give it water on the Sabbath. Now here is this descendant of Abraham whom Satan has kept in bonds for eighteen years; should she not be released on the Sabbath?" His answer made his enemies ashamed of themselves, while the people rejoiced over all the wonderful things that he did.

—LUKE 13:10–17 (GNT)

We have here an account of a healing otherwise not mentioned among the other physical ailments cured by Jesus. It is about a woman who was bent over, who walked about in a stooped position so bent over that she could hardly look up. It is expressly added that this infirmity came from a spirit of sickness, what the Lord calls an evil spirit that had bound her for

Editors' Note: This sermon is dated 1846.

9

eighteen years. What a remarkable thing it is that Satan should play such a direct part in a bent body.

What? Does Satan's power reach as far as this today? Is it possible that the prince of darkness plays such an essential part in something which we today interpret or explain so easily? Don't say anything against this—it is written in Luke clearly. But as reasoning people, with the inclination to search and inquire further, we must ask: Just how far does the authority of darkness extend? This question, dear friends, alarms us. Yet we do not want to forget that the One who crushed the head of the serpent and stands victorious over Satan is the One who also appears in our text. Therefore, we shouldn't limit ourselves to gloomy descriptions of darkness, for we have every reason to praise the One who has freed us from darkness and led us into the light.

Our theme for today, then, will be: How Christ Jesus came to break the power of Satan. We will first say a word about the power of Satan and how this manifests itself in humanity; then secondly, how this power was broken by our Lord; and finally, how we too may be liberated.

O Lord, our Savior, we pray, help us to consider these important matters. Teach us through thy Holy Spirit so we might understand the truth. Grant that what we say and hear helps us to become free of the devil's shackles. Amen!

To begin with, let us briefly consider how far Satan's power has spread. This story demonstrates how darkness is able to ruin a person physically. However, evil powers can also destroy soul and spirit. We easily understand this because we know more about this.[*] But let us not forget what Scripture says concerning what influence spiritual darkness has on us physically.

In Hebrews it says of our Lord Jesus that, "through death he might destroy him who has the power of death, that is, the devil, and deliver all those who through fear of death were subject to lifelong bondage" (Heb 2:14–15). The power of death is here attributed to the devil. This is why the Lord calls him "a murderer from the beginning" (John 8:44). The devil, then, clearly has a hand in death. And in connection with our Scripture story, this power of death is extended to the spirits of sickness that the devil sends; there are countless numbers that stand ready to do the devil's bidding. But let us not forget, death deceitfully crept in—it was never willed by God! The devil achieved this by offering the world the "fruit" that would result in death. If

---

[*] Editors' Note: Blumhardt is here alluding to the remarkable events surrounding Gottliebin Dittus. For this story, see the books cited in the footnote on p. xx.

this is so with death, is it not also the same with most sicknesses, which are the causes of death?

All the sicknesses we suffer are essentially the beginning of death. With each new sickness something dies in us. Sickness kills us bit by bit, robbing us of one ability after another until, in the end, the last flicker of life departs. And even if we are not afflicted by any particular disease or sickness, the spirit of death exists in all of us. In the face of Scripture, we cannot deny that darkness has its hand in death and in sickness—and possibly in everything that touches upon our physical being in so far as it aims at ending our life.

Who sent the great wind that shattered the house that buried the children of Job? Who afflicted Job "with loathsome sores from the sole of his foot to the crown of his head so that he took a potsherd with which to scrape himself and sat among the ashes" (Job 1–2)? It was the power of Satan. True, this only happened with the Lord's permission, but Job was tormented and bound by a spirit of sickness just like the bent over woman in the Gospel. The devil forced her to look downward as dumb animals do, preventing her from gazing up toward the Lord who made heaven and earth. And what can we say today about our sicknesses in this context? I will let you consider this for yourselves, but it is a horrifying truth that we are shown.

Someone will object, "But we are now part of the new covenant." But has that time already come, which is described in Revelation 21:4, where "God will wipe away every tear from our eyes, and death shall be no more, neither shall there be mourning nor crying nor pain anymore"? Sickness and death, which are the last enemy to be destroyed, are still with us (1 Cor 15:26). Are things different now? Doesn't the devil still have power over the many adversities that beset us physically? Is there any spirit of sickness that does not bind us? Doesn't sickness almost overwhelm us at times?

Don't be deceived, the horrible truth is that Satan plays his part in our bodily infirmities. Yes, consider this deeply—as deeply as any truth can penetrate. Our weaknesses, frailties, sicknesses, and the torments of our bodies originate in or are accompanied by influences of darkness. It's important to realize that the power of the enemy extends this far! The afflictions under which thousands groan, the endless variety of such torments and their widespread dissemination throughout the whole human race, the fact that we are beset by one evil after another and that everywhere people are ravaged by disease is proof of how much power Satan still has over us. This is a serious matter and should make us open our eyes!

Oh, you dear ones, we should sigh about the decay of God's people! The sons and daughters of Abraham, of faith, like this woman who was plagued for eighteen years—all of us are afflicted by sickness. These powers of darkness and Satan's authority still rule over the world. But does it ever cross your mind that it shouldn't be like this? It should not! And in particular, it should no longer be like this in the church, which is supposed to be purified by the blood of Christ. This is because, while on earth he himself freed people from the bonds of death and taught his disciples to do likewise. If we profess that a deliverer and Savior has come—One who is victorious over the devil and his works—then things have to change.

Knowing this, we should take a more profound look at our misery. Physical bondage often indicates yet another kind of bondage—that of soul and spirit. How can Jesus free our bodies while our souls are still bound? Not until we come before the Lord as the redeemed will we be truly appalled at the abyss that is at our feet; only then will we be astonished at all that is required for a person, ensnared in so many different hellish bonds, to be made ready to appear before God's presence. If we really understood the condition we are in, we would fall into despair and would hardly even be able to believe in redemption. This is why Scripture only hints and suggests at such things, so that we don't lose courage and become desolate. Nevertheless, Scripture does tell us all the more emphatically that Jesus Christ came to destroy the works of Satan.

How so? The Gospel text shows us how Jesus breaks the bonds of Satan, including those that bind the body. It didn't take much. Jesus laid his hands on the bent over woman and said, "Woman, you are freed from your sickness." At once the spirit of sickness was forced to yield and Satan's power over the woman was broken. Everything Christ did for the sick and oppressed demonstrated that he was indeed the Promised One—the One who would tread upon serpents (Luke 10:19). He alone could give the help that was to be found nowhere else.

Who is this Jesus? Who is he and what did he accomplish? In the Gospels he is called the Son of Man, but he is also the One who came from the bosom of the Father, the only begotten Son of God, full of grace and truth. He saw the terrible misery of people everywhere and how Satan rejoiced at having them under his power. The Son of God was moved by the world's misery. He became flesh and entered into the menacing sea of satanic bondage. But praise and glory be to the One who overcame! Even though snares were set for his body and soul he came through unharmed. By his steadfast resistance, Jesus completely discredited the powers of darkness. If one looks closely at the struggle in Gethsemane, Satan was infuriated and became desperate because Jesus rejected even the slightest evil. The devil tried his hardest, torturing our Lord until blood ran. Finally, Satan's servants nailed Jesus to the cross. But Jesus patiently overcame all this with faith in his heavenly Father. And as the prophets proclaimed, "Surely he has borne our infirmities and carried our diseases; yet we accounted him stricken, struck down by God, and afflicted. But he was wounded for our transgressions, crushed for our iniquities; upon him was the punishment that made us whole, and by his bruises we are healed" (Isa 53:4–5).

This is the way help came. However, we must see Christ's victory more clearly still, because it was as a man that our Lord overcame all the snares of darkness, all the shackles of the devil. The central core of Satan's power was weakened to the very root. This is the victory of our Lord that is meant when it is said of him that he came into the world to destroy the works of the devil. From now on, Satan cannot bind in the same way as he did before. And when he binds, we can resist him with Christ's power. Whoever believes in Jesus the conqueror is free. As Jesus said, ". . . the truth will make you free" and also, ". . . if the Son makes you free, you will be free indeed" (John 8:32, 36).

The victory is won! Our Lord sits at the right hand of God. He has received gifts to bestow—even on those who have fallen away. He fights from above until at last he has laid all his enemies at his footstool; until all those spirits of sickness and all powers that in any way deform or destroy body or soul are removed; until all of creation, all heaven and earth, can rejoice. Oh, who can imagine the greatness of the victory of Jesus, whose heirs we have become when we believe in and learn to grasp that victory laid open before our very eyes!

With this we come to our final point: how we can really be freed from the power of Satan. This doesn't mean that the world is now released from all of Satan's bonds. When Jesus cried out, "It is finished," don't think that all the powers of darkness were forced to cease working; that no spirit of sickness could bind people again; that no one would be held fast by demonic powers or that darkness no longer influenced anyone's spiritual and mental powers. Rather, after the death of our Lord the fight was passed on to his disciples. They were to use the power and victory gained by the cross to bring Satan completely under their feet.

The disciples were commissioned to fight on: "Go into all the world and preach the gospel; [that is, the message of Jesus' victory]. This is the message of Jesus' victory to the whole creation. He who believes and is baptized will be saved [by just this victory of Jesus], but he who does not believe will be condemned [that is, he will remain in the bondage and fellowship of Satan for time and eternity]" (Mark 16:16). In order that the world might believe that all of Satan's powers really were broken, and as a logical consequence of faith, there was to be a visible freeing from the bonds of Satan and the spirit of sickness. For the Lord promised, "And these signs will accompany those who believe: in my name they will cast out devils; they will speak in new tongues; they will pick up serpents, and if they drink any deadly thing, it will not hurt them. They will lay their hands on the sick and they will recover" (Mark 16:17–18). With this command and with this promise the disciples went out into the world. In this simple way they were to complete Satan's downfall. He, the prince of darkness, has fallen; but those who believe are able to fight every battle to the end using the victorious power of Jesus. Jesus' words, which were fulfilled in full measure during early Christianity, prove that it is possible from now on to be victorious over the powers of darkness that bind body and soul.

How do we respond to this today? After such a fruitful beginning we might think that after 1800 years the last stronghold of Satan's power would have disappeared. How very different it has turned out. Why? Why is Satan's power still so strong? I can only imagine that we have had too little faith. For, victory is promised to everyone who has faith. Jesus' words are always true. Of course, we speak a great deal about faith and many people do believe, but it looks as if we have a "believing" Christianity without any real faith. Real faith, and only faith, must have been lacking and still is lacking. Otherwise Satan's mortal wound would not have healed. But sadly, faith is lacking. This is why so many people are enslaved by sin in so many thousands of ways—the boundless depravity of so many of all classes and the shocking ignorance. We don't even want to know what it is we are really being called to believe. The result is demoralization and unscrupulous brutality. This is also the reason for all the calamities that undermine our world. The powers of darkness cover the earth like swarms of locusts (Rev 9:1–3). In their cowardice people have allowed these powers full rein without resisting them in faith. So much so that countless numbers of people now have far more respect for the devil's power than for the power of God.

Should we let it remain like this? Is Jesus Christ's victory futile? Or, do you think that when he has finally "had enough" or when our world has become too evil, our King and High Priest will, without further ado, come and destroy the powers of darkness? Will this actually free "the children of men" from the powers of darkness? Will we receive such a reward for our laziness, for our lack of conscience and faith? No, dear friends, it will never happen like this! We must become children of Abraham, in the way the woman in the Gospel was a daughter of faith. If we do not believe and fight for faith; if in the struggle against sin and the power of Satan we do not, or will not, work hard—then, finally the world will come to a terrible end. The Lord has staked everything on our faith. Faith is the victory that overcomes the world. Indeed, it already has overcome the world wherever it is really present. Shouldn't we take this to heart once more? Can't our Christianity come to know that Jesus is truly victor? Or must it get worse the longer it goes on? Are we too weak to want to gather strength again to oppose the new invasions of the powers of darkness? Didn't Jesus Christ promise to give us strength if only we believed? Are we to be indifferent to all the ways Satan binds people? This occurs daily and in so many ways: when people open their mouths spewing out "all hell," and when others open their eyes, capturing and poisoning souls with a lewd satanic glance.

Dear friends, unless we rise up, take heart and shake off the arrows of the evil one, unless we rise up and stand in his strength, the strength of God Almighty, in the authority of his power, the world will quickly go up in flames. The earth will fall under the curse of utter destruction, which the prophet Malachi describes. Let us be those who believe, and thereby delay this curse—no matter how bleak the present time appears. Let us cling to the promise that God's counsel will prevail in the end. The time will surely come when "the people who are loyal to God shall stand firm and take action" (Dan 11:32).

Let us not delay, dear friends! Let us hold firm and do whatever is necessary! Test yourselves and acknowledge where you might be bound by Satan. I want to impress it upon your hearts: keep an eye on yourself! If the "wolf" but seized only one of your limbs or only your clothing how would you feel? Be aware! The wolf has made us his special target. Do we not tremble? If we really believe that when we fight in earnest Jesus' victory will benefit us, we will be victorious. We know that faith is its own reward.

There is so much within our reach, but we must persevere. Satan himself might well fear us if we would but have that kind of faith in Jesus that grasps the meaning of victory and gives the devil no due! And how many sons and daughters of Abraham may experience how the spirit of sickness disappears! Stand upright and be courageous in the name of Jesus! Let your watchword be, "Jesus is victor!" And we will be victorious with him! O Lord, our Savior, grant us this! Amen.

1. As the Father loves me
God the Father loves — what is divine love? *a Father's love*
God the Father loves Jesus — His precious *sacrificial*
only Son *protective*
provision
preserving
times 1000

2. So do I love you
what is the love of Jesus — The Father's *The Father*
what is the love of Jesus to me — *love* *so loved*
saved me *the world*
taught me
guides me
all by His Spirit

The Son's Love

3. Abide in my love
abide in — how do I abide? live in the knowledge
my love — The HS who love, lights up that I am loved — the
beloved
Son

As the Father has loved me, so have I loved you; abide in my love.

of Christ & Father — me.

—JOHN 15:9

Were the disciples as close to Jesus as he was to the Father? Could Jesus say that he loved them as the Father loved him? The grace that broke in through Jesus is seen above all in that we are as highly valued by the Son as the Son is by the Father. Because Jesus loves us with the love of the Father, the Father also accepts us. How can the Father be indifferent toward anyone whom the Son loves? The Father's love for the Son is so great that he embraces all those who love his Son with this same love, whoever they are. This is why Jesus says elsewhere, "He who loves me will be loved by my Father, and I will love him and reveal myself to him" (John 14:21). See how everything works out according to the Father's will: The Father loves the Son, the Son the Father; we love the Son and he loves us; the Father loves us and we love him. All this came through Jesus who brought God's love into the world again. Consider how we have been rescued by Jesus! Were we not sinners, did we not deserve to be eternally rejected and cast out by God? But our Father in heaven saw to it that if love to his Son were kindled in us, his Son would love us, and thus the Father in turn would bestow his entire love upon us.

The HS to love

There is one thing, however, to remember in all this. Jesus cannot love us fully unless we give him our whole heart. For Jesus' sake the disciples had forsaken everything; no self-denial was too much for them in the light of the Savior's love. They were humble, childlike, and genuine. There was

Jesus stirred love in us
love of the Father

Editors' Note: This sermon is dated 1875.

When we saw Jesus' love we loved him and his Father,

17

nothing in this world that bound them. What compelled them was Jesus—always Jesus. As they grew close to Jesus' heart, he grew into their hearts. Then it happened that the Father, against whom they had sinned—as all sinners do—wholeheartedly embraced them, giving himself to them. Reconciliation was theirs. Oh, we foolish people who will not allow Jesus to be our all in all, who refuse to let Jesus love us as the Father loves him! How wonderful it would be if Jesus loved us as the Father loves him! Then we will share in the glory of the Father and the Son!

But even if we are found wanting, things can still change. The Lord said, "Abide in my love." He wants us to stay in his love, to give ourselves to it again and again. When we do this, he will always hold us in his love. He won't treat us as strangers, even if we stumble and stray from him. But if we reject Jesus, then we reject his love. Thus he pleads with us, "Don't deny love." For when we cease to love him anymore, we forfeit the Father's love. God cannot love us for our own sake. If our hearts no longer yearn for Jesus, then the Father will reject us—we are not worthy of his love. To draw so close to the Highest and then to forsake this love—how terrible that would be! Oh, let us remain in the love of Jesus. Amen.

Jesus stirred love for the Father because love of god was dead. The Jews had loads of theology about god, but not love. The Father wanted to have our love — ad show us his love. This is what Jesus did.

Honor the Son!

Anyone who does not honor the Son does not honor the Father who sent him.

—JOHN 5:23 (NRSV)

If you don't personally know the Son, you will not honor him in your life. And neither will you know God the Father or honor him. If you claim to know the Father and yet reject the Son, you doubly dishonor the Father who sent him. There are two kinds of people who do not honor the Father through the Son: pious people and those who reject what is holy altogether. Those who simply give themselves to the spirit of this world, the irreverent, simply don't understand the Son or the Father and therefore can't honor them in their lives. Yet, they are less guilty than the "saintly," good people who piously claim to know the Son but live no differently than everybody else. Religious people fail to honor the Son because they really don't trust him. They ignore his grace and power, which he has promised us. They don't believe in his compassionate love, that love which is for all people. To know him and yet not believe in his mercy for the sinful world is nothing less than unbelief. The guilt of religious people is therefore twice as heavy. They know all about Jesus and yet refuse to accept him as the Savior of us all. As in the time of Jesus, many Jews realized who the Savior was, but they did not honor him, and consequently loaded guilt upon themselves. They did not change, gaining no greater trust in God, and did not give up their own self-righteousness. This was a disaster.

Editors' Note: This sermon is dated 1878.

May the Lord help us all! May he help each one of us to exclaim: Jesus is my all in all, and for all people!

The Legacy of the Departing Savior

"You are witnesses of these things. And see, I am sending upon you what my Father promised; so stay here in the city until you have been clothed with power from on high."

Then he led them out as far as Bethany, and, lifting up his hands, he blessed them. While he was blessing them, he withdrew from them and was carried up into heaven. And they worshiped him, and returned to Jerusalem with great joy; and they were continually in the temple blessing God.

—LUKE 24:48–53 (NRSV)

Dear friends, today is an important day. It is the greatest day we can imagine. The call to us is, "Out of the depths into the heights, out of the domain of darkness into the realm of the living God to whom we belong!" We are told that our Lord, who took on flesh and blood just like us and became our brother (and doesn't want to be anything else), ascended into heaven. It is as if he drew all of us up with him, and even today everyone who believes in Jesus feels drawn upward toward him. We want to speak in more detail about what happened on that day and will arrange our thoughts about the text under four headings: 1) He ascends to heaven; 2) He ascends with a blessing; 3) He ascends, promising power; and 4) He ascends, and yet he remains.

May Jesus who is raised on high give us strength so that our thoughts will be lifted upward to where he is now! Amen.

Editors' Note: This sermon is dated Ascension Day, 1861.

I

Jesus ascended to heaven. We know that the living God fills all creation; he is everywhere. And thus it is so with the Lord Jesus; he penetrates the whole creation. Because of this, it is written that "he sustains all things by his powerful word" (Heb 1:3). And so his word was quickly fulfilled: "All authority in heaven and on earth has been given to me" (Matt 28:18). Jesus said this while still on earth and even now it is taking place. When he ascended to heaven, authority over heaven and earth was given to him, authority over all creation. From now on, everything is under his watchful eye; his boundless divine power is at work everywhere. What comfort! The Lord Jesus, our brother, is under heaven and in heaven.

Imagine how tremendous this is! It is your brother who fulfills everything. It is your brother to whom all things are subjected; and wherever hostile powers remain, it is this brother who will eliminate them all. He is the Master; everything is under his feet. We all know that this world is in dire shape. From Scripture we learn that the satanic world extends everywhere; there exist evil spirits on earth that fill the air. But the Lord Jesus is still present. He has everything in hand, even the evil powers. Wherever we find ourselves, no matter what situation we are in, Christ comes to those who really want him. We needn't be frightened because Jesus always has the upper hand. We only have to call on him and even the gates of hell cannot prevail. It has been prophesied that Jesus himself will be there when the multitudes from the abyss fill the air. Nothing, not even the smallest incident, can occur without the presence of his mighty hand. He protects, shelters, liberates, and redeems all those who cry out to him. See how important it is that the Lord Jesus took possession of heaven!

And this is not all. He placed himself at the right hand of God and thus opened the gates of blessedness. We too can receive our place in heaven. This is far greater than anyone can imagine; although to imagine that we shall become like Christ Jesus is also incredible—much too much to comprehend. Our way of thinking that in heaven we will somehow sit together in a meeting, as in a room here, is all wrong. It is far too narrow-minded. No. It will be a million times more glorious. It will be a million times greater, far greater than what can fill the whole world now. How wonderful it will be—beyond all our wildest dreams! One thing is certain—we will all see his glory.

But let us leave this for now and let this thought remain with us: Heaven is no longer closed. It is wide open, we can enter heaven into God's glory, and into the beloved Father's heart. We can enter freely, liberated from all dark powers. And our hope is that this is for all people. Jesus' promises will be fulfilled. Even if we can't ascend to heaven right now, we can experience something of his ascension in our spirit. Just as Jesus ascended to heaven so will we, for this is his will. He came for this, suffered for this, arose for this. He ascends not to show-off, as if to say, "Look at the glory that surrounds me!" No, he ascends so that a way to heaven is opened for us all.

II

Now we come to the second point: Jesus ascended with a blessing; he leaves something behind. Our text says: "While he was blessing them, he withdrew from them." Picture this for yourselves—Jesus is seen stretching out his hands when a cloud carries him up to heaven. As he ascends, he stretches out his hands to everyone who is watching, and they are blessed. Something remains behind at his departure. Now, think further. His hands, raised in blessing, encompass a larger and larger circle. The further away from the earth, the wider is the horizon and so the blessing from his hands extends over all nations. This blessing has remained. In this way he comes to every man, woman, and child, to every nation on earth, to all who are able to accept his blessing. We don't understand this, but without this blessing the disciples would not have found open hearts when they began to joyfully proclaim Jesus. From that time on his blessing rests upon the whole earth, even though people still feel lost and frustrated. Nevertheless, the blessing is there and is felt by thousands. He still comes today with blessings for everyone who longs for him.

What does this blessing mean? "To bless" means to wish for salvation. This expresses everything. It is as if Jesus says over and over again: "Salvation will come, salvation will come upon all the people of the earth. Deliverance, redemption, and refreshment will come to everyone who is troubled in heart." He casts a compassionate and loving glance over everyone. He knows and thinks of all our needs and will fulfill them all.

Imagine, dear friends. Jesus is near to each one of us today with his hands raised and stretched forth in blessing. Perhaps his eyes are weeping with pity, wishing for our salvation. Indeed, he is holding out salvation for everyone—redemption for all who want it. He is near to you today, and you will see that it is really true. Believe it! It is true. "My dear child, salvation is for you." His voice can echo in your heart, for he has not withdrawn his blessing. Jesus still desires to lift us from "out of the depths." He wants to help everyone. He longs that the "lost," no matter who they are, will be found. His love and kindness await every person who, in prayer, looks up to him.

It is still the same, nearly 1800 years later. His blessing remains and whoever wishes for it is blessed. Remember, he ascended with a blessing:

> My will shall be accomplished. All the powers of darkness will be overthrown, all things must be renewed. Those who are far from God but who belong to him must be brought back, and all creatures must be helped. Every tear will be dried, every heart refreshed and made glad, everything must be laid into my Father's hands.

That is his blessing, and in this hope we must think of our ascended Savior. Then nothing can lead us astray anymore, even if we feel under the weight of darkness or doubt the appearing of his victory. Think of his blessing. He has not withdrawn his outstretched hands. His blessing remains for all nations of the earth. And when they want it, his victory will be theirs. Therefore, rejoice and be glad. The Savior who blesses us all continues to bless us, fulfilling his every word.

III

Jesus ascended into heaven, not only with his blessing but promising his power. But this blessing must be fulfilled and made reality. From heaven Jesus sends the promised Spirit. He sends his power from the fullness of the Godhead, so that all people will realize that he has truly gone to his Father. From the holiest place, heaven, he pours forth "power from on high, which the Father has promised." What is this power? It is the outpouring of the Holy Spirit. Dear ones, this happened precisely because Jesus ascended. Think about this. With this gift from Jesus' heart, divine power descends on this earth, to us poor, weak, sinful people, who until now have been subject to Satan. Remember, this is completely new, unknown to us. It is a beginning of the heavenly glory that Jesus takes possession and to which we too shall be raised; this came upon the disciples ten days later. Promising this power, Jesus ascended to heaven. The disciples believed. They came together and told what they had seen and heard. One hundred twenty of them met together with the assurance that the Savior would send them something from heaven. He, the Savior, pledged a piece of "heavenly bread." And that is what happened. This great grace, the promised gift was bestowed on the disciples, transforming them into true followers of Jesus.

This promise still applies to us—he did not promise it just for that time. Even though that which Jesus once gave has for the time being receded, let us not forget that he departed promising us power. His blessing and Spirit are for today. He is faithful to his word. If you find it hard to believe that this is still true for today; if instead of power you feel only your weakness; if instead of the blowing of the Spirit you are more aware of the stirrings of your fallen, human nature; if you can't get beyond seeing and deploring your own frailties and those of others—then remember your Savior who, when he ascended, promised his followers power from on high. It is still true today. His promise remains, it will come, and it will come again and again. As long as any part of this promise remains unfulfilled we can know that power from on high will be given. Plead for it!

Jesus' promises will stand for as long as the world exists. "Ask, and it shall be given you; seek, and you shall find; knock, and it shall be opened unto you!" Ascending, Jesus calls these words down to us and continues to call to all who seek him. Who doubts this? Who will deny it? He promised us power from on high. Therefore, we know that these powers will come. Watch. Believe. Pray. Cry out and plead. Knock and keep on knocking. Just as he spoke to his first disciples, he makes the same promise to each generation. His promise remains forever. It will come to pass. We know it to be true, for it can already be seen among those who earnestly seek and long for it. Whatever Jesus has promised will come, and his children will become strong on earth. When the great battles begin, we will see how strong his disciples are and how the devil will have to yield before this new power from on high with which God's children are clothed. Do not let yourself be robbed of this promise by any loveless thought.

IV

Lastly, Jesus ascended to heaven and yet he remains on earth. "And they worshiped him, and returned to Jerusalem with great joy; and they were continually in the temple blessing God" (Luke 24:52–53). The disciples did this not as those who had lost what was most precious to them; they still felt Jesus' closeness. Jesus told them, "Lo, I am with you always, even unto the end of the world." Though he ascended, yet he remained present. Dear friends, he remains! This follows from what we said at the beginning—that

Christ Jesus has permeated all the heavens and therefore the earth as well. Though it seems as if he has left us, for he is not literally seen, yet he is here, your loving Savior. He longs to tear us away from all the devil's snares. He has not left us—no! He remains with us. "Where two or three are gathered in my name, there am I in the midst of them" (Matt 18:20).

Dear friends, herein lay the significance of Christ's ascension. If the Savior were still physically on earth, we would have to constantly inquire as to his whereabouts. Announcements would have to be made everywhere, as with great gentlemen, and it would even be put in the newspapers. But now he is within us and in our midst, "unto the end of the world." Therefore, have courage when you struggle, or are anxious or hungry. You who are tormented inwardly and outwardly—remember that the Lord Jesus is with you. Please try to remember this. Hold firmly to it! Persevere! He will be the victor and will deliver his children from all evil, according to his promise. Amen.

Lord, our Savior, who was raised up to heaven but is also present here in our gathering—help us to believe, help us to hope! We want to be sanctified by your hand of blessing! We want to keep your words of promise in sight. We want to hold firmly to them. You are with us and will stay with us! Establish your glory more and more upon earth, for evil still rules in so many places. Lord Jesus, reveal yourself as victor, helper, and deliverer for all those who call upon you. When we stand outside, looking up into the heavens seeing the stars, let us remember that is where you have gone and where we too want to go! Under all temptations help us to remain faithful and stand firm and true to your Word. We are your children. Lord Jesus, when we offer a blessing, let it be a blessing from your hand! Lord, we look up to you. In life and in death prepare us to see you in your glory. Yes, help us, Lord, that this may really come to pass! Amen.

darkness and lead them into God's light. This is the great gift of God. Without this gift, however, no one is capable of finding repentance or receiving forgiveness of sins. <u>Forgiveness is not possible without repentance</u>. Those who take forgiveness of sins lightly, as something easily obtained, without repentance, only deceive and cheat themselves. <u>Faith without repentance is never enough</u>.

So faith and repentance are both necessary. Sadly, many people today are afraid to respond because they think that they are unable to repent. They try hard to feel repentant, to feel pain for their sins, but they know, deep down, that nothing has changed or been accomplished. They still feel cold and apathetic, not sufficiently grieved and broken. This, in turn, makes them worry and uneasy, causing them to struggle and fight, spending long hours praying for a repentant heart. What they forget is that it is Jesus who freely gives repentance. Left to ourselves, we can't create a repentant heart. We can't force feelings we don't have. We can't heal our sinful hearts. No! Our hearts must be broken by Jesus and by his Spirit. Jesus alone does this and promises to do it. <u>Repentance is finally the Lord's work</u>.

Therefore, let us all become peaceful and quiet. Let us not fret and grieve so much. We must pray, calmly and in hope, "Lord, give this to me." If we feel that nothing is happening, then it must be right. Remember, the beginning of repentance has already come if this is truly what you want. Do not worry—for forgiveness of sins is promised to you as a gift from Christ Jesus. When you feel too poor and miserable to repent, be glad! For this can make you humble. Then when the time of refreshing is given, the innermost feelings of your heart will become right. <u>Just be small and poor in spirit; believe in God's grace</u>—a grace that is always given to the humble.

Oh, how wonderful! Jesus is everything since he gives us all we need for salvation: <u>repentance, faith, forgiveness, hope!</u> Hold to him calmly, without care and grief. Put your trust in him. Keep your heart pure and single, then repentance and a new life will be given to you. Your joy will be made complete. Amen.

SECTION 2
THE CHRISTIAN POSITION

Into the Kingdom of Life

... giving thanks to the Father, who has enabled you to share in
the inheritance of the saints in the light. He has rescued us from
the power of darkness and transferred us into the kingdom of his
beloved Son, in whom we have redemption, the forgiveness of sins.

—COLOSSIANS 1:12–14 (NRSV)

Through faith in Christ we are given strength to take possession of the
kingdom of light. It is through this faith that we are justified. Formerly
we were unqualified, being sinners and unjust, but now we have been reconciled through the blood of Christ. We now can partake in the kingdom
of light. We are now able to leave the dominion of the devil and take part
in God's kingdom.

These two things—deliverance from the dominion of darkness and
being transferred into the kingdom of God's beloved Son—happen at each
conversion. From darkness into light, out of slavery into freedom, out of
misery into joy: truly out of hell into eternal bliss. Ah! What will it be like
when this happens to everyone? There are so many people, including those
whose faith is still shaky, who groan in "harsh chains." They are still completely bound. What will it take before the power of faith completely breaks
into their hearts? Salvation still has to come to the world. For how much
more must happen to all those still heavily bound, who are far from faith.
But we know our Savior is compassionate; he will labor hard to bring all
those who are in darkness into the light.

Editors' Note: This sermon is dated 1873.

Born of God

We know that those who are born of God do not sin, but the one who was born of God protects them, and the evil one does not touch them.

—1 JOHN 5:18 (NRSV)

John is speaking to those who had left paganism and found faith. Without faith in Christ they would not have been baptized; without faith they could not be part of the Christian fellowship. Despite this, there were still many sinners among these believing Christians, as John himself repeatedly testifies in his letter. When John says, "Whoever is born of God cannot continue to sin"—this makes it clear that even then not all "believing Christians" were born of God. It could also be that not all who were baptized received the Holy Spirit in the same way as the very first Christians did. We can't build entirely upon our faith or the faith we assume others have; there is faith by which we are born of God, and there is "faith" by which we are not born of God. Another way of putting this is that there is a faith by which someone becomes a new person, and there is a faith that does not change a person. If believing does not change our thinking and behavior, if we continue to live and think as the world does and give way to worldly desires, then no new person is there, no new being born of God. True faith leads people to become faithful to God. We see plainly, however, that this is not always the case for those who profess belief.

Inasmuch as love of the world, self-interest, pride, envy, and all kinds of wickedness, even sensuality, are obviously in full swing, it is increasingly

Editors' Note: This sermon is dated 1875.

34

difficult to see God's people as we would like to see them be, even those people who—in contrast to the indifferent world that only lives from one day to the next—really want to experience faith. Being born of God through faith is not to be taken as a given or daily occurrence. We must therefore have forbearance—also with ourselves. We must pray for all those who continue to struggle against their fallen nature and who grieve because they fail to follow Christ completely. Perhaps they really are, after all, born of God. It is those who, self-confidently and self-righteously, regard themselves as being good that we must worry about.

Still, let us take comfort in the fact, and in the promise, that anyone who is born of God, by means of a faith that acts on their mind and will, does not keep sinning—that is, they do not willfully transgress God's commandment. The Lord helps them so that even in great temptation they do not commit a sin which will place them outside of fellowship with God. Moreover, anyone who sincerely pays attention to God's divine qualities cannot be touched by the wicked one and be forced against their will to sin. Though this can easily happen to halfhearted people—to those who really live more for the world than for God—we who are sincere are promised victory over sin. There are many over whom the evil one has no power. He protects us from the wicked one in wonderful ways. All we need is a simple and sincere heart, a longing to be born of God—to rightly be called a true child of God. There is, nevertheless, much to sigh about. The Lord, however, will have compassion on those who sigh and will always provide new help. Amen.

Conversion

Convert me and I will be converted, for you are the LORD my God.

—JEREMIAH 31:18 (FREE TRANSLATION)

So many people today long for conversion, and yet conversion never fully becomes a reality. And those who claim to be converted, those who zealously preach about it, are often the least converted of all. They may feel close to experiencing conversion, but still it does not become a reality. Is there any faith? No! People are quick to despair. As soon as there is a spring frost people immediately believe they are going to starve. We only need to hurt a finger and immediately we "go to pieces." Do we really love? No, not really. We love for a short time but when we have to go one step more, when we have to go out of our way, our love ends. We are happy as long as love doesn't cost us anything—as soon as love entails some effort, then that is the end of it. Do we have hope? Ah, we so easily give up everything for lost! Too many of us have forgotten how to hope, in small as well as in large matters. Is there selfless dedication? Oh, what a lot of envy, stubbornness, pride, and other baser things can be found among us Christians! All the more we need to pray: "Lord, convert me, and I will be converted." We will not and cannot change until the spirit of genuine conversion overcomes us. Only when the great Pentecostal gift of repentance reappears, only then will the Holy Spirit personally dwell among us again. Without this, true conversion escapes us. The request, "Convert me, Lord!" coincides with the request for the gift of the Holy Spirit. We want to make this request today for ourselves and for all flesh.

Editors' Note: This sermon is dated 1878.

36

Let us not forget that conversion is much more than a stimulus to pray, to read the Bible, or an eagerness to partake in the Lord's Supper, to gather together with like-minded souls. All this is right and good, but this is not yet conversion. Do I say too much? You must only be sure not to apply this to others, saying, "This or the other one is also not yet converted!" Rather, examine yourself, and if you are humble and honest you will have to say, "Oh—I am not yet converted. Surely everybody else will be converted before I am." This is how we should think of ourselves; this is the attitude that marks the beginning of a real change. As long as we assume that we are converted, God cannot use us. And if we are quick to point out to anyone that he or she is not converted, then be forewarned: that's the end of our relationship with God, even if we might be right. No. Our task is to try to connect with every person, whoever they are. Maybe then God will look down and have mercy on us!

Don't misunderstand what I am trying to say. Many people mean well. Indeed, they desire, even pray for conversion, even though this is not very obvious in how they themselves are. Many people truly want to be changed. Because of this we must never give up hope on anyone. We must believe that the Lord will one day deliver all of us from all that stands in the way of conversion. There is so much that is hidden that holds people back. If we only knew all that hinders people, we would cease being so surprised. We would perhaps even have more sympathy for the so-called "unconverted." Let us turn completely to the Lord and hope for everything from him and only him. Let us hope for his mercy and victory. He must guide everything!

Joy in Zion

And the ransomed of the LORD shall return, and come to Zion with singing; everlasting joy shall be upon their heads; they shall obtain joy and gladness, and sorrow and sighing shall flee away.

—ISAIAH 35:10 (NRSV)

We have no real conception of the time to which this verse refers. It's a time too tremendous, too glorious, for us to think about, especially today when everywhere sorrow and pain try to overwhelm us. It is tempting to explain passages such as this and other sayings of the prophets as mere poetry—flights of fancy. Poets are able to lift themselves and us to the "clouds," delivering from there all kinds of magnificent descriptions. Then we think, "Oh, yes, it is all painted in glowing colors, but it will never become a reality!" Don't we also think of the prophets in this way—that their words are painted in too glowing colors and will not become a reality? Let us be careful and not think this way. Isaiah is referring to when the world is drawing to an end. There will come a time, perhaps in a very short while, when the Most High will appear, which will be the transfiguration, when everything is changed and made heavenly. This is the real gateway to God's temple.

All this can only happen once. In the Bible the expressions "in that day" or "in the latter days" are repeatedly used. The question is whether this promise will be fulfilled or not. Should we even expect it? Should we hope for it? Should we think of it as being close at hand? Or is it far off in

Editors' Note: This sermon is dated 1873.

the distant future? What do we think about this verse becoming reality? This is the point!

Most people look upon this everlasting joy uncertainly, as something that may or may not happen anytime soon. No one knows when. Advent after advent we say, "One day it will be." In the back of our minds, however, we think that this day won't happen, at least not for a thousand years, even for a hundred thousand years. I must confess, I am not satisfied with this! I must think that it is near at hand! But sadly, we lack a prophet like John the Baptist, who can speak to us again, proclaiming, "Now it will come," so that everyone who hears believes. We are so spiritually poor that there is no authority to give us hope for an early beginning of God's promises. We are in an extraordinarily bad situation. Nowhere in the world do we hear anyone exclaiming: "Have you heard what was said in the name of the Lord? Now, be on the alert!" In the whole world no real authority is to be found.

As a result, this passage from Isaiah feels immeasurably distant from us. Anyone who has a premonition of its truth, even when it is based upon a firm foundation, still feels they have to be quiet. Even if they did speak, no one would pay any attention to what they say because they have no God-given authority and no special task to express this. Who really listens to those who proclaim, "I believe the kingdom of God will come soon!"? Anyone who cherishes such a hope is under a tremendous strain; it weighs on them like a mountain. No one else really understands this. They feel they have to be silent. They fear that someone will react and ask, "Who do you think you are?" What are they to do?

But I believe more and more ardently that we stand before the gateway to the prophetic times that all the prophets and also the Lord Jesus spoke about. We stand at the threshold—this is my firm conviction. And what convinces me most of all is the fact that there is nothing in sight upon which we can build. Everything is going downhill, and it looks as if soon nothing will be left. People today live such isolated lives that there is no longer any human fellowship. Of course we do discuss this or that concern together, but we don't find any real kinship of souls; a communion of believers, a heartfelt hope and faith are nowhere to be found. One can discuss and argue, in a kind of superficial sort of way, but then everything becomes a debate! One has this opinion, and another that, and a third says, "Now I believe you." But this is not genuine fellowship. No, we are "harassed and helpless, like sheep without a shepherd" (Matt 9:36). There are exceptional movements and stirrings of course, but none of these lead to true fellowship or community. Why? All I hear is "I," "I," "I." There is no fellowship, no community in this. But it simply can't remain like this. There should be community. So I look up to heaven and cry out, "Lord Jesus, let it happen now!"

We read in our text, "The ransomed of the Lord shall come." This is the heart of our text. All the rescued people come hand in hand, happy with one another, looking into one another's eyes and hearts. When they meet there is real joy in each other. The next part of the text says that, "They come to Zion with singing . . . ." This also points toward a unity that is immediately present when that happens. And where does this unity come from? It is because they are ransomed! Note carefully: They are ransomed. I tell you, this is even more significant than being "converted." The latter certainly appears in Scripture, but being "ransomed" is different. Behind the word "converted" there is a great deal of a person's own working and doing, when a person starts to do all kinds of things and it is said of them, "Yes, they are quite different from what they were." But this is not enough. Oh, dear friends, who of us can grasp what it means to be ransomed? We don't realize how bound we are, how much we lie chained and fettered, how many evil spirits fill us with harmful thoughts. We are influenced by false piety, conceit, self-esteem, by a peace that seems good but is only a delusion. There is no redemption in any of this! Yes, we all want to change, but we need first and foremost to be redeemed. If only we could experience being ransomed from all the shackles that bind us, from all burden of sin, from spiritual bondage. Our fetters continually annul all that is good. However high we hold up our heads, again and again envy, greed, impurity, evil desires enter our hearts and minds. In spite of this, we good Christians act as if we were so special. But evil things continue to rage within us; we are still caught firmly in sin.

The Lord must intervene. We can't redeem ourselves. For this to happen we must trust in the Savior, who one day will place all his enemies at his feet. He is secretly preparing a joy for us so that in the twinkling of an eye we will experience redemption. Therefore we must pray, "Take away from me all that binds, restrains, and defiles my body and soul, so that I may be free of these things." If you are bound by darkness, any darkness, then ask the Lord to free you, for you are not freed just by thinking "Now I believe!" Jesus said to his disciples, "If you forgive the sins of anyone, they are forgiven" (John 20:23). Has this happened to you? Yes, there are many that forgive their own sins and believe that now all is well. But this person is not yet truly redeemed.

I believe that our friend Jesus Christ, the most high and merciful One, hears the secret prayers and the sighs of all those who carry entreaties in their heart, and thus will quietly loosen their bonds. When this happens, life among us will change by leaps and bounds. What will happen? People will come out of their hiding places, out of all those places into which they have crawled, out of the dark pits into which they had descended. This will happen for both the living and the dead, as far as the latter are worthy. Redemption will come everywhere in this world, in heaven, and below. All creation will confess that Jesus is Lord. All those who are redeemed from their graves, from captivity, chains, and bonds will come together through the mercy of Jesus. We will surely experience this one day. Pray for this. "Do this for us, Lord Jesus. No preacher or evangelist is able to redeem us. You alone can redeem and free us. May you redeem us! May you set us free!" I tell you, no one who prays for this prays in vain. We already see small signs and indications of God's great redemption.

When the ransomed return, where will they go? "To Zion!" You must remember that in ancient times the Israelites made their sacrifices at many places, probably thinking, "Why should we run to Zion? Why not just go to the nearest, most convenient mountain?" But this caused many divisions. We too have just as many places—the one here and the other there. This is not right. Those who are redeemed have only one place—which the prophet calls Zion. From Zion the law of the Lord went forth and also the gospel through Jesus. And in time, all people will come to the Savior. Our concern and inner attitude must be toward this one goal—not you in one direction and others in another, but we must all head toward the same goal, Jesus! This is what it means to come to God's Zion. When we are gripped by the fact that Jesus alone is the Redeemer from sin, death, devil, and hell, and seek nothing besides Jesus, least of all ourselves, then we are coming to Zion. I tell you, so few of us know this Zion. Though many believe they are baptized by fire and Spirit, still they have no Redeemer. We can have devotions year after year and still feel no need of Jesus.

Therefore, seek only Jesus, the One who alone redeems—that is what it means to come to Zion! For in that day, people will come together, and when they do we will not hear, "I have found it, I have it!" but rather, "You have found him, you have him; how glad I am that both you and I have found Jesus." And we will know God's redemption: Jesus will wrench the devil out of us, out of our blood. On that day all people will experience this, and there will be joy and jubilation, gladness, and freedom. We will know that it is the Son who makes us free, and there will no longer be any sorrow and pain. When the plan of Almighty God is accomplished, the heavenly choir will descend and join the redeemed in dance!

Now we must focus our thoughts on redemption and on coming to Zion. When we do, everywhere there will be joy, gladness, exultation, jubilation, and bliss! Soon? Soon? O Jesus, let this happen soon! Amen.

Live Not for Yourself!

And he died for all, so that those who live might live no longer for themselves, but for him who died and was raised for them.

—2 Corinthians 5:15 (NRSV)

Before hearing the gospel, each of us lived for himself; this is characteristic of our perversity. This is the origin of sin, for the serpent deluded Adam into thinking that if he ate of the fruit, he would be like God. That is, we lived our own life, unconcerned with whether our will conformed to God's will. We went our own way, ignoring those around us, even God himself. We were, in the words of Isaiah, sheep who had, "gone astray (that is, like sheep who have no shepherd or do not want one); we have all turned to our own way, and the Lord has laid on him the iniquity of us all" (Isa 53:6). Now when we stop to think about it, we know that there is nothing more harmful to us than living only for ourselves, thinking solely about ourselves. A self-centered existence leads only to sin; nothing is set right. It is a sad picture when people come together but are completely unconcerned about their neighbor. We so often act as if nobody else but ourselves were alive or even had the right to live.

Christ came to free us from this sad situation. He did not live and die for himself, rather, he lived for us all and died for us. In this, he showed us that our only help is to get away from ourselves and join with others. And as soon as we start believing in Christ, we see how we cannot go on in our own strength. We realize that we must surrender to the One who died for everyone, and stop living selfishly. For the Risen One now lives for all

Editors' Note: This sermon is dated 1877.

people. Oh, that we might learn to give up our self-will and surrender to the love of Jesus—Jesus who in his death and in his life puts us back on the right track. He shows us how to live together in peace and happiness; we no longer have to torment and oppress and take advantage of others in order to improve our lot in life. God's loving counsel will one day be fulfilled. Every knee will bend before him and every tongue will confess that Jesus Christ is the Lord. Will this ever come to pass? Yes, it surely will! Hallelujah! Amen.

Eyes Turned to the Lord

As the eyes of servants look to the hand of their master, as the eyes of a maid to the hand of her mistress, so our eyes look to the LORD our God, until he has mercy upon us.

—PSALM 123:2 (NRSV)

When David refers to the servants and maids who look to the hands of their masters or mistresses, he means the slaves who existed everywhere in ancient times. David is thinking how, especially in the mornings, they attended the master or the mistress. Standing at a little distance, they would quietly, without a word, simply with a look, show their desire and readiness to serve. Respect, and also awareness of their servitude under which they were not allowed a will of their own, did not permit them to speak unless spoken to. When that relationship was a good one, as was often the case, they served with trust and love. They were treated well and, in turn, gracefully carried out their assigned duties.

This is what our own attitude should be toward God. We should stand before the Lord, devoted and surrendered, loving him and accepting all he gives. This is how we should be when we pray. We mustn't use many words, or make arrogant, presumptuous demands or be self-righteous and complacent. We should be almost silent. If we do speak, we need to do it only to clarify what it is that we wish for or want to request of God. And we must never stand before the Lord defending our own ideas. We must learn how to wait patiently for his command.

Editors' Note: This sermon is dated 1877.

Now what about those who find no words, or find it difficult to know how to pray? What about those who, when they have scarcely begun, lose courage to go on? And what about those who are robbed from all desire to pray, when dark powers deprive them of words and thoughts? What advice can we give to these discouraged people? I believe that the words of this psalm are important for them. It is not always with our mouth, not always with our brain, with its confused thoughts, that we pray. Prayer can be expressed just with our eyes. We can direct our eyes to the Lord in trust and with courage, without saying a word. We can be like the tax collector, who with just a whisper uttered, "Lord, be merciful to me" (Luke 18:13). We can do this right in the middle of all our rush and work. Whenever we direct our gaze to him, we will immediately encounter his gaze.

This silent prayer of looking to the Lord, when we turn our thoughts to him and open our hearts, is the most powerful prayer we can utter. But it takes great humility, modesty, patience, and an awareness of one's nothingness before God. It also demands that we remain in earnest, even if we have to wait a long time—"till the Lord has mercy on us," as David says. I said "earnest," not "pushy." We have to be willing to wait until mercy is given, which often only comes gradually. When the Lord helps us, in response to our quiet prayers, he often responds quietly. However his help comes, ask for the grace to be certain of his will, so that you might know what he requires of you and how you can best serve him. Show the same eager desire as did the slaves of old. How pleasant it is just to look upon the Lord, without idle talk! God also wants to have something from you as his servant, just as you want something from him. And the more he has from you, the more you will have from him. Let us remember this above everything else! May the Lord be merciful to us and to all suffering creation! Amen.

SECTION 3
THE COMFORT
OF THE GOSPEL

Be Strong in the Lord

Finally, be strong in the Lord and in the strength of his power.

—EPHESIANS 6:10 (NRSV)

Christians are to be strong. So if we are weak, we will have to give an account. It is a sad thing if we always feel weak and are unable to pluck up the courage to find strength when it is needed—in the Lord or through faith in him—strength which we ourselves certainly do not have of our own. Of course, not all of us have faith. Yes, there are many who think they have faith, but few of us know whether or not we really have faith until it is tested. If we boast about our faith, yet tremble with fear and lose heart the moment we see a bug, as if it could knock us over, our faith means nothing—it counts for nothing.

Therefore, we have to be courageous in faith, daring to express ourselves. We must not fall back on our incompetence and weakness as an excuse, holding back instead of "putting our hands to the plow." When we act this way we demonstrate how little fellowship we have with the Lord. We are not yet really united with him in faith. Certainly we don't yet find our security in him; he is not our fortress. In fact, we may even be avoiding him.

There are circumstances, especially when it is a question of defying the enemy and the power of Satan, when we must become bold and dare to clothe ourselves in the strength of the Lord's power. God's fighters will not lack this strength so long as they do not tremble before the enemy, behaving as if he were mightier than they, even mightier than the Lord himself. Let us recall how determined the believers in the old covenant were when they fulfilled their great deeds! Let us learn to do this in small ways. Yes, learn to be strong in the Lord, especially in little trials and temptations, and

49

then you will surely be victorious. In this way you will learn to be strong when you are up against great needs. Everything depends on us equipping ourselves with the strength of his might. When we truly desire this, God will fill us with courage. He is never far from those who dare to be strong in him.

God's Mercy

I have seen their ways, but I will heal them; I will lead them and
repay them with comfort.

—ISAIAH 57:18 (NRSV)

The Lord says, "I have seen their ways." We can well imagine what the
result might be, "and I will hurl them all to the ground." Just before this
verse it says, "I was angry with them because of their sin and greed, and so
I punished them and abandoned them. But they were stubborn and kept
on going their own way." But no! God says, "I will heal them." God's heart
was moved when he saw his people, abandoned by him, and how they had
fallen deeply into foolishness and sin. He was filled with compassion for
them. Yes, because of their sin God had turned away from them, but despite
this he wanted to turn back to them again, heal them, and guide them to
a better way of life. The people accepted God's leading and found healing;
they became free from the spirit of darkness. God's good Spirit worked in
them and redeemed them.

How incomprehensibly great is God's goodness and mercy! When nations stray, he hurries to help them with his overwhelming kindness. We
must not lose heart, therefore, even if our times are evil, even if the Lord
has withdrawn his presence and allowed us to go our own way. And what
evil ways these are! Yet these will arouse his compassion. "I cannot allow
my people to go on like this. I must act and see that they change their sinful ways. I must heal their evil spirit with my Spirit!" This is promised to
us. Do we believe this? Why don't we, as Israel did in Isaiah's time, believe

Editors' Note: This sermons is dated 1873.

51

and hope in the Lord? How wonderful it would be if we were allowed to experience this in our time just as Israel did at that time! How much more we should expect and believe in God's redemption because of what Jesus Christ did for us on the cross!

In our text the Lord also says, "I will repay them with comfort." Just imagine how encouraged we would feel if the Lord would lead us, through signs and wonders, to see the Savior reveal himself again and gather his sheep! Truly, everything is not yet lost, not even in our own day. We know we cannot improve our life, but the Lord can intervene and heal our pain and sin! Yes, the Lord is our Master, and he is victorious even when he appears to be far off. All is not lost. The time has come when his compassion heals and he is there to lead us. And there will be a time when everyone will fall down at his feet. May the good Lord bless us! Amen.

Do Not Worry!

Cast your burden on the LORD, and he will sustain you;
he will never permit the righteous to be moved.

—PSALM 55:22 (NRSV)

M any of us enter the New Year with a great number of worries that are
often just so much junk. We would like to leave this trash behind
in the old year and breathe more easily and happily in the new one. But
for some reason anxieties pursue us; they just won't leave us alone. They
cling tightly to us and we can't escape them. What should we do—especially
when our cares become heavy and oppress us? Perhaps on no other day of
the year do we turn our gaze heavenward as much as at the New Year. We
feel, in some way or another, that someone else controls our destiny, that we
are not entirely our own masters. We can easily become depressed, feeling
how powerless and helpless we are.

It is then that we are close to heeding David's call: "Cast your cares on
the Lord." As soon as we realize that we can't do anything, we can boldly
cast all our worries upon the Lord. "Dear God, here it is; I leave it all to you.
I will be quiet and content in my spirit, for I have placed everything into
your hands." Let us really do this! And let us also think of him—Jesus, our
deliverer and Savior—who burns with longing to deliver everyone from the
evil under which we still groan. Christ has already appointed a day in which
he will accomplish this. Until then, he wants to encourage us. What else do
we need or want?

Editors' Note: This sermon is dated January 1, 1876.

"He will never permit the righteous to be moved." Now, don't be dismayed and think, "But I am not righteous." Who knows, maybe you will be—right at the moment when you, with your whole heart, cast your cares upon the Lord. Then the Savior will lift you up and carry away the debris of your sin, along with everything else you long to cast upon him. He takes away sin from anyone who trusts in him. Whoever believes—sincerely believes—will not only find encouragement, but will be changed. If Christ takes your sins upon himself you can then become new; you can be made right. You will not always have to remain in disquiet. He will come at last.

At the start of this New Year, then, instead of good wishes I will give you this advice: "Give up your cares, your sins. Leave them in the hands of your God and Savior. You are precious to him, and he will not fail to be your loving Savior." Amen.

God Is My Strength

My flesh and my heart may fail, but God is the strength of my heart and my portion forever.

—Psalm 73:26 (NRSV)

This is a tremendous word from David. It is hard to believe it came from his mouth, since the hopes of Israelites were mainly concerned with their daily life on earth. A future life had not been revealed to them yet. David might have seen the redeeming Savior in spirit as a prophet, but he did not know him as the One who reconciles us to God. However, David is certain that if his flesh and heart grow weak, God would remain the strength of his heart and his portion. Whether or not he was thinking of a weakness to the point of death we cannot say. Nevertheless he expresses in the sharpest terms that when we submit to God, he always remains the comforter of our hearts. He is the One who devotes himself to us if we trust in him.

We must understand this verse in all its significance. No evil into which we may be led can dismay us, no pain, even if it attacks us in body and soul, can be too hard for us if at all times God is the strength of our hearts and we are certain that he is ours and we are his. The apostle Paul was able to say that nothing at all, no tribulation or distress, could separate him from the love of God which is in Christ Jesus. That is to say, nothing could obscure God's love to such an extent that it was no longer apparent and valid for him. When we become weak and start to fail physically, we can easily think that God has forsaken us. We don't find comfort and strength

Editors' Note: This sermon is dated 1875.

in him anymore. But despite this, nothing can obscure the love of God. It is so important to trust in this. We find this trust by relying on Christ our Savior who sacrificed his life for us. If you cannot grab on to this, if you can't accept suffering—mental or physical—to the very end without losing faith in God, you don't have the faith of a Christian, nor the faith of David.

God has so much patience with us! He doesn't run the risk of our faith being shipwrecked. He is careful not to overburden us. Yet, if we really want the kingdom of God to come, if our desire is to believe wholeheartedly, then God requires us to trust him like he trusted Job to dishonor the devil. Accept this until you are exhausted, even if it seems to be too much for your body and soul. If we are always asking why things move forward so slowly, why the powers of darkness seem to be on the increase rather than on the decrease, who knows maybe one day God may answer, "Why have you been so soft on yourselves? I never dared put a real burden on you because you always felt exhausted and raised such a fuss. I had to stop requesting your help to make things better in this world." Oh, when will strong and firm people of faith arise on whom God can place burdens, without endangering their body and soul?! These are the faithful ones who "shall receive the kingdom" (Dan 7:18). O mighty and compassionate God, accomplish this in your children through your dear Son, Jesus Christ! Amen.

Praise Be to God!

Praise be to the God and Father of our Lord Jesus Christ, the Father
of compassion and the God of all comfort, who comforts us in all
our troubles, so that we can comfort those in any trouble with the
comfort we ourselves receive from God.

—2 CORINTHIANS 1:3–4 (NIV)

Paul's second letter to the Corinthians was written during a time of great
distress. He had endured tremendous hardship and he was heavily
weighed down by grief when he thought about the Corinthians to whom
he was writing. Many situations alarmed him, making him uneasy. Things
weren't going as they should. Paul constantly experienced setbacks and
persecution at the hands of enemies and opponents. As he wrote later, "We
were under great pressure, far beyond our ability to endure, so that we de-
spaired even of life" (2 Cor 1:8).

So Paul was very distressed. Nevertheless he begins his letter with
the words, "Praise be to God!" Praise of God is more important to him
than anything else. He doesn't groan and complain, but offers praise and
thanks. Why? Just to utter the words, "Father of our Lord Jesus Christ"
filled Paul's heart with praise and thanks. What more could he ask for?
When he thought of God who sent Christ, his soul was at peace; all storm
clouds and all distress were swept away. God gave the greatest and highest
gift imaginable—his Son, Jesus Christ. He did not send him merely as a
prophet, as a Moses, a Samuel, or a David, but as the Most High. Jesus is
the very essence of God. His appearance on earth is unique. It is an actual

Editors' Note: This sermon is dated 1880.

visitation by God in person. Christ Jesus, God himself, has come into this poor, sinful world of ours.

Whoever reflects on this and keeps it clearly in mind will never be sad. It takes away all fear, however hard life is and continues to be. The Father of our Lord Jesus is comfort enough. Jesus who came into the world and gave up his life for us is enough reason for us to give praise and to be so greatly filled with thanks that we are unable to say anything more.

Do we give praise and thanks like this? Do we? Why not? Is it not because Christ Jesus is not uppermost in our minds and hearts as it was with Paul! But let us not forget this article of faith: Jesus Christ came from God, from the very being of God. If we really believed, grasping this with our whole being, then we would jump and leap triumphantly over "flames of fire." No tribulation would discourage us. Again and again these words would pour forth from our lips: "Praise be to God!"

How important it is that we believe. Unfortunately, so many people throw so much doubt on this important truth that we no longer believe in this reality. It is as if a "veil" had been thrown over faith. We argue back and forth: "Is it like this or like that?" "How should we interpret it?" "How is it to be understood?" Our hearts have become indifferent, as cold as a block of ice, even though we profess that God is the Father of our Lord Jesus Christ. Oh, if only we would learn to grasp these words with all our heart and soul: "Praise be to the God and Father of our Lord Jesus Christ!" Then, even in all our troubles, joy would triumph.

Paul also calls God, "the Father of compassion" and the "God of all comfort." God, against whom we have sinned, from whom the world is so far away, and whom we must fear as a holy judge and avenger of all evil, this God, through the sending of his Son, has become the founder and creator of every imaginable mercy. By sending Jesus Christ his Son to us, he became not the Father or God of judgment but the Father and God of mercies, the God of all comfort. Nothing but God's mercy pours down from above, and only goodness awaits us! Gleaming brightly before us is compassion and comfort for poor, sinful, suffering humanity. Hold firmly to this. Don't despair!

It is God who "comforts us in all our troubles," for his Son is our very comfort. Paul can say this not only because the sending of Jesus Christ is a comfort, but because God continues to send further comfort to us in our afflictions even now. We can deeply feel his love. We, as his children, already realize his comfort through the Holy Spirit, who Jesus called the Comforter.

We savor it through unexpected protections—through help and deliverance, which the apostle Paul himself experienced again and again. Each time Paul's life was in danger, he was rescued. When he saw no way out, suddenly a little door opened before him and he went safely through. When he felt greatly concerned about different church members, reports were sent to him about others who continued firm in faith, not giving way under troubles. Again and again comfort came to him through the Father. Paul lived between affliction and comfort, between comfort and trouble; this was the pattern of his life. Here is the wonderful thing: with those whom God loves there is no burden that is not also interwoven with smaller or greater comfort—more than any of us needs to survive.

And that, dear friends and precious souls, is how it is in the new covenant with those who glory in the Father of Jesus Christ. Now it all depends on your having eyes and ears and an awareness of comfort in affliction. How often we are discouraged because we are not aware of the many blessings that our God combines with our small troubles! If only we would open our eyes wider and carefully look around! If only we wouldn't see just the phantom of sadness but the angel of peace, the strength of comfort! These are the companions of the cross and suffering. When we learn to really see this, then I am sure that will be enough. Each of us has experienced how God's gracious hand is at work in our pain and distress. It is his very hand that keeps us from feeling lost. God always intervenes and in many small ways renews our courage. Again and again we experience the goodness of our loving God, and this causes us to exclaim, "Behold the goodness of God shines forth!"

Notice how Paul exclaims, "Praise be to God!" He didn't necessarily always receive tangible help, but he always received comfort. Oh, what fools we are! We don't want to praise God until we are released from our troubles. But troubles don't harm us. No, they can even help us. We will never praise God when we think like this. Remember, when we receive comfort we receive help. It's the same whether we receive help, or comfort. God's comfort is immeasurably great; it is all the help we really need. That is why we offer praise and thanks. I suppose it would make you happy if I said to you, "The Lord will take away all your pain." But no one can promise this. But, I can tell you this—you will be comforted, whatever your pain; we are promised help from God. So have courage and bless the Lord. Keep on fighting until you encounter Jesus.

One would think that Paul, an apostle with such tremendous tasks, would remain free from troubles. Didn't he deserve a better life? Why did he, a faithful witness to the gospel, have to suffer so much? Why? Because, as he says, "So that we can comfort others." I have often been told by unhappy, unbelieving people whom I have tried to help, "It's easy for you to talk of comfort—you haven't experienced what I have had to put up with." (People are not even right about this. I have also passed through the fire.) But nobody could have said this to Paul. Why? Because he bore the sign of the cross of Jesus. If Paul gave comfort to a person, everybody would know that he really had the right to do this and that it should be accepted. Thus he says, "so that we can comfort those in any trouble." He also says, "I was comforted. Now, please accept my comfort." Right in the middle of his troubles he says, "Praise be to God!" Doesn't this make us all want to join in this comfort? Yes, praise be to God!

Whatever the trial, Paul stood firm. And so he urges us to let ourselves be comforted. Those who are called to offer comfort are also the very ones who have suffered. It's no wonder Paul had such a hard time. Oh, you dear ones, each one of you may be called to give comfort! Therefore, endure your troubles, and then you will be able to comfort others—the miserable, the sad—because you have also suffered. When trouble comes to you, don't lose heart. Hold firm! Allow yourself to be comforted in the middle of misfortune so that you can say, "Praise be to God!" Whoever wants to be a genuine disciple of Christ must allow themselves to be comforted, they must allow the comfort of God to overpower them so that they in return are able to comfort others.

Well, I think that we have learned something this evening. Oh, may it remain with us and may we never forget it! Amen.

The Lord: A God of Judgment

For the LORD is a God of judgment:
blessed are all they that wait for him.

—ISAIAH 30:18 (KJV)

The God of Israel, who is for us the Father of our Lord Jesus Christ, foresaw a time when he would allow grace, mercy, and pure compassion to come among us. For this reason our verse begins with the words, "Therefore the Lord waits to be gracious to you; therefore he will rise up to show you mercy" (Isa 30:18). The Lord waits, just as we wait. Why does he wait instead of coming right now? Why doesn't he immediately carry out what his heart longs for—what we too long for, we who languish and sigh in the midst of so much distress and affliction? The answer is in the words, "For the Lord is a God of judgment." Because of our sin and unfaithfulness, everything, even his grace, must pass through judgment. We have become so unfaithful that the Lord cannot ignore it. Just think of the people of Israel to whom the Lord is now speaking and of how many, many times they grieved God. The prophet Isaiah had to write it on a tablet. "These are rebellious people, deceitful children, children unwilling to listen to the Lord's instruction" (Isa 30:9). Certainly there were exceptions, but his people were one flock. Israel had to go through judgment before the Lord could send them help.

It is like this with us as well. We too easily assume, "The Savior has borne our sins." But let me remind you that if we go on sinning we cannot simply expect mercy from the Savior. So don't be surprised that the world

Editors' Note: This sermon is dated 1875.

has to go through great judgment; that God's grace, his mercy, are not just freely given to us. Even so, realize that the Lord, even if he is the God of judgment, does not bring on us destruction, but a judgment to prepare the ground for his grace and mercy, to make everything smooth for the coming of his grace and mercy. Let us not be alarmed, therefore, if God judges us. His judgment is not our ruin. If we accept it and humble ourselves under it, God will lead us to his unlimited grace and compassion where our sins are forgiven. "Comfort my people," says our God. "Comfort them! Encourage the people of Jerusalem. Tell them they have suffered long enough and their sins are now forgiven. I have punished them in full for all their sins" (Isa 40:1–2).

We are told, "Blessed are all they that wait for him." You need not be daunted by any judgment. Be faithful, and you will see that God's judgment leads to salvation. Even in our greatest trouble, when we see only judgment, we must wait for his final grace, the final mercy—the great final mercy. We can do this because God himself waits—he waits impatiently for the moment when he is able, at last, to be gracious and have mercy upon us all.

O Lord, break powerfully into our midst, if only this may at last bring grace and mercy! You will surely bring it! God, you cannot break your word! Amen.

God's Goodness

Give thanks to the LORD of hosts, for the LORD is good, his steadfast love endures forever!

—JEREMIAH 33:11 (NRSV)

G ive thanks to the Lord and you will experience his grace and goodness. Although hostile powers have scattered adversity and sin among us, although we are corrupt in our nature, our bodies, in our whole life, although we act repulsively, God's goodness still shines. He has the upper hand and will crush and break all the powers of the enemy. Therefore, we must thank the Lord Almighty, the Lord of hosts.

It would be very small minded to think that God stood alone and all by himself, aloof from the billions upon billions of human souls here on earth. He is the Lord Almighty, the Lord of hosts—that is, the Lord who does not stand alone. He commands great regiments and sends forth servants here and there to help us. He can call one to him and say, "You go to such a person," and to another, "You go to that one," and so forth. There can be one of his servants for each of us and however many he needs, there are more than sufficient. He has servants enough so that he can arrange everything to gain the great victory.

He is gracious, and with his help we can always glean something good from whatever faces us in life, even when so much that is not good is also present. It is his will to do good to us, and it is only our sin that hinders it. Our human will, which asserts itself, is the greatest sin, but it can and will be overcome. Even if God must allow this or that evil, one day it will be different. Death and sickness will be overcome and done away with, since their right to exist lasts only as long as sin is present. In the end, God will rule in and through and over all with his grace and his goodness. We can thus pray, "Deliver us from evil," for this actually means, "Do good to us for evermore." We can hope for the Lord of hosts to deliver us from evil right now, and the more we pray in a childlike way the more quickly our deliverance will come. That we may pray like this, with the absolute assurance of being heard, is something so very great that we can give thanks even now to the Lord. However much of wrongness and adversity there is, God's goodness wants to shine upon us again and again and, one day, it will prevail. All the powers of the enemy are even now being crushed and broken. Therefore we have no alternative but to thank the Lord, for he is good!

PART II
The People of God

———————

SECTION 1
THE CHURCH

The Great Flood of the Spirit

But now hear, O Jacob my servant, Israel whom I have chosen! Thus says the LORD who made you, who formed you in the womb and will help you: Do not fear, O Jacob my servant, Jeshurun whom I have chosen. For I will pour water on the thirsty land, and streams on the dry ground; I will pour my spirit upon your descendants, and my blessing on your offspring. They shall spring up like a green tamarisk, like willows by flowing streams. This one will say, "I am the LORD's," another will be called by the name of Jacob, yet another will write on the hand, "The LORD's," and adopt the name of Israel.

—ISAIAH 44:1–5 (NRSV)

Here the Lord talks with Jacob, with Israel—the people who are descended from Jacob, whose name is also Israel. The Lord speaks to him! This is not a mere figure of speech. It is really true that in Israel it was God who spoke, even if he spoke through his angels as his personal representatives, or prophets who were filled with his Spirit. When they spoke, it was just as though it were the Lord himself speaking, placing their own personality completely in the background. It is unheard of anywhere else in all of world history that God stoops to speak with his people. He does this having in mind all the people on earth. The people of Israel are but a small part of this.

Israel was called to be a servant of God—to be used by the Lord for his purpose—who will help all nations of the earth. Originally, when the Lord said "I have made and prepared you, I have chosen you," he was referring to

Editors' Note: This sermon is dated 1879.

the people of Israel. Since the appearance of Christ Jesus, however, everyone who believes in him belongs to this Israel, to his people. When we love the Son, the Father loves us, and we are allowed to claim all the wonderful and glorious things that were foretold for Israel. We have been chosen just as Jacob was, made and prepared like him; through baptism we are consecrated to the Lord, as Israel was through circumcision.

What does the Lord want to say to us now? We need to hear from him, so we ask, "What does he say?" We would all like to ask this, for what one usually hears on earth today is so very unsatisfying.

First, "Do not fear, O Jacob my servant, Jeshurun whom I have chosen." As God's people, we have to contend with fear and tribulation, just as Israel did. Those who belong to the Lord are often despised and slandered; their life gets attacked or ignored. But those who belong to God have to be true witnesses, especially to those who are far away from him. When we attempt this we will invariably confront many obstacles and dangers. The murderer from the beginning seeks to destroy everything we do. On that score, nothing has changed. Consequently, God's people keep living in fear and cower. For we know that if we dare to stand up against our everyday worldly way of life, we will have to risk our whole life—everything! As soon as we refuse to make any concession to the enemy, danger and oppression encroach upon us. Despite our hope that the Lord will be master over all nations, we are easily overcome with fear: "How can this be?" "What can we build on? We see only ruin before us." "What shall we do? Everything is falling to pieces—it's coming apart." Whether we raise or rest our heads, we fear that sooner or later everything will be lost.

And yet the Lord says, "Don't be afraid my servant Jacob, my beloved, whom I have chosen." When life seems so dim that we can no longer see anything to hold on to—don't worry! Things can quickly change—the Lord will intervene soon. Do not be afraid that all is lost or act in such a dejected and despairing way as though it were the end and the death of everything. No! "Do not fear, O Jacob my servant!" Why not? Because he, the Lord, wants to do something! As soon as we see that he wants to do something, then we are no longer afraid. Fear and worry rob us of sleep when we think that it is we who have to do something. But when we come to realize that he will take things in hand and that his people and servants need only serve, then there is no anxiety!

Second, what does God plan for his people? Just listen: "For I will pour water on the thirsty land, and streams on the dry ground; I will pour my spirit upon your descendants, and my blessing on your offspring."

There you have it! When everything is thirsty and dry, when all hope is lost and all life seems to fade away, when the world languishes and is parched, then refreshing rains fall from heaven. Water comes, first in drops, then increasing until streams overflow on the dry ground. When we read and hear this, we want to jump up and cry out, "What? God will let something come down to us from above? Shall water from above really come to us?" This gives us fresh courage.

On earth nothing more is left; everything is completely dried up. This changes when help comes from above. What God means when he says, "For I will pour water on the thirsty land, and streams on the dry ground" is seen in the following words: "I will pour my spirit upon your descendants, and my blessing on your offspring." What does this mean? It means that the Spirit of God is still to come. Israel had not yet possessed this Spirit, and it was not promised them for that particular moment. But it was to come upon his descendants, his offspring. In other words, "Be patient! You haven't experienced it yet, but your descendants will."

Now listen! We today must hope for this promise and put our trust in it. There is no other way to refresh thirsty people or revive the parched land than that God pours out his Spirit. Why don't we believe this? Is it because it is extraordinary and does not fit into the ordinary thinking of this world? Is it because it is completely beyond the realm of our experience, so new and radical? The apostles, however, certainly experienced it at Pentecost. If we compare this with how we live now—with how we think and feel and act today—we have to admit that all this is absolutely nothing when compared to what is promised to us. For this reason most of us can't grasp this mighty promise. Nevertheless, we must not make what is great smaller or think of it as smaller than it really is. No. The Spirit will come upon the descendants, upon the offspring of Israel, and thus upon the offspring of Christians—upon us! We must confidently wait for this.

To a small extent this was fulfilled at the time of the apostles, but for reasons that we cannot easily explain, this stream of the Spirit retreated. It is no longer present as it once was, but it must come again, and it will be fulfilled in even larger measure. God keeps his word. And we need this refreshing now, for we are a parched people—we are nearly dying of thirst. It is so sad to see how we are dying, both in body and in spirit. But because we need it, God will give it again. Here is his promise, "Fear not, Jacob! Your God knows what to do. He will send the great gift of God, the Holy Spirit, which comes from God and which will make the nature of all people divine, transforming all things."

Third, the impact of the Spirit of God will descend like a stream of life upon the thirsty and the parched. God's people, "shall spring up like a green tamarisk, like willows by flowing streams." Great changes take place as soon as God sends forth his Spirit: great things start to come to life again among those who believe in a childlike way. "This one will say, 'I am the LORD's,' another will be called by the name of Jacob, yet another will write on the hand, 'The LORD's,' and adopt the name of Israel." Children of Israel will rise up everywhere, as grass springs from the earth, until a new Israel will be created from all humanity. All the generations of people will be renewed with God's divine nature. We will be astonished by how quickly the Spirit of God can work among us all. People from all over the earth will gather from all sides, saying, "I also want to belong to the Lord! I also want to belong to the people of Jacob and to be called by the name of Israel!" Nobody will want to stay behind and be excluded from the blessings that flow to the people of God. Then the servants of God will receive the authority to say, "Yes, you belong to the Lord, you will also belong to God's Israel; it is also given to you. Just come!" Oh, what a wonderful time that will be when everyone, even those who are now involved in foolishness and perversity, is filled with only one thought: "How can we enter the realm of grace with the blessings of God and be called by the name of Israel and Jacob!"

Yes, if this could only begin today! Isn't it possible in our poor, parched time? Our heavenly Father has been preparing us. Let us ask him to intervene with his power and to help our dying world. Come then, let the word from the mouth of God give us fresh courage and we will be confident and joyful, awaiting the hour promised to us!

Praised be his name! Amen.

Rejoice!

Rejoice, you nations, with his people.

—DEUTERONOMY 32:43 (NIV)

It is important to keep in mind that this verse refers to the people of
Israel, not the Gentiles. Gentiles were outside God's camp and so were
more exposed to wickedness and darkness than those within the camp of
God. Those outside the camp could not find hope in God; they were unable to achieve anything through their prayer and supplication. But not
so for God's people. The prayers and requests of those belonging to God
were answered, each according to their needs. How does this apply to us,
as Christians, as baptized people? Certainly, with the passing of time there
have emerged many differences among us. But if we refuse to believe and
live like a Gentile, then we stand outside; we are not within the camp of
God. Yet anyone who is baptized can count themselves as belonging to
God's people and can turn to him. Anyone who wants to belong to his
people can feel assured of God's grace and protection. Anyone who has
been brought by Jesus to the Father belongs to his people. They can pray to
God and call upon the Savior who forgives sins. Do we, or do we not, want
to rejoice with God's people? It depends entirely on us whether or not we
will receive our full rights as God's children.

Editors' Note: This sermon is dated 1880.

The People of God's Inheritance

But as for you, the Lord took you and brought you out of the iron-smelting furnace, out of Egypt, to be the people of his inheritance, as you now are.

—DEUTERONOMY 4:20 (NIV)

God calls Israel a people of his inheritance. This is because he wanted a people on the earth that was not at all occupied with the prince of this world. If only he could find a believing person, one who was somehow able to keep themselves free of the prince of this world, then he would have a place on earth to reside. God found this in Abraham and commanded him to go to Canaan. God chose this land, and the people to whom he gave it became "his people." Israel, as God's chosen, received Canaan, which God wrested away from the prince of this world. In Canaan, a land made holy by God, there was to be no idolatry. In this way it would be different from all the other nations. This land was holy, to be God's very own. God laid claim to it again and again on behalf of Israel, even when they defiled it and turned to pagan practices. For this reason there were times when Israel had to leave the land, like during the Babylonian exile.

Since the time of Christ, however, Canaan is no longer the only land made holy by God. Now the whole earth belongs to God. The prince of this world is being cast out. The holy land is now wherever the children of God gather together and pray to the true God and to Jesus Christ whom he has sent. All humanity now belongs to God, bought with the blood of Christ. The entire earth has now become the Lord's. God's people, his inheritance, need not return to Canaan. God, who once was only known in Israel, now makes himself known everywhere through his people. With the angels we now sing, "Holy, holy, holy, is the LORD of hosts; the whole earth is full of his glory" (Isa 6:3). Every land is now made worthy of the glory of God. Jesus spoke of this to his disciples when he said, "Blessed are the meek, for they shall inherit the earth." The whole earth is the Lord's, and one day his people with inherit it. Let us therefore hold firmly to God and to the One whom he sent. Make the whole earth a land for God—a place that truly belongs to his people. He will then surely be recognized everywhere, in his full divine majesty.

The Little Flock

Do not be afraid, little flock, for it is your Father's good pleasure to give you the kingdom.

—LUKE 12:32 (NRSV)

The Savior is speaking to his disciples who were appointed to go out into the whole world and preach the good news to all creation. He told them not to be anxious about their life, their food, or their clothing. They would suffer poverty and thus would have to exercise their faith, even for their smallest needs. These words can serve as a real comfort to those servants of the gospel who are especially outwardly hard pressed.

The Lord also addresses his disciples as the small and insignificant flock. Even so, their vocation is a great one—one that will change the whole world into a kingdom of God. How can this be? How can a handful of people ever be in a position to fulfill such a great task? When one looks at the world, it is easy to become despondent and discouraged! But the Savior tells his disciples, and this applies to us too, not to fear. Instead, he points them to God's good pleasure, to his well-pleasing counsel. He will give them the kingdom of God. The Father himself will be the One who gives it to them. The word, "Seek first the kingdom of God," means that the kingdom of God will come. Followers of Christ must turn all their thoughts toward this so that it comes quickly. If they do this, they will lack nothing. God will meet their needs without fail. The Savior told his disciples, "I confer on you, just as my Father has conferred on me, a kingdom" (Luke 22:29). The kingdom was appointed for the Son before his ascension, although it never came

Editors' Note: This sermon is dated 1876.

about. Now Jesus' disciples are appointed to deliver the kingdom into his hands through their work and their struggles. What a joyful task! Through his help, Jesus' disciples are to bring to him that which is already his; that which he bought with his blood!

We must be careful not to misinterpret what Jesus is saying. It is easy to think that by "little flock" Jesus means that only a very few will inherit God's kingdom. We may also mistakenly think that the kingdom of God concerns only their salvation. But this is not what Jesus meant. No. It will be hard for Christ's followers to bring about God's kingdom. Many people in the world seek to remain distant, even hostile toward them. Even so, his disciples are meant to win the kingdom of God for all people.

In the meantime, it is often the case that only a little active flock remains; so all the more each one of us must work and struggle. Then we can be part of the flock of workers who conquer the kingdom for the Lord. The first disciples did not accomplish this, but when it finally is concluded, we will see that it is our Father who has granted it. Even today, our work, our word, our struggle are the means by which this can be brought about. It will come only with the help of God's Spirit and with those who want to carry it on. What?! Don't you want to belong to this active little flock? Oh ,that our feet were better fitted with the readiness to proclaim the gospel of peace! (Eph 6:15). Amen.

The Strength of the Church

No one shall be able to stand against you all the days of your life. As I was with Moses, so I will be with you; I will not fail you or forsake you.

—Joshua 1:5 (NRSV)

God promised Joshua that no power, no enemy, would be able to defeat him as he entered the land of Canaan. Joshua depended on this. He had no need to measure his strength against that of the enemy for victory was always on his side. That is, on God's side!

Now we who are disciples of Jesus can also become conquerors, just as Joshua was. We belong to the little flock of whom the Savior speaks: "No one shall be able to stand against you all the days of your life." The Savior says, "Fear not, you little flock. It is your Father's good pleasure to give you the kingdom." However, if we stand on the side, if we refuse to belong to this flock, then any enemy can attack us. Who knows what manner of evil may befall us—we can even be completely put to flight. We can only be victorious if we are fully part of the flock—the flock that gathers around none other than the great Joshua, Jesus Christ.

Whoever strives toward the kingdom of God, in and through Jesus, belongs to the people of God. As the land of Canaan was granted to the people of Israel, so the kingdom of Christ is granted to us. Therefore, we need to fear no enemy; we will be victorious through faith in Christ Jesus. When we have this faith, enemies cannot overpower us either from within or without. As the apostle John expresses it: "And this is the victory that conquers the world, our faith" (1 John 5:4). When we have this faith we have the living God. With this faith we also have Jesus to whom all author-ity is given in heaven and on earth. And with this faith we already have Christ's victory.

It is a defeat if we do not believe this, but a victory when we do believe. When we believe we are certain, "Jesus is victor!" That is what should fill our hearts even if the enemy pursues us. His hand leads to victory every-where. For our Savior promises, "I am with you always and will lead you to victory." This makes us secure, and it enables us to go on toward the goal. The Lord Jesus will rule all things. What joy will be ours after all our struggles and tribulations!

Love for Jesus

Those who love me will be loved by my Father, and I will love them and reveal myself to them.

—John 14:21 (NRSV)

When the Savior asked Peter "Do you love me?" he also said, "Feed my sheep." We must never think of the Lord as somehow being apart from his sheep and lambs. In other words, we cannot love God without loving his sheep. If we distance ourselves from his sheep, we do not love Jesus for his sake, but for our own; we fail to consider what is most precious to him. We who want to love Christ will do all we can to care for his sheep. Jesus became the sacrifice for the sin of the whole world. Because of his shed blood, the Redeemer and the redeemed became one. Therefore, if we want to love Jesus, we must love the whole Jesus, that is, Jesus together with his sheep. Jesus would rather recognize those as his own who, without knowing him, care for his sheep, than recognize those who say they know and love him but care nothing about his sheep. This is how God's glory will be revealed, when we show a keen striving and eagerness for the salvation of all people. May the Lord give us wisdom so we are found to be his true and wholehearted followers!

Editors' Note: This sermon is dated 1873.

The Saints—The Faithful

Oh, love the LORD, all you His saints.
For the LORD preserves the faithful.

    —PSALM 31:23 (NKJV)

Those who believe are the faithful, and the faithful are those who believe. They are called the servants of God because they are his chosen ones, those near to him, those for whom he has a special regard, friends taken out from all the people. He protects them. This is because they put all their trust in God. As soon as they become lax in this, they distance themselves from the Lord. They separate themselves from him and become independent. It's as if they try to do everything in their own strength. When this happens, we are no longer faithful. Those who trust in him always acknowledge him; they are his friends. God draws them close to his heart; they are his saints and chosen ones.

Not all of those who are now called believers belong to the saints. For among them there are many who are independent; they are not in fellowship with the Lord. There are many who believe only in doctrine. These, however, are not true believers. Belief in doctrine does not mean that one is a new person, or that one belongs to God. Nor does belief by itself ensure God's protection. If we want to belong to God, then we must have a childlike trust in him and show him unreserved obedience. Then the Lord will be able to protect us—not just today, but every day of our life.

To trustingly obey the Lord means to love him. It means to find our contentment in him, even when what he does is not always what we want. It demands that we love him, even when his ways seem puzzling and incomprehensible. It isn't worth much to say you love the Lord as long as he only does good to you, allowing you to succeed in everything and granting your every request. We must love him as the One who always acts rightly. Even when we are irritated, annoyed, or discouraged, we should love him and all the more so. Those who love the Lord can always be recognized by whether they grumble or not, whether they lose heart and give up hope or not, or become fretful. When one is his servant, the love of the Lord gives us strength, even when the darkest and most puzzling things happen.

Let us hold firmly to him! It can do us no harm. We have to trust in God's almighty power, especially when all seems lost and dark. This is precisely the time to hope and expect the reclaiming of all that has been lost in this world that is falling apart. This is the time to hold firmly to him. If we do, then we will be particularly near to God's heart.

Use Your Gifts for Others

Just as each one has received a gift, use it to serve one another as good stewards of the varied grace of God.

—1 PETER 4:10 (NET)

In the early church everyone had a place where he or she could serve; each person was helpful. All the believers, the simple as well as the more gifted, could serve others. God gave each one "gifts" to build up the community. No one was neglected; everyone was appreciated.

Of course, faithful stewardship was required of each one. This is what our quote from Peter's letter is pointing to. We are to be completely useful by serving one another. We are to use whatever gifts we possess to prove our faithfulness. We must never stand outside the circle with folded arms, criticizing, gossiping and judging, shaking our heads over all we see and hear, especially toward those who have been delegated with special responsibility. No, we are to help wherever we see a need. We are to serve wherever we can and as much as we are able.

We don't have, certainly, the same gifts as the first Christians, but still much is given to us. God still enables us to assist all those around us as the occasion arises, through instruction, admonishment, and warning, through visiting, by cheerful encouragement, or by help through word and deed. Unfortunately most of us act quite differently. If we are not entirely indifferent, then we like to be the clever ones, ready to give our disparaging opinion about this or that. We organize, complain, debate about what is wrong, but without ever personally doing anything to improve the situation. Few

Editors' Note: This sermon is dated 1874.

of us really want to serve or help others. We would rather leave it to others or to the minister to get things done.

Christian organizations of every sort now serve the needs of many and do it very commendably. However, the spiritual care of individuals by other individuals—actually serving one another according to the instructions of the apostle—is almost completely missing in the world. "Good stewards of the varied grace of God" are hardly known, except among those who are active in the ministry. It occurs to very few of us that we too, each one of us, must help out and serve. Those who withdraw from the church are especially quick to criticize and argue. "Now you can see," they say, "the church accomplishes nothing and is under a curse." How can things ever improve if the "better ones," those who have received gifts to serve others, band together against the rest, instead of placing themselves at the service of the whole? The life of the church, yes, the whole church depends upon whether we all learn to serve one another fully, in every way. The future of our wicked, corrupt world depends on whether we band together and use our gifts to serve.

Oh, that we might be more like those first zealous, God-fearing, and humble helpers in the church! Can this still happen today? Hardly, I fear, unless the Lord once again pours out his Spirit. Let us hope for this, for a time of grace in which we Christians become more active and caring for one another. Amen.

May They Be One

I have given them the glory that you gave me, that they may be one as we are one—I in them and you in me—so that they may be brought to complete unity. Then the world will know that you sent me and have loved them even as you have loved me.

—JOHN 17:22–23 (NIV)

O n the way to the Garden of Gethsemane the Savior prays. He prays to his Father expressing how much he longs that his disciples may be one, just as he and his Father are one—perfectly united so that absolutely nothing divides them from one another.

How could disunity among Jesus' followers be in accordance with the unity between the Son and the Father? Can the Father and the Son stand back and watch while those who claim to be disciples separate themselves into groups, exclude and repudiate one another, settle down into their own cliques, and then stand before them expecting to be regarded equally? How is this possible? How can some disciples act in one way and others in another, and both sides say, "We are the ones—we have the right way; these others are not the ones. They do not have it!"?

What does it mean if here on earth Jesus' disciples are persistently disunited, each having their own opinions? The Savior is expected to settle this—judging one right and the other wrong, although such bigotry is reason enough for him to think that none of them can be used by him, because none of them have taken any notice of Jesus' most ardent wish that they be

Editors' Note: This sermon is dated 1874.

united as one. This is the great grievance of our time! Is it to remain like this until the Lord returns?

When Christ comes in triumph from heaven, after having united all the heavens, must he look on while people on earth elbow one another aside, putting themselves forward as if they were the most distinguished people? Must the Lord just look on while we good Christians see ourselves as so important, as if we were the only ones the Savior uses? How can we keep doing this? We have to stop this. Only then will the Lord come!

But will we ever change? Do we as Jesus' disciples really want to become one? We despair about how disunited the church is, and because we despair, we make a virtue out of this need. But what use is despair in the face of God and all the angels? It is utterly wrong to say that the sects especially are the core of God's people. I say, "This all has to change!" We must find a way where what you believe I believe and what I believe you believe. For the Lord says in his prayer, "I have given them the glory that you gave me, that they may be one as we are one." What is this glory given to him which he passed on to his disciples? It is the same glory he received while a man on earth, given to him when the Holy Spirit descended upon him like a dove. It was after this that he performed the miracles that made his glory known. Jesus emphatically promises to give his disciples the Holy Spirit: the Comforter, the guide to all truth, and the One who will unite them. Without this Spirit, they could not become one. This promise became reality. Right from the start this glory was given to the disciples, completely uniting them.

Now I ask, if the Holy Spirit would descend again today in order to unite us completely, would we embrace this gift from heaven? Do we recognize that there will never be unity so long as we rely upon our own human ingenuity and thoughts, relying on our own strength and doing what we think is best? Will we admit that it is only by this one Spirit from heaven, who was proclaimed and promised to us by Jesus, that true unity is ever going to be achieved?

Think about the words of our text. The world will only recognize that the Father sent Jesus and loves them if his disciples are one as Jesus and the Father are one. Nothing has brought greater discredit to the gospel than all the different denominations, sects, and divisions that we now have amongst us. We are rightly reproached; our cause has no value because we are so disunited.

But let us not give up hope. Let us imagine again how fresh an impression the gospel would quickly make through the gift of the Holy Spirit, when at once all our various denominations, sects, and divisions really believed and became united. If only we would drop all the differences that separate us! We would discover anew the love of Jesus. How wonderful it would be if all "isms" would suddenly cease among us and we would see that among all those who really believe, whatever their background, they are our brothers and sisters—all equally just and blessed through Jesus' blood.

Let us then cry out, "Lord, give us once more your Holy Spirit, the Comforter, and teacher of all truth. Make us one, even as you, Father, are one with the Son." Whether it is many or few who would cry out like this, the Lord will listen to them for the sake of the many and, perhaps very soon, he will send us the indispensable gift of the Holy Spirit.

God's Own People

But you are a chosen race, a royal priesthood, a holy nation, God's own people, that you may declare the wonderful deeds of him who called you out of darkness into his marvelous light. Once you were no people but now you are God's people; once you had not received mercy but now you have received mercy.

—1 PETER 2:9–10 (RSV)

One of the greatest things in this passage of Scripture is that not one individual tribe or one man in that tribe is God's priesthood, but that everyone who belongs to God's people belongs to his priesthood. Individually and collectively all of God's people can draw near to him and hear his Word. Access to him is open to all—each one who has priestly concerns to bring before the Lord can personally approach him at any time. It is written, "Let us then with confidence draw near to the throne of grace, that we may receive mercy and find grace to help in time of need" (Heb 4:16). At one time, only the high priest had direct access to God, but now every believer can come to God—we are "a holy nation, God's own people." We have become God's through the Savior. The Jews today can no longer lay claim that only they are the chosen race. Ultimately, only those who belong to Jesus can say this.* Before giving the commandments God said to Israel, "You must be a holy people for the LORD. Keep my commandments and you shall be a holy nation." This has always been God's will. We are to be God's own people, that we may declare the wonderful deeds of him

* Editors' Note: This is an unfortunate and typical expression of classical "supersessionism."

88

who called us out of darkness into his marvelous light (Col 1:13). We must become a holy nation. It must become reality.

By keeping God's commandments we show that we are his people. If our actions do not reflect or proclaim the wonderful deeds of God, we are not members of Christ's kingdom nor are we God's people. The commandments of God remain. From now on God must be honestly represented among his people. Merely believing with the head, without also proclaiming the wonderful deeds of God in our actions, does not make us members of Christ's kingdom, nor does it make us God's own people. If we are his children, then we must represent our Father with our whole life. We must set aside the failings that have marked us up to this time. Only then can we be said to be "the chosen race, the royal priesthood." To want the name only is nothing but a lie. No! The image of God must be renewed in us and only then will we, by our deeds, become God's own people.

Therefore, let us do everything we can so that God will see in us the reflection of how holy, just and compassionate, patient, gracious, and true he is. God, who has called us, must have us as his personal representatives. How highly then we would be regarded. By this we are his people. Oh, that we might really understand and practice Christ's message. May the Lord help us so that in everything we do we may resemble our compassionate and beloved Savior. Let us give ourselves faithfully and wholly to the Lord so he is truly pleased with us.

The Bride

Hear, O daughter, consider and incline your ear; forget your people
and your father's house; and the king will desire your beauty. Since he
is your LORD, bow to him.

—PSALM 45:10–11 (NRSV)

The bride spoken of here is the church here on earth. She should allow
herself to be instructed, she should open her eyes and ears to hear and
understand the Lord, who wishes to speak with her, to reveal himself to her,
and to bring honor to her. She is to forget her father and her father's house,
that is, leave behind the world and its corruption, leave behind completely
all that is perverse so that she no longer appears as a child of this degener-
ate age. She must leave everything, and if necessary leave father, mother,
brother, sister, just for the sake of belonging to the Lord alone. If she does
this, then there will be "beauty" in her. This delights the king, her Lord; he
has pleasure in her and considers her worthy of him. When she has cast off
all the filth of the world and submerged herself in that which is godly and
heavenly, then the Lord will enter with her into eternal joy.

The One to whom she is to belong is the Lord, whom she must follow
in all things, whose commandments she must accept, placing him above
all else. She must worship him as the One from whom she will receive all
things. She must turn to the Lord again and again, entreating him and pay-
ing homage to him and him alone. Then she will be the daughter, the bride,
the church of the Lord. Everyone who hears this and obeys will prosper.
They will indeed receive the highest that the Lord has promised to give us.

SECTION 2
THE POVERTY
OF THE CHURCH

Be Sober and Awake!

So then let us not fall asleep as others do, but let us keep awake and be sober; for those who sleep sleep at night, and those who get drunk are drunk at night. But since we belong to the day, let us be sober, and put on the breastplate of faith and love, and for a helmet the hope of salvation.

—1 Thessalonians 5:6–8 (NRSV)

Dear friends in Christ Jesus, today we celebrate our yearly festival of the Reformation in which we commemorate the great blessing that the Lord conferred on Christendom three hundred years ago, including our fatherland, enabling us to pierce through the rubble of gross ignorance and folly and to rediscover the shining light of the Gospels. Today, we are free, and we can reflect undisturbed on the salvation of our souls and strive for this. We can instruct our young people in this, where they can from their childhood on become familiar with the Holy Scriptures, the fount of all light. We can serve our Savior and trust him in life and death without being led astray under human pressure. For this great grace we can well devote a special day, and so we too want to show our thankfulness by resolving anew to use faithfully the good things given to us by the Lord so that we may not be accused on that day that we who were in the light nevertheless had walked in darkness.

So let us take a closer look at our text. Today, dear friends, we rejoice especially in the light that the Lord gave us with the Reformation. We rejoice in the knowledge of God's Word, which clearly places before our eyes

Editors' Note: This sermon is dated 1856.

God's will for salvation. We rejoice that we have a well-established basis that can easily lead us in all that we need for obtaining the eternal jewel. No longer do we feel pressed by a darkness forced upon us from without. We are free, and we can reflect undisturbed on the salvation of our souls and strive for this. But, in this freedom, the question is: Are we who stand in the light really awake and sober? Or do we act like sleepers and drunkards? This is a serious question.

A look at the Protestant Christianity of our day scarcely gives the impression that our social life is getting any better. In fact, a great deal of sleepiness, indifference, and unconcern delude thousands of people. Too many of us are not sober and thus stagger around. We waste away in indolence and dullness, like dumb brutes whose life passes by without their being able to think any kind of higher thought. Thus, so many of us Protestants go through life as if in a stupor. In our "freedom" we have tragically shaken ourselves free of everything—not only the yoke of human tyranny, but also the commands of God. We have made ourselves into the law-giver, like a god, with no thought of what the true God has made known to us through his Word and which should serve us as a guide to eternal life. We have pushed God and his Word aside. Too many of us are asleep, oblivious of our high calling, and therefore we have become a prey to the prince of darkness.

Dear friends, the Lord did not place us in the light of day so that we should regard day as night, doing as little by day as is usual at night, or even trying to make use of the day for carrying out the horrors of the night. Against this the present day is a powerful challenge: Rise up, you who sleep, so that you are not overcome by a darkness from which no arising is possible.

What are we to do? How are we to escape from our sleep and drunkenness? The apostle expresses it simply: "Put on the breastplate of faith and love, and for a helmet the hope of salvation." The Reformation tried to bring back to us these three things: faith, love, and hope. Life has become much brighter around us because of these three things, and whoever stands in faith, in love, and in hope and has put these on, stands in the light. But if we only voice these things, without really having them within us and upon us, we remain in the darkness, just as though we had never heard of faith, love, and hope. Oh, how essential it is that what we read in the Bible becomes a reality in our midst and not just something we know by rote! Let us therefore speak about these three things.

What then is the breastplate of faith, that is, the faith that serves as a breastplate, as armor against the attacks of darkness? We are well aware that it was chiefly Luther who brought to light the truth that we are saved by faith and not by the works of the law. This comes to the fore in all his writings. The whole structure of evangelical faith is built upon our trust in the living God, who redeems and saves us through undeserved grace, not because of any merit of ours, but through the meritorious work of Jesus Christ alone. We Protestants, especially, often hear this. But hearing is one thing, being awakened to faith is another. Thousands, even millions of Christians comprehend faith with their minds, but not with their hearts. Faith of the head and the mouth do not signify that we are in the light, that we are awake and sober. We must put on this faith so that it fills our whole being.

The faith demanded of us by the gospel is that we, as poor sinners, take refuge in the work of Jesus Christ, that we come to an end of ourselves and entrust ourselves completely to Christ. Yet so few of us reach out eagerly to the Savior, who alone can help. We hang onto our self-love, smugness, and self-justification; we never truly repent and in remorse break down under our sin. Yet we go right on to church and profess that faith brings salvation! No greater harm is caused than by the presence of so many with such a pretended faith.

But, dear friends, if we want to be awake, if we want to be sober, we must be convinced that above everything else, there is nothing good in us—that in our sin we continue to inflict grave sorrow on the Lord. God cannot use us in his kingdom as long as we refuse to feel the full burden of our sin, and thus our own unworthiness. God's compassion cannot truly be grasped until we have felt the unhappiness of being without it. We need once again to humble ourselves. Only by becoming poor in spirit, by bearing suffering in meekness, hungering and thirsting after righteousness, can we walk in the light. As long as we stand impudently before God without any spiritual effort on our part, just wanting to take to ourselves the saving gift of Christ without more ado, then on the final day we will most surely be found wanting.

Let us remember that true faith stems from a contrite heart; it is the conviction that we are absolutely and completely nothing. Let us cease deluding ourselves. Faith is a fight—a fight to live a life based on complete trust, so that all we are and do is penetrated by the vision directed upward. That vision compels us to live our lives in a way that shows that we have a God who delivers us from sin, death, and corruption.

How can we say that we have faith if we think that trusting in a Savior for all our needs is impossible? Do we truly act and believe that God hears our prayers? What then is our faith if we cannot expect something from it, if we cannot trust that God will hear and give us what we ask him? What a heavy burden of guilt we Protestant Christians bear, we who boast of faith, but a faith that, when one looks at it more closely, has nothing to do with experiencing the presence of the living God. Mere intellectual wisdom is not faith. But how much more we could expect and hope for if our faith was truly living!

What about the breastplate of love? The situation is, if anything, even sorrier when we ask: "Have we put on the breastplate of love?" At the beginning of the Reformation what stood out was the conviction that the love of the first Christians had returned. There was noticeable evidence of a devoted love, the like of which had been known only in the time of the apostles. A heartfelt union of all those who had been penetrated by the new light was once again seen; and one can well say that it was just this love that offered the best proof that a ray of compassion had come down from above.

But all too soon things changed—indeed, in two ways. First, in daily life. For where is that special love amongst us today? Today there is a lot of talk about love, and scarcely a Sunday goes by without our hearing a great deal of preaching about love. But where is it? Where is the love that is not irritable or resentful, harms no one, but will rather suffer wrong than do wrong, despises nobody, but humbles itself for the sake of the others, that forgets itself and has regard for others? Do we Protestant Christians distinguish ourselves by this love so that when others meet us they are able to say, "Truly, it is not like this amongst us! We are amazed at how they love one another and bear patiently with one another and no quarrelling is heard; discord is unknown. It's as if heaven has come down to earth!"

Are onlookers today inspired by the "love" we Protestants have for one another? To be sure, there are individual circles where heartfelt love prevails, but on the whole where can we find the love that should distinguish us? Dear friends, in this we must humble ourselves and remember that although we know full well what belongs to love, nevertheless there is so little of it to be seen. How can we claim to be in the light and how can we say we are sober when we wound and hurt one another, when we wrong, rob, and abuse one another? Is that being a Christian? Oh, that our merciful God would remind us of our obligation and of the great frailties that lie within our daily and social life!

And there is still another way in which we fail in love. How much bickering, envy, anger, enmity, hatred, even deadly hatred is there among us Christians—especially among just those who want to differentiate themselves from the so-called world. It has gone so far that in some places a person is not reckoned a good Christian unless he continually rants and raves, unless he flies into a passion about something and brandishes a sword against those who think differently on this or that issue. It has gone so far that a difference over even one small point brings about a mutual exclusion of one another. We can see no way out as to how things can ever be different, for the longer it goes on, the worse it gets. One faction after another arises, claiming, "We are the ones! We alone are right!" And in this way they cast all others from their hearts, regarding as enemies anyone who does not go along with them. How much quarrelling, hate, envy, and rage there is just because of some so-called points of faith! Instead of exhorting one another continuously—at least not to depart from love—just the opposite is the case, and we think that for the sake of God's honor it is all right to hate one another. This has happened a thousand times in our church.

We plainly do not wear the breastplate of love and should deplore the fact that we fall so far short of what the Lord so urgently wanted when he said, "A new commandment I give to you, that you love one another." Therefore, guard yourselves against any and every factional spirit! As soon as we are filled with a zeal that wounds, offends, and repudiates other souls, surely and truly evil is at work. It is part of a satanic spirit that wants to divide and destroy us. It hates nothing more than those who have a Savior and want to unite with one another, because it knows that this is an impervious power against the prince of darkness.

We must grieve, however, that we lack such a power. Ah! If we do not come more into the light and become sober, what can the Lord do with us? He can only accept into his kingdom hearts that are full of love, compassion, mercy, gentleness, and patience. This also shows that our faith does not rest on a proper foundation, for if our faith had grown out of a genuine repentance, which recognizes that we are nothing and have deserved only death and hell, then lovelessness could not be the fruit of this faith, and hatred and conflict could not be its consequence. For those who do not know love are in the dark; they deceive themselves no matter what they think they have. Without love nothing is of any use. "Though I speak with the tongues of men and of angels, but have not love, I have become sounding brass or a clanging cymbal. And though I have the gift of prophecy, and understand all mysteries and all knowledge, and though I have all faith, so that I could remove mountains, but have not love, I am nothing. And though I bestow all my goods to feed the poor, and though I give my body to be burned, but have not love, it profits me nothing" (1 Cor 13:1–3).

Let us guard then against the loveless spirit of partisanship and learn to treasure each other and to treasure especially anyone who has any regard at all for the beloved Savior. It is the saddest thing to see people who claim to love Christ cast each other out because they do not agree on every particular thing; they should thank God if even a trace of faith in Jesus is present. Therefore let us keep awake and be sober. Let us seek in every way we know how to stand in the love that one day will be the sole test of our faith!

Finally, there is the helmet of the hope of salvation. It belongs with faith and love, and without it we cannot stand in the light. But here too, my friends, the actual New Testament understanding of hope is something that almost everyone has forgotten. What is this hope? It is nothing other than the expectation of Christ's coming, through which everything will be put right. Our hope is that Christ Jesus will at last become Lord, that he will conquer all his foes, and then come again to lead his people into his kingdom, whether they are alive or dead. The hope of the New Testament refers to the expectation of the end of all things when all things will be brought into harmony, when all pain ceases, all mysteries are revealed, and the fullness of God's mercy in Christ Jesus will unfold over all creation. This will be revealed to the children of God when the groans of all creation are quieted. The "hope of salvation" is not just the hope for life after death. No, it means the final deliverance of all groaning creation from its torments and need, its misery and distress.

But as a church today do we possess such a hope? How does the Protestant church of today view a hope such as we have just described? Ah, how self-seeking and egotistic our hope is! Most Christians think very little about anything other than that which concerns them, and them alone; they are not concerned about any other hope. Who today truly cares about the whole of humankind, the whole creation? So much is about how "I" may be saved—"I," "I," and nobody else but "I!" But how unchristian this is! The Reformers never thought this way! No. They strove to see that entire nations might be snatched from the fetters of darkness. Let us remember how large hearted Luther was, how he sent epistles in all directions and cried daily to God that he might bless his whole gospel. The spirit that extends to all humanity, which inspired the Reformers, can be seen in so few people today! So many Christians know of no other hope than that of working for forty to fifty years and then lying down and dying peacefully.

Ah, that we might be more zealous, but zealous for all. We need to be filled anew; our hope needs to be gripped more and more so that the arm of Jesus can clear the way for the deliverance of all creation and the conquest of the satanic powers, until at last comes the great refreshment of his countenance. If we do not have this hope, then we are not in the light. How deadly dull it is if this goal is not before our eyes! Generations come and generations go, and each generation has to struggle through the same battle, with Satan on top and Christ below. We, however, would not be sober if, on looking at our children, we thought of nothing but: Ah, now they must wade through all this and see how they may be saved—one after the other—and so it goes from generation to generation! Whoever does not have real hope lives inebriated and is not in the light, for if there is to be light, there must be light over everything.

Believe me, nothing will be right in the church until we Christians are wholly filled with this hope. For with such hope we would naturally reach out more to the One who has gifts to give to humankind. We would also pray more and in so doing draw further divine powers down to our poor, groaning world. Instead, we too easily allow everything to waste away miserably, convincing ourselves that this is how it has to be.

Just imagine if we had this hope! Why, we would also be able to cast a loving glance in the direction of other denominations with the thought: Be of good courage! When the Lord really does burst forth upon us, we will all experience that there is no other salvation except in the name of Jesus. Oh, may the Lord shed more light upon us. May he help us to become the children of light, never again asleep, but people who stay awake with eyes that survey the whole world and remain sober until the end. Amen.

Concerning the Pitiful State
of the Church

From the ends of the earth we hear singing: "Glory to the Righteous One." But I said, "I waste away, I waste away! Woe is me! The treacherous betray! With treachery the treacherous betray!"

—ISAIAH 24:16 (NIV)

These words call us to lament. God's people, to whom God has revealed himself, bemoan their barren condition, while ever and again from afar can be heard songs of praise to the glory of the Righteous One. They complain that many treacherous ones are in their midst who even mock and despise the holy of holies instead of rejoicing and giving praise and thanks because of it. Now doesn't this apply to us today, dear friends? Truly, there is probably no one here who did not think right away—yes, that applies to our day! It should not be the concern of just the individual congregation when a place of worship is dedicated, although it is chiefly they who should remember that a house of God is given them wherein the Word of God will be proclaimed. But all the churches are linked together, and if they all collapsed, would ours alone remain standing? Or if the entire Protestant church, even the whole of Christendom, were destroyed—which will never happen—would we be the only ones standing? We celebrate a Christian festival today because a church has been founded that will stretch out her arms to all corners of the earth and in which one congregation will always support and care for the other. We celebrate because in every parish where

Editors' Note: This sermon is dated 1846. The sermon was delivered at the dedication service of a new church.

Christianity flourishes, there stands a church and a preacher, and many services for worship are held. Today, therefore, I want to take a general look into the nature and condition of this Christian church of which we are a part.

In a larger context, let us think of Christianity, or our fatherland, or of our Protestant church, as one single person. In what frame of mind are we—happy or sad? Do we give praise and thanks, or do we complain and sigh? We should soon be clear about this and know where we stand.

Yes, we can be thankful that God's Word is still being proclaimed, but we also need to grieve that things are not so well in the Christian church. Nowadays we hear all kinds of songs of praise from the ends of the earth and hear many stories of what God is doing around the world, in far distant places. People everywhere are hearing the gospel, people who until now have known nothing or very little of Christ. In some places they come running with joy and do not know how to be sufficiently grateful for the message of salvation that has been brought to them. And there are even many old churches that are being reawakened. [. . .] Songs of praise can be heard everywhere, and their sounds are loud enough for us to rejoice in them, from however far they come.

But how are things with us? What is the matter with us? Has there ever been a time that has given rise to so many shameless despisers of the divine truth as ours? Soon it will even be a disgrace to believe in simple Christianity. A note of contempt, both from the wise and scholarly as well as from the working classes, can be heard today. It has become the fashion to think that Christianity is entirely insignificant and irrelevant to practical matters of life. Oh yes, there are little circles here and there that are sincere. But they are few and far between. But the Christian church has by and large become utterly feeble. [. . .] We think that we are rich and have become well satisfied. But, as it says in John's Revelation, we do not know how wretched, pitiable, poor, blind, and naked we are (Rev 3:17). At a church dedication, aside from gratefulness for the great things that the Lord has done, has not each one of us cause to sigh, "How pitiable I am! How constantly in need I am!" Today, dear ones, it is especially important for each one of us to examine ourselves. We have to see how guilty and barren we have become. It is just on account of this guilt that people see so little that is genuine and powerful amongst us who profess to be Christ's followers. No wonder this provokes so many taunts and sneers and such contempt. It is just as the text says: because things are so pitiful, the treacherous ones gain the upper hand, aspiring higher and higher, and finally appear to destroy everything completely.

We need to see how impoverished our Christianity has become and why each one of us has to recognize how very small our concerns are. We must, of course, differentiate here, since we are not all alike, although we cannot now emphasize these differences. However, I would like to ask that each one modifies what is now said to fit his own situation, and then perhaps all will note that in nearly all of the points to be touched upon, there is a great deal of wretchedness to be found among all of us, some especially in regard to one point, others in another, and many in all points. We ask then: Why has our Christianity become so barren? There are two things that stand out. First, we have so little understanding. Second, so little power. Let us, in turn, explore these further. In these two points—understanding and power—the church of God today is lacking in every respect. Because of this, things look so miserable, wretched, and pitiful that we can hardly believe any longer that the Word is what it claims to be.

O Lord our Savior, for that which is now to be brought before us, we ask that you give us understanding and that we take it to heart. And let us grasp deep within our true wretchedness, and let each in his own way learn to do what is necessary at this critical hour. Amen.

1. I waste away! Thus speaks the church in the words of our text. We will first examine more closely to what extent there is so little understanding and discernment among Christians. So very much comes to my mind in this connection that I just do not know where to begin or where to go on or where to stop. It would be necessary to speak shortly about everything that belongs to Christianity in order to show how ignorance has come to prevail everywhere. I will try to do this as succinctly as I can.

Firstly, how many of us truly know the Holy Scriptures? Most of us only have a superficial knowledge of God's Word. Granted, we have thousands of churches and preachers and books and church schools. But our children grow up, get married, dress up on Sunday, and twice a year go to Holy Communion. But what do they really know of Scripture? Do they know who the prophets are or the message of individual books? But the church rests on the treasure of God's Word. It is simply frightful to see the ignorance of so many Christians who nevertheless claim to believe in the Bible. We may have knowledge but remain ignorant.

We are so ignorant that we have fooled ourselves into believing that holding onto certain forms and practices is sufficient for being a Christian.

I don't need to discuss this. We go to church, come in, sit down, and leave when the service is ended. But—we have been to church and are therefore devout people. Others partake of the holy Lord's Supper, but it doesn't occur to them that they must become changed people. We even go to prayer meetings, but neither we nor our circumstances change.

Nowadays many complain about the lack of commitment to the church, and of course in many places church-going has declined. All too often one finds empty churches, although at Easter or Christmas they may be better attended. Many ways are sought on how church life can be improved, all kinds of suggestions are made, and people want to try—but how can this be tackled? All the while, people keep on clinging to external things; they imagine that if something attractive were offered from the pulpit or in some other way then everybody would come running, things would suddenly change. Dear souls, what is all this? Is this not the height of stupidity? How is satisfying peoples' need in such a superficial manner an answer? "If only the churches were filled!" What a farce! It is the most tragic thing to try to turn practical changes into spiritual answers.

Practical changes leave people just as they are. They have no more spiritual or moral discernment than before. [. . .] Think about it. Granted, the very crudest things are still considered immoral, although this too is changing, but how many thousands of matters come up in daily life that are never regarded in the light of being good or evil! Genuine discernment has been lost. There are countless things that come up in daily life regarding, for example, honesty, or compassion and respect, regarding impurity, even in marriage, that people simply ignore or turn a blind eye. Even in the court of law, where we so easily and unashamedly do a favor for someone by giving false witness.

People's conceptions of good and evil seem to be completely distorted. We no longer know how to distinguish between light and darkness. [. . .] Many, for instance, simply do not want to understand how it can be a sin to use and wear magical pieces of paper and then use God's name in various magic formulas.[*] They say, "But it is prayer!" We cannot shudder sufficiently at the horrors into which most people have plunged themselves. But we still have much to say. Certainly the Word of God has become passé, that Word which, if allowed to, strikes so piercingly upon the conscience. It is no wonder we have fallen into such a miserable state.

---

[*] Editors' Note: Blumhardt is referring here to folk magic practices that were widespread among his parishioners. See Zündel, *Johann Christoph Blumhardt*, 148.

This lack of discernment is further seen by how little we grasp God's judgments. We pass over them and never consider that here and there the chastening hand of God might be at work. When a fire breaks out, or a hailstorm destroys a whole harvest, or there is a crop failure, or if an epidemic, pestilence, or contagious disease occurs—without exception people never think that this might be a punishment from God; that it is a judgment carried out against us. [. . .] But it is not only these more universal acts of God—which in truth already cry out loud enough and which must perhaps increase in number until people finally realize that the Lord has spoken— but how many thousands of things do we encounter in the course of daily life, how much sickness, curable and incurable, how many ailments, how many thousands of such things are constantly taking place, and who stops to think of where they have incurred blame or been off track?

We no longer feel free to say that sin is the cause of this or that accident or sickness. However, if we look at the Bible and see how serious it is then there can be no doubt as to why the world is full of such misery. Unless we recognize what the Scriptures say, we cannot say that we have any true Christian understanding; we only persist in our ignorance and live as if there were no God in heaven. Because we no longer want divine justice, we have ceased to long to be converted from all that is contrary to the will of God. As such, we remain in our pitiful condition.

Our whole approach to faith has become twisted. [. . .] For example, many relish in the fact that, "Christ has broken the power of the devil, crushed the head of the serpent, judged the prince of this world, who is now just about done for, and therefore the devil has no longer any power." And then, without further ado, the existence of all powers of darkness is flatly denied. Somehow, all those who are subjected to the power of the devil are now suddenly rescued. Their problems can be explained in other ways, and thus they cease to have strength to fight. We no longer feel the need to fight because the Savior has already fought the battle. What nonsense! Is it any wonder that Satan gains ever more power in this world? Or then there are those who boldly profess that they are justified by faith, not by works. "I believe, therefore I am justified." They think that as long as they don't deny anything in the Bible and join with other believers in worship, then that's that. Simply by believing they think their sins are all forgiven. What a sham! This wonderful truth that we are justified by faith has become completely misunderstood and misapplied.

Or consider how so many people today pray. How many times have I heard, "I pray and therefore I will be helped," and then when an answer doesn't come people conclude that their prayer has not been heard. Such a pity! It doesn't occur to people that praying requires something, and that when our prayers are not heard it is because there is something in us that hinders God from answering them. While others simply think that they only need to stammer out a few words and then God will protect them. [. . .] Or they think that since God alone forgives sins, they no longer have to confess their guilt to one another, completely ignoring the ministry of the "keys," according to the word of John 20:23: "If you forgive the sins of any, they are forgiven; and if you retain the sins of any, they are retained."** These are words that are now completely excluded from the Christian church; "Nobody but God can forgive sins." Yes, that is how the Pharisees also acted, and today people have only a pharisaical understanding of forgiveness. In that case, how can things ever improve in the Christian church? This is the universal priesthood—everybody wants to forgive sins. We do not take into consideration that with this we override the last words of our Savior, that there must always be particular members who help the others.

Nowadays everything gets turned around—taken in the wrong way—and consequently everything is thrown into confusion. We simply refuse to accept and understand the Word of God as it is, and therefore everything gradually deteriorates. Must the church waste away like this, until at last she lies there breathing out the last of her miserable life?

2. The church's lack of understanding is ultimately proven by her lack of power. Even for those who want to give themselves to the Lord, so often they feel within themselves no strength for inner renewal. They fight and pray and try in every way to overcome a vice, a temptation, a bad habit, yet however hard they fight, nothing really ever changes. [. . .] Even when they repent of this or that, time and again they fall into great need and concern about it.

So now we have come to believe that we are the way we are. God has somehow ordained it that certain people have to struggle in life like this and hence carry with them certain weaknesses even to the grave. But this is completely opposite to God's Word and his promises. We must cry out and lament this miserable state—we must cry out and sigh, "Dear Savior, how is

---

** Editors' Note: Blumhardt is referring here to the controversial practice of confession and the laying on of hands, which he instituted after the revival that followed the exorcism of Gottliebin Dittus in the winter of 1843. See Zündel, *Johann Christoph Blumhardt*, 162.

it possible that you can leave us in weakness and poverty such as this?" Yet, this is where the church has come. For centuries now we have not desired anything more than this; we have just become poorer and poorer—and so we lie in our misery without knowing how to pull ourselves up.

But it is not right to let it go at that. No. That is just the point at which we must fight until the situation changes, until more strength from above is given. We must not believe that God has decreed our condition—no, it is not so! If we would but consider God's mercy and remember the Comforter, the Holy Spirit, and the situation of the early Christians, would it be in keeping with his glory and grace that a power that came from him should, in the course of the centuries, become weaker, like an aging man? Look! It is as clear as day! We must win back what has been lost, and when at last God's blessing is restored to his people, we shall then celebrate a joyful church dedication. But have courage and faith! We can gain the victory; we have only to unite with one another and see the critical state we are in. The time will surely come in which God's people will again be clothed with power from on high, and every single person will experience to the full the strength, the peace, and the compassion of God's heart.

This lack of power is perhaps the reason why our witness is so dismal. We sing songs, utter prayers, and many zealous preachers stand in the pulpits. All our institutions breathe the Spirit of God and are of the truth—and yet, how many people are really alive, how many have become new beings? How many are inwardly kindled so that they are intent to change their ways? Is it possible that so few want to be instructed, so few want to be true believers, so few allow themselves to be guided into a Christian life? What is it that is lacking?

The church on earth lacks the witnessing power of the Word of God. His Word is more like an echo than a power. Although stony hearted people hear it, they remain stone and iron! Everywhere messengers stand and preach the will of God—and yet the world becomes increasingly corrupt. Why? Here, truly, we see what a pitiful state we are in—how the power from on high has been withdrawn and how much things have to change before the Word may be kindled in us again. But that is how it is. Many true and lively voices ring out, but there is still no fruit.

I could tell you about many men of God who have preached for years but who have not seen one soul converted. Isn't this a tragedy? [. . .] We must desperately pray that the Lord will pour out his power as it originally was and that this may capture and burst hearts open everywhere, bringing people from hell into life. When we look back to the first Christian church—what strength was astir there to heal the sick, to open the eyes of the blind and the ears of the deaf! What strength was astir to restore the lame, to drive out the devil, and to comfort all those who were under attack! What a promise Christ the Lord left behind for us: "And these signs will accompany those who believe: by using my name they will cast out demons; they will speak in new tongues; they will pick up snakes in their hands, and if they drink any deadly thing, it will not hurt them; they will lay their hands on the sick, and they will recover" (Mark 16:17–18).

Where are these powers today? Just look at all the misery that has penetrated human society! Just look at how many people are confused, tempted, and possessed—our age abounds with them! Look at all the wretched people of whom we all know enough examples in our immediate neighborhood. What attitude does the Christian church take to this? Oh, where is the strength to overcome this need? We weep, we pray, we try by all possible means, but it is of no use. The suffering remains.

Dear souls, what is wrong? Can we say that we are rich in strength, that we have abundance, and that we do not lack for any good thing? Oh, who does not know the many sighs that perpetually rise up to God—and still there is no strength to help! Where in all of Christendom are there people who believe that we should have more strength? We have interpreted Jesus away and preferred weakness to strength and would rather see people waste away than do good to them. Ah, must the church not also say, "I waste away! I waste away! How impotent is all my strength!"? Can there be any doubt as to why the church is so terribly ridiculed and mocked? When one makes so much of Christianity and yet nothing is to be seen, is it any wonder why skeptics increase? Are they right or wrong? Yes, we must groan that God's strength, his power has left us, but not as if it were God's will, as so many say—no indeed! Our lack of power is to our shame, and this should move our hearts so that we turn back to the Lord and pray that he might come once more to make an end to our misery.

There is much more I could say, but this should suffice. And I think you will all agree with me that we have reason enough to cry out with the prophet, "I waste away!" May the Lord have mercy on us and may he let the spirit of his grace come down again and urge us to cry out, to pray and to fight, each in his own way, until the heavens open once more and give us what is our own, fought for through the blood of Jesus! The time will surely come when the Lord will again comfort his people, and then the whole world will shout for joy and rejoice over all he does for us. Amen.

When the Lord Comes

When the Son of Man comes, will he find faith on earth?

—LUKE 18:8 (NRSV)

We often think that the Savior has far too little confidence in people. But what would it be like if nobody believed any longer? I mean, really believed? It seems actually that we are very close to this today. Who truly believes? Dogmatic belief—orthodoxy—yes, many accept this, but what else? Who believes in God's intervention in decaying humankind? Who has faith in the return of Christ and in God's drawing closer to us through him? I hardly dare mention such thoughts, even among people who are believers. In our generation biblical faith means nothing. Our world is filled with believers, but not with faith.

But, wait. When God intervenes things change. Even if nobody wants to believe this! People will see how they don't have faith. Today we view everything from a natural point of view only. Hardly anyone sees how God is working, either in the physical or spiritual realms. Our age is one of unbelief. This is why we seriously must ask, "Do I have faith?" Do I believe that a living relationship to God is possible and that he really will make himself known? Do we really believe God will break into this world and change it? When the Son of Man comes, will he find faith on the earth? Who has the faith that he will come, and is coming?

Real faith demands a tremendous struggle—a fight against the forces of unbelief and doubt. Without this fight, we lack faith. We must remember the widow the Lord speaks of in the Gospel of Luke who kept calling out,

Editors' Note: This sermon is dated 1878.

"Vindicate me against my adversary!" (Luke 18:1–8). Yes, one day the Lord will suddenly burst forth and deliver his chosen ones and justify their faith before the whole world.

God Answers Our Prayers

Therefore I tell you, whatever you ask for in prayer, believe that you have received it, and it will be yours.

—MARK 11:24 (NIV)

We Christians easily misunderstand the above promise. We imagine that we can ask for whatever we like and get it. Stop! It says, "Whatever you ask for in prayer." Who is meant by you? Not just anyone. Jesus is speaking to those who are most closely united with him, who live in his strength, and who abide in his Spirit. These are the ones who pray with hope, who pray and believe that their prayers will be answered. They ask in hope, believing that whatever they ask for in prayer will be given to them.

Today it's hard to find anyone who is as deeply united with Christ as the disciples were. Who of us are truly submitted to him and filled with the Holy Spirit? If we are honest, can the Savior say to us, "Whatever you ask for you shall have, if only you believe?" Just try it—nothing will happen because we are not deeply united with Jesus.

The reason for this is not because the promise has been weakened. No. It remains, but we are not ready for it! Yet there will be a time when apostolic voices are heard once more, filled as they are with the Holy Spirit and in complete unity with Christ, and it will then be possible to move mountains and uproot trees. For the time being, however, let us be glad if the Father in heaven even hears our prayers. And when we pray, let us implore God to help us pray in his power only, in his grace, in the way in which it is taken for granted in this verse. Then evil will completely disappear.

In God's Time

But as for me, I will pray to you, LORD; answer me, God, at a time
you choose. Answer me because of your great love, because you keep
your promise to save.

—PSALM 69:13 (GNT)

There is an acceptable time and a time that is not. The acceptable time
is when heaven is open wide and reveals every grace and wonder.
Heaven is closed, however, when we fail to honor God. When this happens
we cannot receive anything from him.

We are often very quick to believe, but then it happens that we begin
to doubt and are left on "short rations." It seems then that everything is lost;
nothing seems to open up. Even when we pray, we do not receive an answer.
That is how it actually is now—although for my part I cannot say this, it
does apply generally. We feel that God's countenance no longer shines fully
upon us; it's as if he is hiding his face from us. We don't experience the grace
of the Savior. God even seems angry with us.

We find it hard when we ask and don't receive what we ask for—we
think we ought to at least receive something! Then we recall the words,
"Ask and you shall receive," as well as other promises made by the Lord to
his disciples. Why doesn't God do something?! But we forget that God has
a time for everything, a time he has chosen. We also forget that often we do
receive what we ask for and find what we are looking for. But this is not the
norm. No. When it does become the norm again, then the acceptable time
of God's grace has come.

Therefore, we must not harp on certain words Jesus said. Jesus promised that the sick would be healed (Mark 16:18), and that all things are possible to those who believe (Mark 9:23). We can find many such verses in the Bible. And they are completely true, but only as long as it is God's time. When the time of God's mercy recedes, it is different. Jesus' promises always refer to the acceptable time, to the favorable time when heaven is opened up and we can reach up and receive all we need. The acceptable time is that time when we all really believe. But do we? I long that the veil of sadness which covers the whole world is removed. But this will happen only when the powers of darkness are removed. The powers of darkness are what stand in the way, not our Savior. Then our requests to God will be answered immediately. He wants to help us, but he can't because of our sin and guilt, which have spread and covered over everything like a thick blanket of darkness. Only when the clouds of darkness are driven away will there be a clear, benevolent heaven shining down on us.

David prayed, "I will pray to you, Lord; answer me, God, at a time you choose. Answer me because of your great love, because you keep your promise to save." He prayed for a time when he would be accepted and could approach God with his request; a time in which he was sure of being heard and sure of God's faithful help through his great love. He prayed, "You will help, O Lord, and be faithful to your promise to answer in your acceptable time." But he understood that he would have to cry out, pray, and implore God with patience. He prayed, "Lord, let it be according to your will. You always remain faithful: your help will finally come."

In fear and trembling, we must be grateful for every help given to us from God. But God gives us help as he sees fit. I always hesitate before saying this, because someone else might have come to God with the same request as I and it was not granted to them. Nevertheless, we must ask that God's acceptable time will come soon, when all of us will be able to ask for and receive just what we need. The Lord is compassionate and gracious, even if the rest of the world isn't aware of it or able to experience it. At the chosen time, his countenance will shine upon the whole world.

Prayer and Supplication

I love the LORD, because he has heard my voice and my supplications.
Because he inclined his ear to me, therefore I will call on him as long
as I live.

—PSALM 116:1–2 (NRSV)

My heart is heavy when I think of the misery, the need in which so many people live today. This time of great confusion is so terribly difficult because hardly anyone knows what Christianity is anymore. So few of us have the slightest notion of what Christ demands of us. How this can change without the Lord's intervention, I don't know. At present people live in sorrow and muddled anguish. God will have to judge us before we come to our senses. Yet, God's Word gives us comfort and hope.

There were times when David experienced specific proof that the Lord heard his call for help: God inclined his ear to him. Now most of us rarely feel that God is so near, even if we believe he hears our plea. Yet the Lord slowly, secretly, inconspicuously answers our prayers. We know he is gracious [this we confess], and yet we wonder why he doesn't fulfill our specific requests. This is when we must call on the Lord and ask him to plainly show us that he hears us—that he is "inclining his ear" to us. [. . .] What is most important about prayer is that the Lord himself comes close to us, and that we allow him to be heard more clearly amid all our distress and misery. Whatever may happen to us we must seek his abiding peace and patiently hold on to faith. We must know that God hears us and inclines his ear to us. Even more, that he has been exceedingly kind to us all, and that he remains the caring and listening Savior. Even when we suffer distress, we must be able to say with David, "I love the LORD, because he has heard my voice and my prayer."

As long as I am alive I will call upon the Lord and I will do this more fervently, more faithfully each day. I will always bring to the Lord the misery of his people, praying for his compassion. Any separation between him and me, between him and others, must stop.

Let us truly pray. For we all need a deeper relationship with him. A new outpouring of the Holy Spirit is necessary; pray for this without ceasing, day and night! This is what we really need.

True Churches

These are the words of him who holds the seven stars in his right
hand and walks among the seven golden lampstands.

—REVELATION 2:1 (NIV)

The seven golden lampstands are the seven churches, and the seven
stars are the angels and their elders, among whom the Lord walks.
True churches are meant here, churches who have allowed God's Spirit to
work within them. These are churches that have a living fellowship with the
Lord and receive his instructions; they are in direct communication with
him through the angels. The Lord communes with them, he is united with
them. Even when they are weak he walks among them.

We know the Savior complained about these seven churches. He
threatened to knock over the lampstands and give up his communication
with them and let them only deal with him in the regular way. This is what
is told to us in Revelation. We are astonished and hardly know what to say
about it. Where can we find churches here on earth with whom the Savior
has direct communication? We sigh when we hear this. This is just what we
lack. Think about it! If only the Savior would walk among us as he once did
so long ago! If that were to happen, it would be the sign of the breaking in
of the end times, when the Lord will gather his people on earth. The devil
would be master over us all if this didn't happen!

Because the letters to the seven churches precede the other prophecies in John's Revelation it follows, it seems to me, that churches will arise
again where the Lord is found. Angels, who like the prophets were in direct
contact with the Savior, will be found. Yes! This will happen again! The Lord

will come closer to us and walk among us, even if only among a faithful few. But these few will influence us all, and the Lord will gain power on earth. We must pray for this.

When this occurs, John's revelations will unfold and all the prophecies will be fulfilled. Yes, we yearn for the personal nearness of the Savior. However, the Lord calls us to seek and find him amidst the sighing and frustration of his whole creation. God allows nothing to go to waste. He will gather his flock and they will be a light in the world—shining like stars and leading all the peoples of the earth from darkness into the light.

God's Power in the Gospel

While the people pressed upon him to hear the word of God, he was standing by the lake of Gennesaret. And he saw two boats by the lake; but the fishermen had gone out of them and were washing their nets. Getting into one of the boats, which was Simon's, he asked him to put out a little from the land. And he sat down and taught the people from the boat. And when he had ceased speaking, he said to Simon, "Put out into the deep and let down your nets for a catch." And Simon answered, "Master, we toiled all night and took nothing! But at your word I will let down the nets." And when they had done this, they enclosed a great shoal of fish; and as their nets were breaking, they beckoned to their partners in the other boat to come and help them. And they came and filled both the boats, so that they began to sink. But when Simon Peter saw it, he fell down at Jesus' knees, saying, "Depart from me, for I am a sinful man, O Lord." For he was astonished, and all that were with him, at the catch of fish, which they had taken; and so also were James and John, sons of Zebedee, who were partners with Simon. And Jesus said to Simon, "Do not be afraid; henceforth you will be catching men." And when they had brought their boats to land, they left everything and followed him.

—LUKE 5:1–11 (RSV)

The Lord wanted to give Simon Peter courage for his new calling. Peter would be taking on a great responsibility; trying to win others for Jesus.

Editors' Note: This sermon is dated 1857.

But he would also have to face many obstacles along the way, hindrances that could easily make him fainthearted. What lay ahead of him? [He did not know.] He might even get discouraged by the fact that he, among others, would turn away from him—that some of Jesus' former admirers would even cry out, "Crucify, crucify him." [. . .] For the coming struggle, then, he would need encouragement and inner strengthening.

The Lord indeed strengthens Peter and his partners with a miracle. It seemed especially great to Simon Peter, although we don't really understand it. Simon was a fisherman, and he knew that the time to catch the most fish was at night; that most fish are found near the shore. The whole night long he had tried to catch fish by the usual methods, but caught nothing. Now, contrary to all the rules of fishing, he cast out his net during the day and into the deep. He'd never caught so many fish! He immediately understood the miracle.

Peter had an open heart to receive the Lord's gifts, including his miracles. This enabled him to be a man for God's cause. He realized that the hand of the Lord was at work, and this shook him up powerfully. He was so overwhelmed by the thought that here God had intervened that at first he could not even bear to be near the Savior. The Savior was too great for him, and so he wanted to get away. He thought that it could even harm him if he, a sinful man, would stand so close to him. Thus he fell down at Jesus' knee, crying, "Depart from me, for I am a sinful man, O Lord!" No wonder a shock came over the other disciples. They couldn't just think about the profit the fish might bring! Only one thought filled them now: "God has done this." God's presence terrified them.

This, dear friends, should really be our response to all the Savior's miracles. But more importantly, we must see how this miracle changed Peter's whole life. Unfortunately miracles don't impress people anymore. Even in Jesus' day, the Lord had to rebuke cities that had seen so many miracles but still did not repent. [. . .] On the day of judgment it would be more tolerable for the cities of Sodom and Gomorrah than for them!

And what about us? So many times we refuse to acknowledge God; we even deny that God's voice can be heard. For instance, when tremendous events take place in nature everyone, instead of recognizing that "here is a deed of God," just explains everything in terms of natural causes. We simply refuse to believe that the living, personal God of creation directly intervenes in our world. This is also why miracles, like those in Jesus' time, hardly ever occur anymore. [. . .] In our scientific age, God has been "dethroned." He is no longer "permitted" to work anymore. But all the more, we must trust in the intervention of the Savior who said, "I am with you always with all might and power." His miracles can [and do] continue today.

But let us take a closer look at the story itself and see what the Savior said to Peter. Jesus performed a miracle. [Peter and his partners made a huge catch of] fish when it seemed impossible [to catch even one.] And then Jesus turns to Peter and says, "From now on, you will be catching men." With this simple word, Jesus tells Peter that from now on he would be gathering throngs of people into the kingdom of God. This is incredible! For the time was anything but favorable for such a thing. The Jews, in their hypocrisy, could not understand it. The Gentiles couldn't grasp the gospel either, with all their supposed wisdom. Conventional people were also all wrapped up in their everyday affairs, too busy to have an open ear.

How would Peter, not to mention the others, gather in throngs of people for God's kingdom? With their eloquence? With their learning? No. Nothing would come from these. The power of the gospel would not be found here. Like Paul, they knew from the start that one could not rely on persuading and convincing people. The servants of the gospel would have to build upon something entirely different. And this "something different" would have to be a power that could conquer hearts. But how would it come?

This "something different" actually lay in the very words of Peter himself, who prior to the catch of fish said, "But at your word I will let down the nets." Yes, "At your word I will try it," Peter replied. It was by his simple obedience, though contrary to his instincts as a master fisherman, that Peter experienced such an extraordinary happening. With that simple obedience he was building upon a hidden strength, a strength that came from the One who had ultimate authority and power: "If the Lord commands it, then it must be right." Without realizing it, Peter was already unleashing God's hidden power, which flowed out from Christ Jesus himself, even to this catch of fish.

What then must a disciple of the Lord build upon then? He must build upon the power of God. It was this power that accompanied the disciples' preaching later on. When the Lord, having identified himself as Son of the living God, told the disciples to go out into all the world and proclaim the gospel, they understood that the Lord himself would be with them. His immediate presence in their work would bear fruit for the kingdom.

Dear Friends, today we resist the idea that it is the Lord who must unlock hearts; we believe we can do his work with our own "power." Oh, we say that the gospel is a Word of God and that when we speak his Word hearts are opened. But to be truthful, we put more importance the manner of our speech, the human, dogmatic way we teach the gospel—not on the direct power of God which alone can break in. This is so human! We don't let the power of God enter our lives or through our words. And because we fail to put our sole trust in God, the Word can't work miracles. Oh, many of us work tirelessly for God for decades, even with tremendous zeal, but at the end we have to say, "We have toiled the whole time and caught nothing." And why is this? Because we do not cast our nets at his word! Sure enough, we cast out our nets, but not in the way in which Peter expresses it here—"At your word." "At your word!" This means trusting in Christ's quiet power alone, trusting his immediate presence, in his Holy Spirit, which he promised to send. All of us must renounce our self-importance, together with all our "wisdom," and trust alone in the Holy Spirit, which seeks to work deep within our hearts.

It is high time we change our whole way of thinking! But we must also recognize how little all our eloquence and knowledge has accomplished. We need to come to the realization that something is really missing! Nobody feels this more than those who truly serve the Lord and the kingdom of God. However zealously, thoroughly, or concisely, however long or often we proclaim the Word—"cast out our nets,"—something is missing, because we catch nothing. We and our listeners hear, but we don't respond to Jesus' command. And our nets remain empty. Granted, here or there we see someone who responds to the Word. God be praised and thanked for this. But if we are honest, something is still missing. [. . .] When we "cast out the nets" no miracle occurs.

What is missing? Surely it is the presence of Jesus himself, with his all-embracing power. This is what is missing! The disciples toiled all night, and everything they did was correct and good, yet Jesus was not with them. They were doing everything in their own strength. Yes, they knew that Jesus was the One John the Baptist preached about, the Lamb of God. They had even seen Christ do miracles. Nevertheless, they were still lacking—he was not with them. But when he was, and when they truly obeyed him, they caught such large quantities that the nets began to break.

Oh, dear friends, let us not forget his promises. Jesus promises us the Comforter, the outpouring of the Holy Spirit. This should make us long for all the miraculous and divine happenings to come again. In the beginning such happenings brought about great miracles, especially when the Lord opened the hearts of thousands. People fell down, repentant, pleading, "What shall we do to be saved?" The Holy Spirit changed the hearts of those who heard the good news; they immediately broke down and followed his word. When they heard the message everything that was proclaimed to them was fresh and new.

Isn't this what is missing today? Don't we also need this powerful gift of the Holy Spirit for the final fulfillment of the kingdom of God upon earth? Shouldn't we avail ourselves of all God's promises and work toward the return of the Lord? Jesus must come again with his signs and wonders—most of all with the mightiest of miracles, where hearts of stone are softened and when we all accept the salvation offered to us.

Let us not be discouraged! For hundreds of years now, at least since shortly after the Reformation, one can say that there has been very little power by which the gospel has been able to accomplish what it could. There are far too few among those who have heard the Word who actually have a sense of being disciples of Christ. There are hardly any who even show interest and still fewer who really come to a true conversion. Nevertheless, great pains are taken by many people to ensure that the gospel may reach all hearts. Perhaps the Savior has wanted to show us that there are times when nothing, or very little, is achieved, although a great deal of work has been done. And perhaps our time is a barren time of "darkness," when everything is attempted yet the fruits of the gospel are hardly noticed. It is a sad, dark time we are in, but let us not forget that it is one that will surely pass away.

In spite of it, let us live in hope. Let us be people who return to a [simple, obedient] faith in Christ, who pray for the great things of God, which the Lord Jesus told us we should pray for. For surely a time will come when Peter's "catch of fish" will come true—for all those who listen to his call. A time will come when "at his word" God's people will cast out their nets and a great catch of fish will be taken. Many thousands will come, urgently crying out, "What shall we do to be saved?"

Yes, a time is coming when the Word will be proclaimed and hearts will be shaken: turned upside down and toward Jesus. His time must come again! Multitudes will be won for him, and they will go forth victoriously to meet the Lord as his very own people. We believe that God will win! Amen.

To Those Who Are Fainthearted

Say to those who are of a fearful heart: Be strong, fear not! Behold,
your God will come with vengeance, with the recompense of God, He
will come and save you.

—Isaiah 35:4 (RSV)

The prophet Isaiah said this thinking of the future, in particular of the time before the final coming of the Lord. We know that the Lord has already come as a baby, poor and lowly. That happened when most people were without hope and didn't think it was possible that the Promised One would ever come; only a few faithful ones kept waiting for the consolation of Israel. Most, however, went their own ways, abandoning anything that pointed toward God. They kept to the outward forms of life and resigned themselves to their momentary whims, burying themselves in worldly pursuits. They were discontented for sure with the regime they lived under, but when they thought about life and death they were without comfort.

Isaiah's words should have been a comfort to them: "Say to those who are of a fearful heart: Be strong, fear not! Behold, your God comes!" But only a few found comfort, like the shepherds to whom the angel said at the time of the Savior's birth, "Be not afraid; for behold, I bring you good news of a great joy; for the Savior is born to you this day."

The Savior had come. His comfort gave great encouragement to all who listened! But they also crucified him! However, as the Risen One, he inclined himself graciously from heaven toward his fighting disciples, who had no cause to lose heart, for the Living One was with them, making them

Editors' Note: This sermon is dated 1875.

strong and joyful for every battle. How times have changed! The first witnesses all died, and the first powers of the Spirit all but disappeared. The first life-powers of the gospel dried up under the faithlessness, inertia, and indifference of those who initially possessed them. Century after century has come and gone. Heaven seems to be more and more distant, as there are so few signs of the Savior, the very One who promised to always be present, even until the end of the age. Yes, sometimes there are signs, glimpses of God's glorious future, but they are hardly perceptible and seem to quickly disappear.

We are thus afraid and tormented. The powers of darkness are brazenly obvious; they appear to have the upper hand. Who of us has any courage? Who of us can be cheerful or have hope? Who of us can have any real peace and joy? Ah, things should be so different among us!

But then there are the words of the prophet, and we must turn to them again and again. Now is the time. We are nearing the end times, and they demand our utmost. We must therefore boldly believe that the time has come when we must raise our voices and cry out: "Say to those who are of a fearful heart: Be strong, fear not! Behold, your God comes!" We must believe that preceding him will be God's mercy, which wants to grip our hearts. O come, come, Lord Jesus, that we may know you are here, that you are really here! Bring your new graces and powers. Come again, come and show yourself! Our faintheartedness will end when we see and feel your power.

Oh, let us realize this power. Then we will really cry out, "Say to those who are of a fearful heart: Be strong, fear not! Behold, your God comes." Yes, he comes and makes all things new. He will do it! Amen.

Blessed Is He Who Comes!

For I tell you, you will not see me again, until you say, "Blessed is he who comes in the name of the Lord!"

—MATTHEW 23:39 (NIV)

The context in which these words were spoken sounds strange to us. The Lord is speaking to Jerusalem, his children whom he wants to gather together as "a hen gathers her brood, but [they] would not." He says, "Look, your house is left to you desolate," and then he ends with these words, "You will not see me again, until you say, 'Blessed is he who comes in the name of the Lord.'"

The time indeed seems close when his followers would see him again after his death. He is talking to people who are right there with him, telling them that they, if they are still alive, will exclaim, "Blessed is he who comes." Here we see how his task on earth, the salvation of the world, was completely fulfilled with his death. From now on it would grow under his invisible guidance. He also encourages his followers to be faithful and expectant in the task they are given. Their faithfulness will be a comfort to him.

But, something must be lacking to prevent Jesus' coming. Since that time, all of us have been slow to respond and therefore the Lord has had to suffer a long delay. It even appears that everything has come to a standstill. But when the "wheels" start to turn again, as we see from Jesus' words, events could develop rapidly. All the more, we must remain expectant. For suddenly things could come alive! Who knows, it may be us who say at his coming, "Blessed is he who comes in the name of the Lord."

Editors' Note: This sermon is date 1876.

It is wonderful how gently the Lord spoke these words. He continued to care for his people, even though they would later reject him and their "house" would be punished and left desolate. Despite this, they would experience a great longing for him. For power from heaven would descend and change everything. His people would attain a new faith in Jesus whom now they do not see.

This is how it always is. When Jesus' powers are freely at work, everybody begins to long for the coming of the Lord. The word of the Lord shows us this. So let us have courage even in the face of great corruption. It can all become different. There will be thousands and millions throughout all the nations of the earth who, when at last they see him coming in the clouds of heaven, will cry out in joy, "Blessed is he who comes in the name of the Lord." May this come soon! Amen.

The Greater Works

Very truly I tell you, whoever believes in me will do the works I have been doing, and they will do even greater things than these, because I am going to the Father.

—JOHN 14:12 (NIV)

These words of Jesus are ones we hardly dare to take in as they are written. In fact, this passage is rarely discussed. We are afraid to speak about it, especially in any specific way. Yet, the Lord says, "Whoever believes in me will do the works I have been doing, and they will do even greater things than these, because I am going to my Father."

Anyone? Certainly! But the Savior does not mean that every Christian—if only they believe—is capable of these greater works. No, the faith spoken of here is absolute and completely founded in the Lord. Few people possess this kind faith; it belongs to a specific kind of relationship in the kingdom of God upon earth. Nevertheless, the Savior speaks of "whoever" and does so because he does not want to exclude anyone who truly believes. He wants to make sure that we all realize that it does not take an extraordinary person to understand his Word.

Anyone can do great works according to his faith. James, speaking of the works of Elijah, makes it plain that the earnest prayer of a righteous person has great power. Elijah was a man just like us (Jas 5:17). Yet, Elijah was given great tasks by God. Greater works always entail a definite personal assignment entrusted by God—an assignment that does not belong to everyone. The Lord knows the people who can accomplish something

Editors' Note: This sermon is dated 1876.

special for him. God can call anyone. But we must not presume we are called when we are not! This verse applies only to those who have been chosen by God. And yet, each of us should still personally expect to receive wonderful gifts from the Savior. For these gifts are meant to help us do even greater works than Jesus did. Yes, greater works. For while Jesus was on the earth, he lived in lowliness; he made only a beginning. But now Jesus is with the Father and is clothed in divine glory and power. As his disciples we are meant to do his very works here on earth. And the closer his kingdom comes, the greater will be the works—far greater than those he performed while on earth.

Until now such great and even greater works have not happened. It even seems that the advancement of God's kingdom has stopped. Even though the gospel continues to spread, the miracles, including those that Jesus did on earth, appear to have ceased. And so we are thus puzzled by this Bible verse. Are not these just words? No! We must have patience! These works Jesus promises will come. They may not have happened yet, at least not like they will occur in the last days, but God's power from above, the renewed outpouring of the Holy Spirit, will come again. His kingdom will fill the earth. Then we will see how Jesus' words are true—how great and even greater works will be done by those who believe. His works are not confined to the promised land. No, no. They will extend over the whole world. God's glory will be revealed to everyone, and then we will understand that not only deeds such as Jesus did will be performed, but that still greater miracles will be done. God will let Elijah-like people appear everywhere, and hard hearts will be melted and called to eternal life in the kingdom of God. Just think, if Elijah did great works, what more can we expect of the new prophets, when every tongue acknowledges Jesus Christ as Lord, to the glory of God the Father? We all must look forward confidently to this time, believing that it will come soon. It will surely come! Heaven and earth will pass away, but the words of Jesus will never pass away. Amen.

The Coming of Jesus

I will not leave you orphaned; I am coming to you.

—JOHN 14:18 (NRSV)

Imagine what it must have been like for the apostles when Jesus was no longer with them. Jesus, God's very presence, had been their sole support. Through him they had direct contact with the Father himself. But now Jesus was gone. They had to live and struggle on earth without his direct counsel and help. After his death and resurrection, they must have felt like orphans who had lost father and mother.

But no! Jesus told them that they would not be without his presence. He promised to send them a divine substitute greater than his visible presence. He would still come to them, and they would still have him in all their need, perplexities, and weaknesses. He would personally send them someone from God—the Holy Spirit, representing him. They would not see Jesus as before, but he would be with them nevertheless. This promise must have been precious to the disciples. Indeed, how glorious it was when it was fulfilled within just a few days after his ascension to heaven. From that time on they had no feeling of ever having suffered a loss; they were not orphans!

How is it with us? How do we understand this gift, this promise? Or have we become more like orphans? Does the Holy Spirit speak to us? Does he dwell within us and work amongst us just as he did at the time of the apostles? Do we feel Jesus himself in our midst? Why do we lack what was given in those early times? How often we are left desolate, looking for guidance from the Savior that we so much need. How often we lack discernment,

Editors' Note: This sermon is dated 1876.

help, and comfort. How helpless we feel in the face of today's evil. Instead of rejoicing, there is "weeping" in the church. It can be heard throughout the land—a weeping like that of orphans who have lost their father and mother.

But does this have to be? Can't this be changed? Today, at this holy feast of Advent, which brings us into the time of expectation, let us once more prayerfully wait for the Lord to come to us again through his Holy Spirit. For we want to feel deeply his presence and to understand what it really means to have him and what we have in him. Then our lives will be peaceful and content, patient and joyful. We must yearn to be given this grace again—the gift of his Spirit, which prepares the way for his new age of salvation. And when it comes, the Lord will not be far off. But let us turn our eyes upward! Even with all the pain and need that surround us, we must eagerly wait for the Lord. Let us be filled with such deep longing that it overwhelms us. The word of the Lord, "I will not leave you orphans, I will come to you," must prevail. He will come to us! He will come with comfort and help for us all! Jesus is faithful and true! Amen.

Increase Our Faith!

The apostles said to the Lord, "Increase our faith!

—LUKE 17:5 (NRSV)

We are confronted here first of all, beloved listeners in Jesus Christ, by the prayer of the disciples, "Lord, increase our faith!" The disciples experienced, as we also often experience, a lack of faith. They understood, as the saying expresses, that "Faith is at times great and strong, full of confidence and joy; and at times it is small and weak, because much doubt and fear and much despondency creeps in." When the twelve disciples were together with Jesus, they behaved like we often do—they discussed ideas and argued with each other. Each of them still had his own opinions. But this dampened the spirit, leaving them dull and empty. Their spirits couldn't rise to a firm and living faith, which they knew was necessary. Hence their plea, "Lord, increase our faith!" It is just the same with us. We also allow ourselves to be distracted. We also let our thoughts wander, and so our hearts become weary, doubting, and mistrustful. This happens again and again among us.

The apostles prayed, "Increase our faith!" Likewise, we also must ask for more faith. When we realize our lack of faith, we must ask for more. Don't drift! The father of the boy who was possessed, said, "I believe, dear Lord, help my unbelief" (Mark 9:24). The request for faith is not enough; when we pray for faith we must prepare ourselves for more of it. We must confront our unbelief, turn away from all that interferes with the power of faith, and gather together our thoughts and spirit and our faculties. We

Editors' Note: This sermon is dated 1846.

need to do everything we can to be united in spirit with those around us. We cannot be frustrated or torn. Faith will be given, but it must find a "doorway" where it can enter your heart.

But what kind of faith are we to ask for? The faith that helps us feel close to the Savior? For one thing, we need to ask the Lord to increase our assurance of faith, the assurance that our sins are forgiven and that by his grace we are found acceptable to him. When people say that they lack faith, what actually weighs them down most is the feeling of being separated from their Savior. Consequently, they become uncertain as to whether they can really bear this uncertainty courageously. This is a need, but we will not talk further about this today. The disciples certainly meant something different when they asked the Lord for more faith. The Lord had already given them power to drive out unclean spirits, to heal the sick, and to perform many deeds in his name. What they needed most was more power from him to do this. They had accomplished many miracles, but there were situations and occasions when they lacked these gifts. And this must have troubled them; they knew full well that the lack of power was on account of their lack of faith; something in them was insufficient. This is why they prayed to the Lord, "Increase our faith!" They did not want to lack what was needed when the time came to call upon his name, which happened when they could not cast out a certain demon from a boy.

The question now to us is this: How do we apply this to ourselves? What does it mean for us to pray for this kind of faith? First, we must not pray simply for ourselves! No, we need to pray that this faith is given to the church. This is our obligation, our main duty—"Increase the faith of the church, of the people of God, and especially of your laborers that they will come to know a genuine apostolic faith!" This should be our prayer. Will we do this? It's a shame that so few of us dare anything in faith so that Jesus' name is glorified. In fact, most of us live and think in a way where faith is no longer necessary. We have turned our need, our lack of faith into a virtue and therefore no longer believe that anything significant can still be done in the name of Jesus.

So much is argued and explained away; miraculous signs are now completely unnecessary in the Christian church. Anyone who expects God to work with power is considered presumptuous or else as some kind of fanatic. All the while, the church is downcast. [. . .] But I say, without faith all else is useless. "Increase our faith that the time may come again in which signs will be performed to the glory of your name. Break our hearts again and again. Lord, choose the people by whom this will come about, but let it come to the church somewhere, for therein lies hidden the glory of your Son."

Signs and wonders will come again, and when they do they will demonstrate that God's kingdom embraces all people. The Redeemer will come, especially to languishing souls. For God will give his people the strength to spread the good news of his kingdom everywhere. But presently, there is practically nothing of this glory to be seen. It should make us weep, like the widow in the Gospel, dressed in mourning because she had lost her husband. She cried out, "Lord, save me from my adversary." The entire Christian church should be in mourning like this widow; it should lament to the Lord, day and night praying that he would restore what has been stolen—that he will again increase our faith. We all know what our obligation is. Allow it, therefore, to speak directly to your hearts. Let us heed Christ's call and join with the widow: "Save us from our adversaries, Lord. Increase our faith!" Amen.

SECTION 3
THE CRY OF THE
CHOSEN PEOPLE

Prepare the Way!

Build up, build up, prepare the road!
Remove the obstacles out of the way of my people.

—ISAIAH 57:14 (NIV)

The way must be prepared for the Lord so that he will draw closer to us. He must be more fully present, with his gifts of grace, powers of the Holy Spirit, and with his miracles. But is this Lord wanted? Is he really wanted here? It seems to me he is not. When he looks down upon us, is he not saying, "I am not wanted here—why should I dwell among you? You want nothing from me. You will only throw me out, just as my people did long ago. You are an ungrateful people!" In so many ways we set up obstacles that prevent the joyful coming of the Lord. Nevertheless, he says, "Build up, build up; prepare the road! Remove the obstacles out of the way of my people!" If we would but listen and repent then this could actually happen; so let us stop everything we are doing and turn in longing to the Lord. We must hope for this, because without it there will be nothing but destruction. We must "arm" ourselves with faith, hope, prayer, and conversion, then we will be able to prepare the way for the Lord's coming. Therefore, let us remove every obstacle that hinders him from helping us. Oh, if we would only yearn for him, await and long for his promise. Then he would come. The Lord will meet us on the way when each of us sighs and weeps for him, hopes for him. He will not rest until the entire earth is full of his glory.

Without Ceasing

Pray without ceasing.

—1 THESSALONIANS 5:17 (KJV)

"Pray without ceasing." We must never stop praying. A man who had cut his foot with a hatchet told me once, "But I prayed just this morning!" But his praying stopped as soon as he said the Lord's Prayer. We often rattle off prayers like this and with the "Amen" move on with the rest of our day. We don't even think about God, although we take it for granted that God is thinking about us. We are good at reeling off our prayers morning and evening, imagining that we have honestly prayed, but then we don't really remain in a prayerful attitude. But Paul exhorts us to pray without ceasing. We are to continue in a prayerful and beseeching attitude to the Lord throughout the day, praying expectantly that everyone will be saved. This is what it means to pray, and to pray without ceasing.

So let us be people who believe, who continually thank God. Let us not cease praying. Yes, with our last breath, let us pray and hope that our prayers are heard. Whoever dies praying for the great restoration will not be found wanting when he passes over; he will not have prayed in vain.

Editors' Note: This sermon is dated 1880.

The Lord, Our Father

You, O LORD, are our father;
our Redeemer from of old is your name.

—ISAIAH 63:16 (NRSV)

Isaiah prays from a deeply moved soul. He feels all the harm that has permeated his people. He sees that Israel has sunk to the very lowest level, into sin and corruption of every kind. In the previous verse, Isaiah cries out, "Look down from heaven and see, from your holy and glorious habitation. Where are your zeal and your might? The yearning of your heart and your compassion? They are withheld from me" (Isa 63:15). God has great compassion. Has it become hardened against us? He does not seem to intervene or stop the corruption in which we live. Is it possible, thinks Isaiah, that compassion can be withheld—"You, O LORD, are our father, our Redeemer from of old . . . ." Further on he sighs, "O that you would tear open the heavens and come down, so that the mountains would quake at your presence" (Isa 64:1). This happened before when the glory of God was revealed before all the people on Mount Sinai.

When we understand Isaiah's pain and sorrow, we can't help but take his words literally and cry out to heaven. It seems like we too can't endure the distress and misery that we feel right now—it's unbearable. Yet the depths where we find ourselves are not deep enough. It feels as though everything will become completely black, completely dark. Not even a spark of light can penetrate our darkness. But the prophet's prayer is written for our time, for us. We are nearing the last days, where a very great darkness

Editors' Note: This sermon is dated 1875.

will set in. Let us cry out, then, day and night! We must declare it: "Turn back, turn back! O Lord, do you make us stray from your ways and harden our heart, so that we do not fear you?" (Isa 63:17). Come change our erring, hardened hearts—or should we allow people to go their own way, believing that it has to be like this, that all will be lost, and that there will be nothing but eternal ruin? Never! The revelation of the glory of God is our promise.

We hold firmly to this one thing: "The Lord is our Father, the Lord is our Redeemer; that is his name from of old." His Son is with us and lives and rules at the right hand of God. Above him is the Father of all compassion who gives us complete consolation. Let us therefore continue to be courageous and joyful. But let us pray—yes, cry out! Then, the Lord's compassion will break through and the right hand of the Most High will change the world! Amen.

The Lord, Teacher of the Gentiles

"So then," says the LORD, "once and for all I will make the nations
know my power and might; they will know that I am the LORD."

—JEREMIAH 16:21 (GNB)

Jeremiah had been speaking of the Gentiles who would come to the Lord
from the far ends of the earth. Until now their gods had been worthless
and had not helped them, but henceforth they would seek refuge in the
God of Israel. For the time being this coming to the Lord is only an approach of heart and mind, only a longing and prayer to him that they also
might be allowed to accept him as their God. In the last days, such longing
will increase among the Gentiles. In our own time we hear about people
coming to the Savior from all around the world—that is, the unbelieving
world. This awakening is but a forerunner of the approaching Holy Spirit,
which certainly will be poured out on all flesh. Even among established
churches, there is a growing yearning for renewal; there is a greater and
greater longing and hunger. In the last days, we will all leave our homes and
seek out those who will tell us the message of salvation.

This longing will only intensify, for millions of people have not yet
found help for their need and suffering. But help will come from God when,
even if only through vague rumors, it finally becomes known throughout
the whole earth. The merciful God will come to meet the world's longing.
Jeremiah says: "I will make the nations know my power and might." In the
end, God will not leave it to halfhearted people to point the way, people
who have only words but are unable to show God's power in deeds. Words

Editors' Note: This sermon is dated 1875.

alone offer little help. It is not enough to talk about what Christ is able to do, or testify how he is strength and power, a refuge in need, if there is nothing to show for it. "I will make the nations know." God himself will be our teacher and will show us what he is able to do. "Once and for all I will make the nations know my power and might. They will know that I am the LORD."

The Lord will not only teach us, but he will perform all kinds of signs and wonders. He will not instruct us in the usual way, having everything explained, but without any tangible examples. No. We will truly learn from him. Just imagine seeing the very works of God again. How quickly would we all learn!

O Savior, what a loving teacher you are for the sick, for those who are so sorely afflicted—for the blind, the lame, the deaf, the crippled. When you speak one word, how much is given. When you speak, how tremendously much we experience and learn from that "one word." Oh, if only you, Jesus, could teach us again in this way. If this were but possible a second time, it would bear infinitely more fruit than the first time. And you, O Lord, you say it yourself that you will teach us. We know this time will come, and so we wait patiently for you. We will wait and keep on waiting until your hand and your might are revealed to us. We will experience that you are the Lord, our Savior and our all! Amen.

The Cry for Help

Oh, that salvation for Israel would come out of Zion!
When the LORD restores his people,
let Jacob rejoice and Israel be glad!

—PSALM 14:7 (NIV)

For all those who sigh in Zion, who see the wretchedness of God's people and look toward something better, which was promised to them, help will come.

"Out of Zion." This means that help shall come right from the holy place of the true people of God. Christ himself came out of Zion, inasmuch as he took upon himself suffering and death there for the salvation of the world. But complete help is not here yet—only the preparation for help. We thus have as much reason to sigh as any Israelite had before the time of Christ. "Oh, that salvation for Israel would come out of Zion! When the LORD restores his people." In Luke's Gospel Jesus quotes Isaiah 61 and points directly to himself: "The Lord has anointed me to preach the good news to the poor. He has sent me to bind up the brokenhearted, to proclaim freedom for the captives and release from darkness the prisoners" (Luke 4:16–18). The whole world is captive and bound. We have little command over ourselves and consequently have fallen into countless follies, which have resulted in so much misery and pain. If we are sincere in our worship, then we must long with everything we have that the great day of redemption will come, the day that will change everything.

We must stand before God, together, and cry out to him for help. God himself tells us, "Call upon me in the day of trouble, I will deliver you"

(Ps 50:15). So our chief task is to live for the kingdom of God completely. We must cry out for the Lord to deliver us from every need. And we must do this with one voice, not just for ourselves, but for all people—for the redemption of groaning creation, for the renewal of the entire universe. We must pray for the deliverance of the whole creation. Even in our most dreadful need we must cry out to him and sigh for help to come out of Zion. This promise, "I will deliver you," applies to us.

So let us pray for this, for nothing will come by itself. We need people who pray, who implore God heart and soul. And if only a few of us are praying, then all the more let us be that much more dedicated. For divine help must ultimately be prayed for. Then when the year of redemption, the year of grace, comes at last, we will truly praise him, glorify him, and thank him for his mercy. When at last this great redemption is completed, "Jacob shall rejoice and Israel shall be glad."

Lord, Have Pity!

Thou wilt arise and have pity on Zion;
it is the time to favor her; the appointed time has come.

—PSALM 102:13 (RSV)

We all hope that God will have mercy on Zion, on the people of God and subsequently on the whole world. This is nothing new. It is already three thousand years old. Even back then people looked expectantly toward heaven, hoping that the Lord might intervene and relieve the misery of his people and of the whole world. David and the prophets believed in this profound vision. They knew, "It is time . . . the appointed time has come." There is no more waiting. And so we rightly think it has to be right now. But we, like they, have to be ready to wait and even be satisfied with "crumbs" for now. Historically, a period of quiet came over Israel. This period continued beyond the time of Solomon's reign. This calm was a symbol that God had provided for his people. The yearning of that time was thus fulfilled in a certain sense and to a certain extent, but it was mostly confined to Israel.

With the coming of Christ, however, God's compassion for Zion has been revealed more fully. How beautifully did Zechariah, the father of John the Baptist, and the faithfully waiting Simeon sing praises. They rejoiced that the time of God's gracious visitation at last had begun. God had once again come close to Zion, yet not only to his people, but to the whole of humankind. The time was fulfilled.

But, what about us? How does it stand with us? Every stone cries out, "Arise and have pity on Zion!" The feeling, "It is time to favor her; the appointed time has come," penetrates the world more and more. But how long must we still wait? We do not know, but when the Lord reveals his will through signs from heaven, then things will start moving. Even then, we must be prepared for the Lord to say, "No, not quite yet." All the more we must pray and bear this on our hearts. The church needs more "Simeons." Only then will the time come—the time that all creation sighs and longs for. This is our greatest expectation—nothing less than the transformation of all creation, a new heaven and a new earth. This is the goal of our faith. Be patient and await its coming! It will and must come! Amen.

The Lord Answers Our Cries for Help

The LORD says to his people, "When the time comes to save you,
I will show you favor and answer your cries for help."

—ISAIAH 49:8 (GNT)

It takes time for the Lord to answer us and give us help. Hence, when we pray today we cannot assume that our prayers will be answered immediately. The Lord hears our prayers and indeed will show us favor and answer our cries for help. But he will do this only in his appointed time. Our prayers bring the day of salvation closer, but when we pray, "Your kingdom come . . ." we cannot expect an immediate response. We must wait for the day of salvation, the time of the Lord's favor. Despite this, our prayer "Come, Lord Jesus" still has an effect. It prepares the way for his approaching and brings his coming closer.

The day of salvation and the time of his mercy and compassion are not fixed times; they can change according to how we pray. When we stop praying the coming of the Lord stops and cannot go forward. But when we seriously pray and fight, then he draws nearer to fulfilling his goal; we help to bring the time of his favor and the day of his salvation nearer. If we want to be true children of God we must honestly work toward this. Our conception of time is not only limited but so often an obstacle. We think that this or that will happen today or tomorrow or next year. Such thinking, however, prevents us from being wholehearted. As soon as we believe that certain things will happen regardless of how or whether we pray, we are finished! God's coming, his compassion, his acts of grace are answers to actual prayers—to our prayers. They won't come unless we pray and sigh for them. How else can our prayers be answered unless we actually pray?!

The Israelites in Egypt groaned in their tribulation and, God heard their lamentations and groaning and took pity on his people, and sent Moses as their deliverer (Exodus 2:23–25). Without such devout sighing the people of Israel might have waited even longer before God would have raised up a Moses. It is always like this—right down to the smallest detail. We are called to pray in all circumstances. And when we do, our requests will "mature." One situation will lead to another and one thing will make another one possible. Then God's time comes. Always keep this in mind. The more honestly we pray and ask for help, the sooner the day of salvation will come.

The Waiting of the Righteous

When the time came for the purification rites required by the Law
of Moses, Joseph and Mary took him to Jerusalem to present him
to the Lord (as it is written in the Law of the Lord, "Every firstborn
male is to be consecrated to the Lord"), and to offer a sacrifice in
keeping with what is said in the Law of the Lord: "a pair of doves or
two young pigeons."

Now there was a man in Jerusalem called Simeon, who was
righteous and devout. He was waiting for the consolation of Israel,
and the Holy Spirit was on him. It had been revealed to him by
the Holy Spirit that he would not die before he had seen the Lord's
Messiah. Moved by the Spirit, he went into the temple courts. When
the parents brought in the child Jesus to do for him what the custom
of the Law required, Simeon took him in his arms and praised God,
saying: "Sovereign Lord, as you have promised, you may now dismiss
your servant in peace. For my eyes have seen your salvation, which
you have prepared in the sight of all nations: a light for revelation to
the Gentiles, and the glory of your people Israel."

The child's father and mother marveled at what was said about
him. Then Simeon blessed them and said to Mary, his mother: "This
child is destined to cause the falling and rising of many in Israel, and
to be a sign that will be spoken against, so that the thoughts of many
hearts will be revealed. And a sword will pierce your own soul too."

There was also a prophetess, Anna, the daughter of Penuel, of
the tribe of Asher. She was very old; she had lived with her husband

Editors' Note: This sermon is dated 1847.

seven years after her marriage, and then was a widow until she was eighty-four. She never left the temple but worshiped night and day, fasting and praying. Coming up to them at that very moment, she gave thanks to God and spoke about the child to all who were looking forward to the redemption of Jerusalem.

When Joseph and Mary had done everything required by the Law of the Lord, they returned to Galilee to their own town of Nazareth. And the child grew and became strong; he was filled with wisdom, and the grace of God was on him.

—LUKE 2:22–40 (NIV)

Beloved brothers and sisters, here are two people, Simeon and Anna, who waited longingly for the redemption of Israel. There must have also been many other people who waited quietly like they did. Imagine how they must have felt. [. . .] They felt the burden of the times; they felt their bondage and captivity. But they also knew what the prophets of old had witnessed to. They were extremely troubled and yet also longed that their lives would improve. [. . .] Hundreds of years had passed, and with every passing year things only became worse. And so, like Simeon and Anna, people were driven to pray: "Oh, that deliverance for Israel would come out of Zion." At the time of the Savior's birth there must have been many devout Israelites who were in this troubled state of mind. We are now reminded of Simeon and Anna, two of these devout Israelites. We will now speak further of them.

But first let me ask the following: Has everything Simeon and Anna wished and waited for been fulfilled? Is the kingdom of God now in its full bloom as promised? No. Are we, then, like Simeon and Anna, yearning and praying for deliverance and redemption? Even though the Savior came long ago and now sits at the right hand of his Father, have we reached the point where our hopes are fulfilled? Ah, who of us can say that Israel's hopes have been fulfilled? God's time has begun. Our Savior laid the foundation for the coming eternal peace, but not all of God's "enemies" have been overcome. The struggle continues.

In the last 1800 years the dragon or the seven-headed beast has somehow recovered from its wounds. And why is this? It is we who have allowed it to overcome the saints (Rev 12:9). And so the powers of darkness appear to have the upper hand. Just look at all our attempts to address human misery. Human suffering seems to only grow worse. It's almost impossible to envision how souls can be set free. It seems as if the waves of the sea pitch and roll just as they wish (Ps 93:4). The "garden" is ravished almost at will. And millions languish in darkness, crying out for peace. When, oh when, will God's hour come—when will the day come for which we have travailed through suffering and death? When will the adversary be overthrown? We are still waiting for the consolation of Israel. We must do this quietly, for most of the world won't hear it, does not want to comprehend it, or grasp it. So many people love the darkness more than the light. They will not allow their minds and hearts to be opened to the drastic measures of the Spirit.

Now as to what the prophets foretold—now, that gives us much to hope for! At whatever page we open the Book we can only look at one another and marvel. "We see nothing of this and never have seen anything like it." Will this still happen? Will this still come? This is the reason why believing souls like Simeon and Anna sigh, "O Lord, let the day of grace, the year of thy favor break in at last, to save the desolate, proclaim liberty to the captives, to give a garland instead of ashes, the oil of gladness instead of mourning, to give garments of beauty to the fainthearted and freedom to all the afflicted and brokenhearted" (see Isaiah 61). It is true that there are many people who hang onto the hope that things will improve. But this has little to do with God's consolation. It is perfectly understandable why people want to be spared suffering. But this is not enough. It does not make us a Simeon or an Anna. Sin and pain are in our homes; and we sigh and complain. But even this is not the same thing as standing expectantly before God.

So we must find out how to wait for the consolation of Israel, how it was that Simeon and Anna bore themselves in quietness. For we have much to learn from them, and much to learn from these short passages from the Gospel.

1. In order to be a Simeon we must be as devout and God-fearing as he was. He possessed a most fervent love and awe for the name of the Most High, and without this we cannot truly wait for the coming of the Lord. Anna too. "She never left the temple but worshiped night and day, fasting and praying" Thus, her waiting turned into joy. In the same way, we must daily lift up our eyes and hands to God in true devotion, in true earnestness—not as a matter of habit, not with idle or right words upon our lips. Our prayer must be heartfelt, whether

alone or together. We must walk in the fear of God, guarding against anything that will grieve God's Spirit—whatever hurts and offends him. Whether in our thoughts or in our words, we must be faithful watchmen, alarmed by every temptation that wants to lead us to sin. The day of his redemption will certainly come, "For he is like a refiner's fire and like fullers' soap; he will sit as a refiner and purifier of silver, and he will purify the descendants of Levi and refine them like gold and silver . . ." (Mal 3:2–3). "Then I will draw near to you for judgment; I will be a swift to bear witness against the sorcerers, against the adulterers, against those who swear falsely, against those who oppress the hired workers in their wages, the widow and the orphan, against those who thrust aside the alien, and do not fear me, says the Lord of hosts" (Mal 3:5). Let us flee far away from evil or else the coming day will not bring us joy like it did for Simeon. Let us truly fear the Lord, otherwise we cannot be a Simeon or an Anna. Without this fear we will become hardhearted.

2. Simeon looked for the consolation of Israel. He believed in the prophet's promised consolation. We must speak about this in more detail. First, Simeon recognized Israel's need and secondly, he believed in the prophet's promise of consolation. In these two things we learn from Simeon that we must take this need to heart, realizing how deeply people are ensnared—also we ourselves. That is the first thing that belongs to real expectation. However, we mustn't let this recognition make us fainthearted; rather, the knowledge of this misery must be followed by a believing hope in which we firmly hold to the fact that not one word of the promise will be lost. Let us think more about all of this and learn from Simeon. Oh, might we all become true Simeons and true Annas!

3. Whoever has this divine longing will soon be rewarded. Simeon believed that not one word of the promise would be lost. And thus, the Holy Spirit was upon him. The more he quietly served the Lord in earnest, the more he prayed and trustingly hoped, the more the Spirit of God was upon him. He was comforted in his waiting and in turn was able to hope with deeper and deeper joy. This can be our experience too whenever we are ready to serve the Lord like Simeon and Anna. The Lord will refresh our souls; the Holy Spirit will clarify our lives so that we do not become fainthearted. And like Simeon, who was assured that he would not see death before he had seen the Messiah, a

special grace, an assurance, can be given to us, which no one can ever take away. And even when such assurance is not given to us personally, we will be able to draw courage from the firm faith of others, who are so blessed. Whoever lifts their eyes unto the hills will receive help.

4. Simeon possessed something else—something that was not given to those who waited as he did. It was something that remained the possession of very few, only for those whom God had chosen. It is written of Simeon: "It had been revealed to him by the Holy Spirit that he would not die before he had seen the Lord's Messiah." That was a very special grace that Simeon received, a grace that was not necessarily given to others. [. . .] And so, to one or the other, an assurance can be given that can never be taken. This assurance is not given equally to each person—one may receive more. But then those with less assurance should draw courage from the firm faith of those who have more. In any case, we can see that those who look up to the Lord, those whose eyes are lifted to the hills from where help comes, receive much grace from him. Many of you can testify that the Lord indeed does not fail to manifest himself to those who look up to him.

5. Simeon was inspired by the Spirit to come into the temple. At the right moment the Spirit urged Simeon to go into the temple. Though not knowing why, he felt that he must enter. The impulse was so strong that he just had to go. This is how it is for all those who long for the day of salvation. God opens up a way for everyone who sincerely believes in him. He knows how to let each person hear what should be heard, see what should be seen, and experience what should be experienced. So great is the goodness of our God and so inconspicuously and quietly does he guide his children that we can only shout for joy and be glad because of his great kindness. Simeon is in the temple when he sees the child. Within him there is a feeling that becomes an overwhelming certainty. "Here is the Redeemer who will save Israel!" He took the child in his arms and praised God, saying, "Lord, as you have promised, you may now dismiss your servant in peace. For my eyes have seen your salvation, which you have prepared in the sight of all nations, a light for revelation to the Gentiles, and the glory of your people Israel."

In a very similar way this can happen today. For when Jesus comes again in his glory there will be light long before he comes. He will make us aware of the time in which we stand, and we will either reject or take this time, like a little child, into our arms. Oh, you dear ones, we have actually seen signs and indications of this, even if it they are inconspicuous. [. . .] But how is it with us—really?

Blessed are those who stand in the fear of the Lord, so that they are certain in hope and constant in prayer that the Lord will fulfill the promise he made to his people. Simeon praises and speaks prophetically—so does Anna. Peace and joy entered into their souls, and all those who heard them received a spark of consolation for their tired souls; once again they could wait with hope and trust. Come, then! Don't become weary, but wait patiently for our Lord. He will not tarry. His day approaches! Happy are they whom he finds awake when he comes! Amen.

Vindicate Us from Our Adversary!

And he told them a parable, to the effect that they ought always to pray and not lose heart. He said, "In a certain city there was a judge who neither feared God nor regarded man; and there was a widow in that city who kept coming to him and saying, 'Vindicate me against my adversary.' For a while he refused; but afterward he said to himself, 'Though I neither fear God nor regard man, yet because this widow bothers me, I will vindicate her, or she will wear me out by her continual coming.'"

And the Lord said, "Hear what the unrighteous judge says. And will not God vindicate his elect, who cry to him day and night? Will he delay long over them? I tell you, he will vindicate them speedily. Nevertheless, when the Son of man comes, will he find faith on earth?"

—LUKE 18:1–8 (RSV)

Beloved, this parable teaches us to always pray. But the Savior doesn't want us to pray without us really knowing why we are praying. It's not formal prayer that he wants from us, not long drawn-out prayers with many words and with all kinds of pious airs and gestures. This is not pleasing to God. Before going further, we must consider why it is we should be in constant prayer and what it is we should be praying for. We need to do this so that we don't grow weary and so we might also grow in an unceasing desire to ask God to act and to grant our prayers. For we shall see, that what the

Editors' Note: This sermon is dated 1860.

Savior desires and what should concern us is not something that will come immediately. No, it is something that is often long delayed, which only comes gradually, depending on how faithful and steadfast we are in prayer.

So then, what are we to pray for? It is clear that Jesus is thinking of his future coming, and our gaze should be directed toward that coming, toward the mighty, universal deliverance of all creation. This will happen when he returns. All our prayers and imploring should echo the cry, "Your kingdom come. Your will be done on earth as it is in heaven!" Never grow weary when you pray for this. All our other prayers are of secondary importance. What the Savior wants to impress upon his disciples and upon us as well is that all our prayers should be concerned with that which is still to come. Now we want to say a few things about what the church must do according to our Gospel text. Our basic theme will be the time about which the Savior speaks and for which it is always necessary to pray. The Savior speaks about three things: 1) About a time in which the church on earth will be a widow; 2) About a time in which there will still be a chosen people representing the widow crying out unceasingly; and 3) About a time in which faith has almost disappeared.

1. Let us turn our attention to the grieving widow. Jesus is actually referring to his people, the church, which is like a weeping, oppressed, and forlorn widow who has lost her husband and is left desolate. Now Jesus promised his disciples that he would not leave them as orphans, but would come to them (John 14:18). It was never the Savior's intention that his children be abandoned like widows and orphans. He promised to send a Counselor, to be with us forever, One who would remind us of everything he had said (John 14:16, 26). Jesus did this when he poured forth in richest abundance the Holy Spirit at Pentecost. The church lacked nothing, for she was the Lord's joyful bride. She felt the promise of divine powers in her midst and lacked nothing. But let us look more closely at this. In what way, according to his last words in John's Gospel, does the Savior remain present? Answer: "I will pray the Father, and he will give you another Counselor, to be with you forever" (John 14:16). "But the Counselor, the Holy Spirit, whom the Father will send in my name, he will teach you all things, and bring to your remembrance all that I have said to you (John 14:26). " In short: "The Holy Spirit will be with you in my place." And when Christ says, "I will come to you and not leave you orphaned," he is referring to the outpouring of the Spirit, which came at Pentecost. At that time the

Lord Jesus came to his children bringing with him the divine powers and divine graces of the Holy Spirit in richest abundance. The first Christian church thus had the full glory of God in their midst and could never again say that they were forsaken, that they were widows and orphans. Ah, how blessed they were to be able to say, "We lack nothing, there is no gift we have not received, and now we only wait until he himself comes" (free translation, 1 Cor 1:7). The church of God was the Lord's joyful bride and had constantly the deepest and most blessed fellowship with her Savior; she lacked nothing and felt everywhere the promised divine powers in her midst.

Did it continue like this? Did the Lord remain with his church in this way? Do we still have these glorious gifts of grace? I think it is easy enough to see that we don't. All we have to do is look at the manifold afflictions that have everywhere eaten into Christianity and for which we can find no help. We can do nothing other than to speak frankly and confess that with us things are different. Inasmuch as our Lord has withdrawn so much of grace we have the feeling of being forsaken, as though he has left us. We are tremendously lacking in what the Lord wishes to give us and to be to us—so much so, that we can say with every justification that the Christian church is like a poor, desolate widow, deprived of her glory, who must in her mourning sigh and pray that God may again be merciful to her and give back what has been taken away; in other words, that her Lord may return to her again in all his original kindness, until the time when he himself will again appear in person. We must seriously consider this. The widow sighs because she has an adversary, an enemy. She lacks protection, she cannot defend herself. She is powerless—at the mercy of anyone who wishes to treat her violently or unjustly. And this is how it is with us today. The church languishes under the yoke and chains of the enemy—the adversary who wreaks so much ruin, corruption, and disunity. Dear friends, open your eyes and see how the church today is very much like a widow. Unless we become like the widow who rushes to the "judge" and wears him out until he rebuilds our faith, the Lord's promise will remain unfulfilled.

2. We can be glad that there are still chosen people who cry out to God day and night. Among the tormented—however forsaken, hampered, bound, and miserable they are—there are still some who cry out to God. These are the ones who also are being robbed and feel forsaken

and pressed down by the adversary. These chosen ones have one thing in common: they feel that they must pray and keep on praying if the world is to get any better. They know that evil should not be allowed to continue as it has and that the devil, who lays hands on everything and wants to seize everything, must no longer be permitted to go on plundering. They feel that they must keep coming to the Lord again and again, without becoming tired, and in so doing save for the future and salvage the truth. There still exist people like these, praying, hoping, and believing that the world will change. In light of the Savior's admonishment in the parable, we must always pray and not lose heart. We who believe, we who see signs of his love, even if they are only a "glimmer of light" shining through a crack, we are all called to keep seeking the Savior. Let us turn to him and allow ourselves to be cleansed by his blood. Let us rely only on his grace and mercy, assured that he rejects no one. Jesus listens to everyone who asks, he comes to all who trust in him. Whoever sincerely struggles against sin, whoever strives faithfully to withstand worldly temptations so as to not be "hewn down" as others are, can be assured of his love.

These constitute the little band who look to Jesus, who are not entangled in earthly affairs, but turn again and again to God. These are the chosen ones who cry out day and night, who are constantly concerned because there is so much tribulation. They cry out under the weight of Satan's bondage and yearn for the redemption of creation. They always pray and they don't lose heart. Many of us try to pray, but then soon give up when we see no immediate result. We assume that since everything is corrupt, we can do nothing but save our own souls. There is nothing more we can really do. We think, even if we don't say it outright, that God's final judgment is upon the world. The world with its widespread corruption cannot be salvaged. We think that the best we can do is to keep ourselves free from sin and evil. But this is not at all what the Savior wants! If we would but take up the widow's task, we would experience again what was once given long ago to the church, and not only partly. Satan wants nothing more than to dominate the world. We must therefore struggle and fight against this day and night. We should do this even if it appears that nothing more can be done. We are called to persevere in prayer or else we will incur a heavy guilt. The Lord commands us to pray—all opinions, all misgivings, and all prejudices must go! We must obey and keep praying for his coming, for his kingdom, for the gifts of grace, for an abundant outpouring of the Holy Spirit. We must be alert and see where we can intercede to achieve his victory. Even if no progress is being made—still we must go on. Even if the judge seems to reject us and says, "Why are you crying? Get away from me, I have no use for you!" we must repeatedly come back to him. Yes, even when it seems that heaven is closed and that God's compassion is slow in coming, when it seems that even from above there is no help for this corrupt and abandoned generation—even then we are required to come again and again, and ever again to God. If we do this, the impossible is made possible. Remember, in the parable the judge is unjust. He doesn't care. The widow should have actually stayed away and remained sighing in her little chamber, "It is all of no use!" Nevertheless, she kept coming, despite the fact that her adversary became more and more impudent. Yet, all the more she hurried to the judge, until at last he gives in, "This woman has gone too far; she gives me no peace. I will have to give her satisfaction." He finally helped her.

When we set out to work and try to obtain decisive help from heaven, we are soon aware that it is hard, a serious and difficult situation. In urgent cases we pray and implore ten times, a hundred times, but it seems as if all our prayers drift away in the wind. It's as if—as pictured by the prophets—heaven was like iron (Lev 26:19). And so we soon grow weary, for it seems that nothing works. But this is what the Lord foretold would happen. In the dark times, when the church is like a widow and the adversary is a hard master, it takes great effort, sacrifice, and hard "fighting" before we are heard. All the more we are to give ourselves up body and soul—all our external comforts and even our inner peace. We must exercise true faith and pray, not with words only, but with our whole being directed toward the living God and his promises. If in our parable the unrighteous judge was at last made to relent, then what about God? Surely the holy, just, compassionate, and gracious God will yield to our entreaties. He will certainly provide aid and deliverance to the church that pleads to him. Surely he will give her all that she needs and set her free from bondage to her adversary. That is the promise offered to us by the Lord. But we must follow his advice and never lose heart. For he says, "Will not God also vindicate his elect who patiently cry to him day and night? Truly, I tell you, he will vindicate them speedily."

At last, at last, the great day of salvation will come. And when it does, it will come quickly, even if for a long, long time it seems as if our prayers are achieving nothing. God's kingdom will at last break in and great things will take place. Suddenly the almighty hand of our God and Savior will break off a thousand chains and burst open a thousand fetters that bind his children. God will show that he is the Lord and will completely shatter the power of darkness. My beloved friends, we who are devoted to him should pray. Jesus' first disciples understood this better than anyone, for what did they have? They had absolutely nothing. They had left father and mother, brother and sister, friends and relations, house and home—what else could they pray for than that the whole world should belong to Christ. This too must be our one and only desire: that every knee should bow and every tongue confess that Jesus is Lord. Everything else is trivial, and when this becomes our supreme wish, then praying for and expecting God's kingdom will naturally grip our hearts and minds. [. . .] We will no longer rest our heads to sleep without also thinking of sorrowing creation, nor will we awaken without feeling the burden of all humankind.

3. There is one more thing that is important in this parable. Christ ends this parable with a sigh, "Nevertheless, when the Son of Man comes, will he find faith on earth?" Dear ones, there will always be people who praise the Savior, who speak of a faith that justifies, who love the Holy Scriptures, attend church, and have received grace and the forgiveness of sins. There will always be people who come together for godly conversation and devotions, who also give themselves in a practical way to work for the kingdom of God, being active in mission at home or abroad. They work to convert others and are always praying. There are many who admonish and encourage one another to follow Christ. And there are always people, both in the past and now, who have left the world for Christ's sake, who mortify their flesh, and who withdraw from all that is displeasing to the Lord. We should give praise and thanks to God that there are such people even in the darkest times. But, this is not what the Lord refers to here. When Jesus asks, ". . . will he find faith on earth?" he is referring to the kind of faith that expects unlimited help. He is referring to the faith that is unswervingly convinced that the Lord will at last redeem the world. [. . .] This faith fights and struggles so that the Lord rules heaven as well as earth. [. . .] This faith is absolute trust in Jesus and in his promises. [. . .] This

faith has no room for doubt—not the slightest room. My dear friends, the worst thing is to have "faith" and yet disbelieve. Yes, we can have faith and yet have no faith. The faith Jesus looks for demands courage to pray earnestly for what has been promised. It gives absolutely no credit to what the devil can do. [. . .] When the Lord's coming draws near, the adversary will seize hold of everything. The Antichrist will powerfully tread everything underfoot so that no one dares oppose him. Hundreds and thousands will be killed, bound and tormented by satanic powers. With his horrible dragon claws the adversary will seize all he can, far and wide. But then many thousands will turn to God and pray to him earnestly. "Watch out—all this will end in a day. A day will come in which a trumpet will sound from heaven and then all the enemy hosts and the dragon will be cast into the abyss!" What is hindering this day? Why hasn't it come? Isn't it partially because of our lack of faith? Who knows for how long? Oh, how near help often is, how quickly and suddenly help would be given if we had unwavering trust in the Savior. Jesus is our brother who sits at the right hand of God. All authority has been given to him. He has the power to help his children. Why aren't we convinced that he really lives for his church, that he lives for those who believe in him and who call out to him? Why won't we believe that Jesus lives for us now while we are on earth and that he is redeeming us and all his suffering creation?

If we do not have this kind of faith, then we must pray for it—a faith that completely relies on the Savior. Only with this kind of faith will we be able to accomplish great things. With this faith we can conquer the powers of darkness. Oh, our age desperately needs this faith. Only through this faith, through our sighs to heaven, will Jesus rescue all who are held captive. With this faith we can call down God's powers so that the wretched of the earth can find true life and lasting peace. Yes! May the Lord look down and hear our cries. May he grant us his counsel and may he destroy the schemes of the adversary. Jesus can and will bring this about. His blood will not be shed in vain. He who was raised from the dead and who sits at the right hand of his Father will be victorious. The victory is his! Amen.

PART III
The Return of Christ

SECTION 1
TRUST IN THE PROMISE

The Delay in the Coming
of the Lord

For it will be as when a man going on a journey called his servants
and entrusted to them his property; to one he gave five talents, to
another two, to another one, to each according to his ability. Then
he went away. He who had received the five talents went at once and
traded with them; and he made five talents more. So also, he who had
the two talents made two talents more. But he who had received the
one talent went and dug in the ground and hid his master's money.

Now after a long time the master of those servants came and
settled accounts with them. And he who had received the five talents
came forward, bringing five talents more, saying, "Master, you
delivered to me five talents; here I have made five talents more." His
master said to him, "Well done, good and faithful servant; you have
been faithful over a little, I will set you over much; enter into the joy
of your master." And he also who had the two talents came forward,
saying, "Master, you delivered to me two talents; here I have made
two talents more." His master said to him, "Well done, good and
faithful servant; you have been faithful over a little, I will set you over
much; enter into the joy of your master." He also who had received
the one talent came forward, saying, "Master, I knew you to be a hard
man, reaping where you did not sow, and gathering where you did
not winnow; so I was afraid, and I went and hid your talent in the
ground. Here you have what is yours." But his master answered him,
"You wicked and slothful servant! You knew that I reap where I have

Editors' Note: This sermon is dated 1869.

167

not sowed, and gather where I have not winnowed? Then you ought to have invested my money with the bankers, and at my coming I should have received what was my own with interest. So take the talent from him, and give it to him who has the ten talents. For to everyone who has will more be given, and he will have abundance; but from him who has not, even what he has will be taken away. And cast the worthless servant into the outer darkness; there men will weep and gnash their teeth."

—MATTHEW 25:14–30 (RSV)

We are approaching the end of the church year, and our Gospel text fits very well with the thoughts that move us at this time. These verses from Matthew make us think how we have spent our time. We are faced with the question: Have you and I used the talent or talents that have been given to us? Have we made something for the Lord with them? Have we made enough in proportion to what we have received, or have we fallen short or not even used what has been given to us, bringing the Lord no profit at all?

We should take these questions very seriously because whether or not we have made something will be of greatest significance on the day the Lord returns. The text says that whoever does not add to what was given will lose everything, even what was given to him. What was promised to the worthless servants? They will be cast into "outer darkness where they will weep and gnash their teeth." I can tell you one thing. None of us will want to be there when any unworthy servant is expelled into outer darkness where there is weeping and gnashing of teeth. Therefore, let us take the words of the Lord deeply to heart. Let us try to understand this parable.

The one who gave out the talents is compared to a master going on a long journey. He thus entrusts the management of his property to others. This master is obviously a reference to Jesus himself. While he sojourned here on earth, he had managed his property alone, so to speak, taking on the lonely task of the redemption of humanity. As it happened, he was killed by human beings, which resulted in his leaving this world. Though this did not result in his remaining dead, it did come about that as the Risen One he went "on a journey" so to speak, entering into heaven without appearing again on earth. The Lord departed with the promise that he would return again. This is what our parable wants to tell us. "Now after a long time the master of those servants came and settled accounts with them."

It is of great significant that Jesus says: "Now after a long time . . ." We often read in the Scriptures that he will come "soon." That little word "soon" occurs repeatedly, puzzling us because we have had to wait such a long time. How much longer? We do not know. But we can only understand "long" differently, since after his resurrection, Jesus' life is long. We cannot measure his life against the span of a human life—it could be a thousand, two thousand, or more years. And because the Lord so emphatically uses the expression "after a long time," it could be an indication that according to our conception, there might be a really long delay. If then, at the conclusion of this church year, we become serious because another year is past and the promised future of the Lord is still awaited, and we can say now that he will probably not come in this next year, we can to some extent be comforted by these words of the Lord. It might delay yet another year, but even so we can feel the beginnings of his coming. We sense in the atmosphere the beginnings of the end, when finally the Lord himself will come. And so we should expect Jesus to return anytime. Even if we have to wait, we can still believe, despite what the Lord said about being gone for "a long time," that he will come soon. Hence, we must be ready for that day.

What, then, should happen while we still wait for this? He is in heaven and we are on earth. He left us talents and distributed them in diverse ways, all to be put to work. The master gave to the different servants five, two, and one talent. [. . .] He gave them something that has to be won. What is it? What are these talents? Didn't the Lord say, "Go into all the world and preach the gospel to the whole creation. He who believes and is baptized will be saved, but he who does not believe will be condemned" (Mark 16:15–16)? The talents, therefore, represent the ability to proclaim the gospel [with power]. With the gospel, people are led into the kingdom of God. This distribution of the talents was actually given to the disciples when Jesus breathed upon them and said, "Take with you the Holy Spirit." These talents were distributed further and more completely at Pentecost when the Holy Spirit was poured out over the disciples and all those who believed. The Holy Spirit, a gift from above, was given to the early followers of Christ. They were given power to proclaim the good news of Christ. At first everybody who believed received it equally. Later on, it came to people in different ways. Not all were filled like Peter; not all were like Paul. They did not all receive the gift of the Holy Spirit to the same measure as the apostles did. Only a few received five talents, the largest sum—the fullness of the Holy Spirit. However, all received something. As Paul would later write in his letter to the Corinthians, one was given one gift, while another was given a different gift. Whatever the gift given to us, we are called to use it faithfully and make full use of it for the good of everyone. And when everyone does this, these gifts, these talents, will be used so that the whole world will hear the gospel.

So then, why hasn't the Lord returned? Why is his coming taking so long? We can never know for sure, but the question arises: Doesn't the guilt lie on our neglecting to spread the gospel? How many even know the gospel? Even in countries where the gospel has been preached there is so little or significant participation in the kingdom of God; it seems hardly noticeable at all. The main reason it has taken so long, therefore, is because Jesus' intentions haven't been fulfilled—his servants have neglected the task that was given to them. The Lord will delay his coming as long as things are not what he wants them to be. Hereupon we can, of course, wonder how long it will continue, how many thousands of years it will be delayed, considering that not more has been accomplished in the past two thousand years.

Now think again about the little word "soon." That word implies that the Lord could return quickly, but only if the newly appointed servants of the Lord would fulfill their obligations completely. In other words, a "long time" could be replaced by "soon" if we, his servants, would do our part to complete the task. Every age has its servants, and when all of them fulfill their obligations then the Lord's return can happen quickly.

In our time it seems as if the gifts and powers of the Spirit of God, his talents, which lead to swift answers, have not been given. We could well feel that our present generation lacks talents. Still, there must be some who have received at least one talent to trade for the day when Christ comes again. Even with one talent we can pray for more, for an increase of gifts and for a renewal like that in earlier times. Christ's great work must be completed.

Remember, it depends very much on the talent-bearers truly conducting their business. Are they making use of God's grace and the gift of the Gospels they have received? Each one of us must therefore plead with the Lord to sow his seed and again bestow his gifts with the power they had in the beginning. We can only increase effectively what we've been given if we petition the Lord, asking him again and again to give, distribute, and renew all the powers to finish the great work of the conversion of the world, gathering all people into the kingdom of God.

God gives talents to each person differently. One is highly gifted to speak out and proclaim publicly what is important for us all; others serve God and their fellow men in a practical way. These various gifts are also apportioned in different ways. Therefore, take a closer look at your situation and be determined not to go away empty handed. Don't try to estimate how much you have received, thinking others have received more and thus are able to do more. No. We are each called to increase whatever we have been given. And if we do this, we will win others for the Lord.

Every follower of Jesus is to "bear fruit for others." [. . .] It is important that our Christianity is firmly rooted in our hearts, so it can become strong and bear fruit—however much we have been given, whether five talents, or two talents, or only one. Those of us who have but one talent have just as an important part to play for the kingdom of God as those who have five. All are needed! Whether our field of activity is small or big, God needs all of us to do our part.

But here is the question: Do you let people pass by you without acknowledging or greeting them? Do you offer something of yourself that will help and encourage people around you? Are you inwardly active within your family and with those in your broader circle? Have you received one talent and are you putting it to use, or not? Listen carefully. Do not compare yourself with others. Be busy with what you have been given and let yourself be used to the limits of your capacities. Use your talents with as much devotion as you can. For there are many who have a large field of activity, and are busy, but who are actually not devoted enough. They are zealous, but they are not necessarily as zealous as those with a lesser task, with fewer talents. There are countless people who have a great deal of knowledge and yet have no talents; they have neither eagerness nor enthusiasm. Whatever the case may be, let us each ask that more gifts and more powers are given to us with which to work.

It is interesting that in our parable no one with five talents is idle, not even one with two talents. It is striking that no one is seen as lazy except the one who received one talent. And perhaps they received only one talent for a reason. For the challenge here is not strictly speaking whether one receives one or two or five talents. [. . .] The problem is one of indifference and laziness. Those with the least talents are those who fail to "stir" themselves, who do nothing and bury their talent.

This should give us a lot to think about. Very often those who have little, even among the poor, don't know how to use the little they have. They are idle and indifferent and leave this world just as "poor" as when they entered it. [. . .] This is why we must encourage and inspire each other. But, this takes effort! And for those of us who have only one talent and pray quietly, are we taking the trouble to speak a good word to those we live with, or to speak with our neighbors and any others we meet?

Most of us have but one talent; our circle of influence is small. We too easily think we are inadequate for the work of the gospel. So we pass it off to others and do nothing. We bury our talent. We are too lazy, too comfortable, and too proud. We hide and do not let anyone challenge us to do more. Our lives are such that even the power of God comes to a standstill against our fear and apathy. [. . .] Yet, Jesus warns us that a great responsibility rests upon those who, though having received little, do not use their talent to further God's kingdom. Indeed, one talent is important, that's why the punishment is so great.

When we fail to invest our one talent we actually hinder the Lord from coming. Our duty and task is to make the Christian life flourish. When we are enthusiastic, everyone around us becomes more alive. So then what would it be like if all of us who profess to follow the Savior were actually alive? Surely God's gifts would increase; surely more and more of this world would come under the influence of the Spirit of God!

Lord, guide our hearts so that we may truly see what you have given to us. We long to bring forth more fruit. Forgive us for being so indifferent to your love and for how little we have to show. God have mercy on us. We do not want the little that has been given us to be taken away. Amen.

I Make All Things New

"... and God will wipe away every tear from their eyes, and death
shall be no more, neither shall there be mourning nor crying nor
pain any more, for the former things have passed away." And he who
sat upon the throne said, "Behold, I make all things new."

—Revelation 21:4–5 (RSV)

The prophets spoke of the great year of redemption, which John describes as beginning with "tears being wiped away from eyes." Whoever embraces God will no longer cry or mourn. Death shall be no more. This can happen even in our time. The horror of death can be removed. But even more than that can happen. Death will be no more! We will all be changed and go to meet the Lord. Today sadness and torment are part of our daily life. However, when the great year of redemption begins, all misery, distress, fear, and sickness will be overcome; sickness will retreat more and more. Instead we will be comforted and refreshed. Despite many imperfections, it will seem like heaven.

He who sat upon the throne exclaims, "Behold, I make all things new." He will accomplish what God had in mind from the very beginning. We know that it is not like this today, but we trust that God will make all things new. He will let us see, taste, and experience his complete love for us. A "new year" in which the history of humanity will be brought to an end is awaited by all Christians [. . .]; a "new year" in which the powers of darkness are weakened, even abolished; in which the will of God alone shall rule and the will to evil be banished; a "new year" in this age in which outwardly everything will continue, but which will reflect God's will for humankind since the beginning of time—God's will, which had been blighted by Satan, the serpent of old.

We are eagerly waiting for this "new year," which will come shortly before the return of the Lord. All sorrow brought by the powers of darkness will be overcome when Jesus comes. Then we will meet him joyfully. The prophets and the good news of the gospel promise this. But are we ready? A sudden change right in our time may happen, when God commands us, "Stop! You cannot go on like this. I am going to change everything!" The powers of God will be revealed, and God's mercy for all creation will come closer; for a great deal is going to happen that humankind has never dreamt of, and mourning will be no more. Despite trials and tribulations, a golden age of God's goodness is promised us. Oh, if only the Holy Spirit and his renewing strength would rule in all creation now! Then we would all recognize the signs in heaven and upon earth. Ah, how different life would be! All the sin and evil that tries to bind us would be gone!

All of us have experienced fear, and the needs of this past year often haunt us. But we also know and experience God's mercy. We must hold on to this, comforting and encouraging one another with Christ's word. It is actually very wonderful to reflect back on all the grace and goodness God has bestowed on us; it is simply wonderful! This keeps me joyful as I wait with deep certainty for the great day of salvation. The Lord is faithful and keeps his promises. Christ's every promise will be fulfilled at his time. Therefore, we will not enter into the New Year with mourning and faint-heartedness, but with the joyful faith that Christ Jesus is the Savior who will soon set everything right.

Persevere!

For still the vision awaits its time; it hastens to the end—it will not
lie. If it seems slow, wait for it; it will surely come, it will not delay.

—HABAKKUK 2:3 (RSV)

A t the time of "the awakening," when Jesus was victorious over the
devil, I had this passage placed on the wall of the Möttlingen Church;
you can still read it there today. We hoped that this vision would be fulfilled
very soon, but the vision reads, "If it seems slow, wait for it; it will surely
come." So we still wait, and we wait with confident, unfaltering hearts. This
promise ends in the final liberation of all creation from its bondage to darkness. We have had to wait a long time, and we still wait for the fulfillment
of this promise.

The beginning [of the fulfillment of this promise] came six hundred
years after Habakkuk, and now almost 1900 years have transpired, and it
still has not been fulfilled. A long time has passed! We still wait. But we can
be cheerful; we are nearer our goal—it will not be long now. The great time
of redemption is near. What God has promised will happen, no matter how
much time goes by. This is our faith, our hope. The words of God will not
fade away; they will become reality. God would have to stop being God
if the words and promises that he has given to suffering humanity aren't
fulfilled. Yes, one generation after the other has waited. We must wait also.
But let us truly wait, wait without relaxing. A time will come—perhaps it is
in some way already here—when God's redemption draws near.

Editors' Note: This sermon is dated 1878.

The Lord Is Faithful

For Zion's sake I will not keep silent, and for Jerusalem's sake I will
not rest, until her vindication shines out like the dawn, and her
salvation like a burning torch.

—ISAIAH 62:1 (NRSV)

The Lord is speaking here of the time when he will reveal himself in the
glorious future that is to come. This future, when God's plan of salvation is fulfilled, is all related to the kingdom of the Savior and to the people
he wants to redeem for the day of his return. This is the Savior's future, the
Savior as he was and will be. The first interruption of God's silence was
the arrival of Jesus, of whom we are especially reminded at Advent. Up
until then God had remained silent for hundreds of years; he had ceased to
reveal his personal testimony. But prophecies such as this made the people
of Israel an expectant people who cherished hopes of the Savior's advent.
But then God sent Jesus—the Messiah! That was indeed an interruption of
God's silence and a fulfillment of this promise—at least a beginning of its
fulfillment. Since then, a long time has transpired. We too long for his coming; we are dependent upon hope, and we celebrate Advent as people who
await a word from the Lord that will usher in his return for the fulfillment
of all things.

This promise has not been cancelled—the Lord will again break his
silence and will not withhold his word. Because the Savior's birth was the
beginning of the fulfillment of God's promise, there is more to come! So

Editors' Note: This sermon was published posthumously in 1881; it is identified as an
Advent sermon.

176

Christ continues to prepare the world for his second coming. He won't re-main hidden; a New Zion, a New Jerusalem will be built. A time is coming when "her vindication will shine out like the dawn, and her salvation like a burning torch." A time is coming when finally all sorrow will end, when all resistance by the powers of darkness will be defeated.

In the meantime, we deeply sigh and cry tears. And we will continue do so until "the last time" comes—when God's everlasting encouragement comes. This is promised to us, and we will not allow it to be taken from us. The Lord is faithful and he will fulfill his promise.

The Lord Comes!

The Lord is not slow about his promise as some count slowness, but
is forbearing toward you, not wishing that any should perish, but that
all should reach repentance.

— 2 PETER 3:9 (RSV)

Dear ones, you may wonder why I have chosen a text like this for today.
But as we celebrate the Reformation, we must remember that Luther
was convinced that the coming of the Lord was near. He actually believed that
his work directly paved the way for Christ's coming against the Antichrist.
His writings are full of this. A special little book of Luther's words has even
been put together and published in order to show how Luther should be
regarded and treasured as a prophet—a prophet who spoke in a stimulat-
ing and profound manner about the future and of coming judgments, and
of the promised coming of the Lord. It shouldn't surprise any of you why
Luther's thoughts have been singled out now to celebrate the Reformation.
We too may look with him upon the "last things." God did not let the new
light of the Reformation come just to achieve a purified Christian outlook,
some religion or confession by which man should live, but to prepare us,
in deed and in truth, for the Lord's future. This is why the Reformation has
never been anything more for me than an example of a spiritual renewal
meant to spread throughout the whole world. It is an example of the rising
of the light and glory of God upon all people to call them to a new, divine
life.

Editors' Note: This sermon was given on Reformation Day in 1879.

Looking at the Reformation, it would be a mistake to think only of Protestants, Evangelicals, Lutherans, Calvinists, or whatever else they are called. No. The Lord had much greater and more far-reaching purposes in mind with the Reformation. He had a far greater purpose than to lift up Evangelicals as being the sole bearers of salvation, as if other people and churches did not exist. Sadly, Evangelicals have thought of themselves as being the new Israel, dreaming only about themselves in an egotistical and self-loving manner. But that is certainly not right; and even if today such thinking quietly persists here and there, we should not believe that this is the Lord's chief intention and purpose.

The Lord is coming! This, in essence, is what Luther nailed to the church door at Wittenberg. The Lord comes as he has promised, and if we think back to all that has happened since the time of the Reformation it echoes back to us, "The Lord is coming!" This promise stands firm, even if it seems to be delayed. At that time God knocked hard on the doors of the church, and every heart felt, "The Lord is near!" But then, everything fell quiet again. It had been the hour of midnight, and the watchman cried out, "The bridegroom comes!" But when the bridegroom tarried, the people went to sleep again. What one had hoped for was again delayed, and for a good two hundred years nobody thought any more about the Lord's coming. Only in the past one hundred years has the idea come to life again in our fatherland, but there are still large districts, also Protestant areas, where belief in the promise and faith in the Lord's coming is dormant. True, we have been awakened, but not sufficiently. Renewal is talked about, of course, but ever again as though it were something which we can only talk about but not experience. That is how it largely is in our Protestant districts. But let the thought of the Lord's coming awaken us, and let us speak about his coming today: 1) How the Lord broke in during the Reformation; 2) How, since then, his coming has again been delayed; and 3) How, at last, his promised coming will be fulfilled.

I.

The promised future of the Lord has broken in; that is, it breaks into history from time to time, and the way for it was especially paved through the Reformation. That is, and remains, a tremendous thought that may not be disregarded when we recall the great work of God at that time. Firstly, Humankind and Christendom was liberated from the shackles that held them captive; a new spirit was set free to move and be active. People placed themselves under the authority of the Holy Spirit, and as a result they prepared themselves for the great event of the coming of the Lord. What had been bound was freed. Fetters were removed. Suppression of God's Spirit stopped. With the Reformation, this all suddenly happened.

When Luther nailed up his theses, a feeling of freedom swept throughout the nations, especially through Germany. A wonderful feeling of freedom was also aroused when, on the 25th of June 1530, the Augsburg Confession of Faith could be openly read out. [. . .] Souls were freed for the Lord—no longer bound by other people, but free for the Lord and his Spirit. People were free to find an inner fellowship with Jesus and anything that was opposed to this unity with him had to be cleared out of the way. A tremendous amount was given at that time, for God's Spirit enabled people to come with a free heart to the Lord. Everybody applauds that side of the Reformation, which permitted people again to breathe more easily so that they could go to meet the Lord with lighter hearts.

Secondly, there was also a new recognition of the Word of God. The Bible was hardly known and even less was it taught. Consequently, the will of God for the salvation of humanity remained hidden. God's great plan of salvation was unknown; even the great event of Jesus' first coming remained hidden. The people didn't understand why Jesus came, why he performed miracles, why he died on the cross and rose again. Nobody knew who Jesus was anymore! His resurrection was a beautiful allegory, but its significance for the world was no longer known. His ascension into heaven, his sitting at the right hand of God, his second coming—all of these things were so covered by darkness and obscurity that it seemed as if the whole Savior, as he has been revealed to us, had never existed.

At the time of the Reformation, however, Jesus was brought back to us; right into our hearts. He was brought close again. His gospel—his life, death, resurrection, miracles, ascension—was revealed again, full of salvation and light. His miracles, as we read them in the Gospels, were to show us how he is present in all our need. His death on the cross was to show how he shattered the power of darkness and wiped out guilt. The splendor of his resurrection and his ascension into heaven, his seat at the right hand of God, and the sure hope of his return all came alive again through the Reformation; without it, this would all have remained dead and buried under rubbish. In this too a further preparation for his coming was given. If he should come, people should know who it is that comes on the clouds of heaven. Through the Reformation, Jesus was brought back into the light for us so that we could have Jesus, trust in him, and with a deep longing now wait for his return.

Now to mention a third thing which, at the time of the Reformation, prepared the way for the coming of the Lord: It was laid on people's hearts how Jesus and his salvation could be regained and certainly would be regained. Previously, in a very mechanical way, people thought they had to make themselves pleasing to God and the Lord Jesus by all kinds of pious deeds, trusting in the infallibility of such means. An example of this was the purchase of salvation with money, and the belief that by making one or the other sacrifice or by practicing some form of self-denial it was quite enough to ensure them of a God, a Savior, and a heaven in the hereafter. It is not necessary for me to explain all this; you certainly know it.

Luther, and thousands after him, showed us that faith in Christ alone, a childlike faith and trust in him, could open the way to heaven and to God. Only then would our hearts be lit up. Light and freedom would come into our hearts only when we learned to trust, pray, and hope, being guided by the commandments of God and taught by the Spirit. Light and understanding comes to us through Jesus' own word, his life, suffering, and death. It is these that uphold and comfort us in the adversities of life and the storms that break upon us. And in this sense, the Reformation prepared us for Jesus' coming—to fill our lamps with oil, light them, and go to meet the Bridegroom.

However we may view the Reformation, one fact remains: namely, that it was directed toward the Lord's coming. Thus, as I have said before, the revival of the Christian church in the early years of the Reformation is a picture of what must come before the Lord can come again—a breaking through in order that he can come.

Unfortunately a great deal of darkness has descended on us again. We may not be enslaved as we once were, but we are still bound. We are in bondage to bad practices, wrong conceptions, false teachers and prophets, to all kinds of secret or open alliances. And much of this is because we have demanded unrestrained freedom instead of real freedom, the freedom that comes only through the Lord. Yes, we have the Holy Scriptures—but who reads them, or even knows them, let alone obeys what is in them? Who really knows Jesus, the real Jesus? Do we understand him? We talk about him and how he "shook" up the world once, long ago, but this seems to have little or nothing to do with how we live today. [. . .] So few of us even long for what was given at the time of the Reformation. Ah, how all this would change if the Spirit of God would descend upon us once more! A life of faith is still open to us; no one is barred from this. The Spirit of God need only descend anew upon us; thousands of people can still be gathered together and be made ready for the coming of the Lord.

II.

Why is the coming of the Lord so slow in being realized? Why the delay? Well, if the Lord had come suddenly, or if he were to come now, whom could he gather to himself? He wants no one to be lost. He wants true repentance and new life for each one of us. In other words, the Lord's delay shows how patient he is with us and that he has not given up hope in us. Yet we are still too far away from God for him to come and have joy in us. We are not prepared to meet him. Thank God that he has delayed in coming and that he still gives us time to repent. What would happen to us if the last trumpet sounded today?

Let us take a good look at ourselves. The delay has come about necessarily and especially because all the light that was given at the Reformation has been channeled into very narrow confines. Districts that long ago became Protestant or Evangelical have remained as they are. No progress has been made. Everything has been kept within narrow bounds. Even in regions that are called Evangelical, the actual Evangelicals are isolated in certain towns and villages and remain that way. Everywhere there is isolation. The Evangelical light does not break through and beyond this. In addition to this isolation there is something even sadder: the exclusion of one another. There is a great deal of exclusion of the other churches in Protestantism, in a way that should not be and is not in keeping with the spirit of the Reformation. There is little feeling, little sympathy, for other churches. It is now possible to dispute and wrangle relentlessly with the members and leaders of these churches about all kinds of matters, both publicly and privately. As a result, a wall of division exists that even the Protestant church, with its light, is unable to break down. Everything is cheerfully left as it is, as if hate and enmity between churches simply belonged to Christianity. It does not occur to any of them to let their light shine out so that others may be won. God's light must shine into this situation, however deep the division. Even the Evangelicals are divided among themselves. Some isolate themselves in one fashion and others in another, each keeping to itself. The mutual concern and working for one another in a way where each stands for all and all for each is missing.

Luther sent messengers as far as Constantinople in order to create greater unity among all Christians. There was nothing so contrary to his vision than the idea of separation or of splitting. But today each church is wrapped up in its own existence. And so, hardly anyone is preparing the way for the Lord, the way for the moment when the trumpet of heaven will sound out loudly, "He is coming! He is coming!" So the Lord waits. He waits because, as our text says, he is patient with us, not wishing "that any should perish, but that all should reach repentance."

Who are the "all" and the "any" who shall not perish? Protestants are accustomed to think of themselves and of nobody else. I would only like to ask how much feeling does the Evangelical church have for other churches, a longing that everybody should come to repentance? There must be a delay before the light, given us by grace, penetrates as a light, instead of as a light that is a cause of controversy. When that uniting light shines it will penetrate all those who are divided and separated within the Evangelical church; it will penetrate all the Catholic lands as well, although—and I say this explicitly—it will be as a light, not as some outward confession of faith. Only then will all come to repentance on the day of Jesus Christ.

A great calling came to us through the Reformation, but we have become unfaithful to it. We should be a light throughout the world, but we are not; we are not a blessing to the nations, as it was said of Abraham that he and his seed would be. Truly we could be a light, we certainly have all that is necessary to prepare the way, but we are not. Every nation on earth now lives in differing degrees of darkness. Millions upon millions need to repent and experience a conversion. Countless people walk according to the lusts of the flesh and are sunk in idolatry. So few truly know who Jesus is because so few of us care enough to tell them about faith in Jesus or to show others Jesus' light. The light given to us has not, and cannot, do its work because we have not placed it upon the "candlestick." Thus we continue to hinder the Lord's coming.

In today's churches, we now have preachers who are practically atheists; they aren't concerned about bringing hope and light into the dark lives of people. Their concern is to keep the church functioning. [. . .] O Light, where are you? Under a bushel! Almost every church is a "bushel." The light, if there is any, shines beneath this bushel, but not beyond it. Whoever seeks light must go underneath the bushel; otherwise, he will not get it.

God, however, does not want anyone to perish. As long as our light is hidden, we will have to wait a very long time before the Lord will come! He will not come until the light shines, not only in the churches, but in the world. As long as we remain unrepentant, he can never come. There would be no abyss great enough to contain the unrepentant of the world. This is why the Lord delays and why there has been such a delay since the Reformation.

III.

But the Lord will come! In spite of all delays, at long last, the coming of the Lord—for which the Reformation paved the way—will reach fulfillment and become an accomplished fact. What should I say about this third point that we have undertaken to consider? I just have to say something that I know few will want to hear. Here I come again with the deepest concern of my soul, and I cannot refrain from talking about it. I am thinking, in short, of the repeated new evidence of God's power, of renewed powers of God and the Spirit following on from what was given at the time of the Reformation. What I hope and wish for is nothing more than what they hoped, wished, and longed for at the time of the Reformation. It is this light that Luther longed for, and it will come again through the Word of God, in power and in Spirit.

Some of you will hold it against me for saying this. But let us not forget, it was a stream from above that was poured over the Reformers. How else can one explain it? Within four weeks, without railroad, telegraph, and newspapers, Luther's theses kindled a fire throughout the whole of Europe! A stream of fire came down from above. The wind of the Spirit swept the fire through all the villages and towns and kindled it in people's hearts. Unless we see it in this way, it would be one of those inexplicable things that happen in the world.

How tremendous it would be if this same stream would repeat itself. Why not? Let us wish for this stream to come again, and to come with even greater power. Pray that it is poured out afresh, so that it can flow together with that stream that started at the time of the Reformation. If that which was begun in the Reformation, and which later came to a standstill, is to flow once more—as it must if the future of the Lord is not to become as nothing—it can only happen if the stream from above is poured out afresh, flowing together with that stream that started at the time of the Reformation, causing it to flow anew. Yes, I hope for this and will testify to it as long as I live. With my last breath I will pray, "Lord, bestow on us the stream of your Spirit and grace so that the whole world may be overwhelmed and renewed by it. Wherever there are people worthy of your mercy, Lord, let them receive a glance from you, a glance from the Savior that promises everlasting peace." For this I stand. I will cry to the Lord until all nations receive this light and turn in repentance in order not to perish.

Those are my thoughts for today, dear friends. So pray with me that this stream will flow unhindered through the whole world. Then the Lord will say, "I am coming!" And when God comes, it will be glorious! Grace and mercy will announce his approach. Therefore, let us rejoice in his coming! Amen.

The Blossoming Desert

The wilderness and the dry land shall be glad, the desert shall rejoice and blossom; like the crocus it shall blossom abundantly, and rejoice with joy and singing. The glory of Lebanon shall be given to it, the majesty of Carmel and Sharon. They shall see the glory of the LORD, the majesty of our God. Strengthen the weak hands, and make firm the feeble knees. Say to those who are of a fearful heart, "Be strong, fear not! Behold, your God will come with vengeance, with the recompense of God. He will come and save you."

—ISAIAH 35:1–4 (RSV)

Isaiah is looking into a glorious future. He cannot imagine anything good, nor anything just upon the earth until God himself comes. Soon after Isaiah's time, Israel was destroyed and the inhabitants taken to Babylon. Later, the Jews returned, but it was of no importance, even if they did return; God himself was to come and must come. Yet Isaiah knew that God would come. He does not say in what way, but only that he must come. Now, let us recall how he did come. He came in great lowliness, in human weakness. That is how he came. [. . .] Immanuel, "God with us," was in our midst, and that was good—but not enough. The Lord came in weakness and lowliness. [. . .] When Isaiah envisioned God's majesty he was looking ahead to the time when he would appear in glory and in power, transforming all things in an instant and bringing them to fresh bloom. In all his descriptions, contemplations, and visions, the prophet continually points to a time when God will come in all his glory. His Christ did come, but first

Editors' Note: This sermon is dated 1873.

in the lowliness of the flesh. However he will return, and when he does he will come in his heavenly glory. We know this.

Christ, who came as an infant, in humility and weakness(but also in God's strength) doesn't fully satisfy our deepest longing. But his coming does give us hope, for we know he will return in power and glory. Many want to take away even this humble Jesus, crucify him again, and cast him out, even more humiliated. What they want to do to Christ they want to do to his followers. Those who love Jesus are always persecuted and trodden underfoot by those in power. They are trampled upon and persecuted by the rebellious, the hardhearted, the godless. [. . .] Since Christ first came into the world—and God's glory did appear—his adherents have taken the lowest place. In the world, knowledge is arrogantly paraded, but when it comes to the lowly Savior, people turn away. Yet the Lord will be revealed in glory, and all those who resist him will be judged (Isa 35:4), and the Lord himself will be raised up. Those who follow him will finally be freed from grief. This is why Isaiah declares, "Your God will come with vengeance." God will come to judge all those who resist his counsel—those who reject the Savior and who pierce him. The powers of darkness, all who deliberately confront Immanuel and do what they choose with him—they will be judged. The misery inflicted on God's children will not continue. All who resist repentance will be turned away, and everything that lifts itself up against God will be demolished.

In the meantime, the Lord gently beckons, "Come here, you sinners. Come! I will not judge or cast anyone out. I want to gather you. I will deliver and uphold all who seek my help so that when the time comes, they will not be engulfed by my judgment, but will be preserved for eternal life." He continually calls out, "Be reconciled to your God. Listen to my voice, pay heed to my Word, and things will go well with you. He who believes in me will not see judgment." We believe this, for the Lord came to save sinners and deliver us from evil.

But one day he will come with vengeance, vengeance against the rebellious. At the same time he will also come to the aid of those who are oppressed and subjected to all kinds of pain, sorrow, and affliction. What has been said is not meant to frighten us, for it concerns only those who torment the children of God. It applies above all to the devil and his company and all dark powers, which continually corrupt and strive to prevent good things from arising. These must be overcome. Anyone who "lifts a hand" against the Lord must be conquered and told, "You have been cruel, godless, and rebellious. Now you must pay for this, for you would not follow the Savior who wanted to lead you from hell to salvation." Isaiah says, "Be strong, fear not! Behold, your God will come with vengeance, with the recompense of God. He will come and save you." He will save all those who are tormented, attacked, and tortured.

And he will delay his coming until all who rebel against him confess Christ as Lord, to the glory of God the Father. All the more we should make sure to be counted among those who love the Lord. [. . .] What will happen when this comes about? Isaiah says, "The wilderness and the dry land shall be glad, the desert shall rejoice and blossom; like the crocus it shall blossom abundantly, and rejoice with joy and singing." Isaiah compares humankind to a wilderness or a desert. We are dissolute and dreary; our natures are such that we bring forth nothing fruitful. What is noble and good has been overgrown by thorns and thistles. Everywhere there is "wilderness" and "desert." Just as the Israelites wandered in the wilderness, so we find ourselves in a world of evil, carrying in our hearts wherever we go only grief, misery, and sorrow. But now, says Isaiah, "The wilderness and the dry land shall be glad, the desert shall rejoice and blossom; like the crocus it shall blossom abundantly, and rejoice with joy and singing." A time is coming when suddenly we will rise up in the fear of God. Then the world will become fresh, bear fruit, and have joy in God. It will be like spring, when all nature revives and breaks forth into glad songs. Humankind will experience renewal. Before he comes it will happen to the extent that countless disciples of the Lord will preach the gospel, their word will be like a wind of pure goodness rushing from nation to nation, from land to land—all this will happen before the Lord finally comes.

In order for this prophecy to be fulfilled, we must make sure that a deep faith in Christ is awakened in our hearts. [. . .] We must experience a new understanding of God's grace in Christ; a new realization of his great salvation for all generations—such as has never been before. This must take place before the Lord appears—or else he will come as a complete stranger. A relationship must exist between him and us all so that his coming is immediately seen as the fulfillment of our hopes and longing. We have to expect a renewal. How essential that is! The wilderness now lies there in sadness, but when God makes the barren land fruitful once more, humankind will all at once be different—we will all be striving toward new faith.

This new blossoming of the people through the gospel, which will happen before the Lord comes with vengeance, is further expressed in these words: "The glory of Lebanon shall be given to it, the majesty of Carmel and Sharon. They shall see the glory of the Lord, the majesty of our God." What a glorious and beautiful scene this is! The most beautiful gardens shall blossom, the blessing of the Lord will be everywhere, and there will be no desolate place. The blessing of the Lord will be felt everywhere. It will be beyond measure, even if it does not last long. For Satan's mightiest opposition will rise against it. But, our Lord and Savior will yet come and take revenge on all who have devastated his beloved garden and ruined his vineyard.

We must therefore remain courageous and hope. We must cry out, "Strengthen the weak hands, and make firm the feeble knees." This cry has rung throughout all the ages, from Christ's first coming until now. Let us keep crying this out to God. Even if we grow weary and despair and stumble, that cry must never be silenced. Especially not in our time! Even if we lose all courage, don't forget that the Lord put these words into the mouth of Isaiah three thousand years ago: "Strengthen the weak hands, and make firm the feeble knees." These words should give us a fresh heart again and again. However evil, sad, and stormy things may seem, and though it looks as if everything is being sucked into the whirlpool of darkness—be of good cheer! Soon the Lord Jesus will suddenly change everything.

Oh, you dear ones, open your hearts to this message! Any of you who are weary and despondent, grieving and sad, listen to this: "Strengthen the weak hands, and make firm the feeble knees." Accept the words of Isaiah, "Your God will come!" He is at the door. He will help you make new all that has become corrupt. And more, he will save millions from every nation and every creed. His Word will penetrate everything and it will benefit all creation until that time when he creates his new heaven and new earth. Do not despair or forget this, "Happy is he who trusts in the LORD" (Prov 16:20). Look up! With Christ we will win. The battle is won as soon as we lift up our eyes to heaven. Don't neglect this. Remain true to the call to lift your eyes to heaven. Wait patiently until the Lord's promise is finally achieved. Amen.

Hope

... and hope does not disappoint us ...

—ROMANS 5:5 (RSV)

To have faith in God is to have hope in him. Since the Reformation stress has been laid upon faith and bringing people to believe; one must become a "believer." Yes, one must believe, but it is a great mistake to think that with faith we have everything—we don't unless we also have hope. So-called "believers" tend to stagnate, going on in the same old way without moving one step ahead. We must be people who hope, who confidently believe and expect that the Lord, who ascended into heaven, will return in all his glory. Don't consider yourselves perfect through your faith, but through your faith, have hope.

Few people understand this. Their Christianity is thus very trivial. They say, "We have what we need," but then remain unhappy. This is because they lack hope. In this way their Christianity rots away. Let us take note! Paul speaks very highly of how much is given to one who has been justified by faith in Christ. But he also strongly emphasizes that we must continue to have hope! In the text it says, "Suffering produces endurance, and endurance produces character, and character produces hope, and hope does not disappoint us." That is to say, [hope will sustain us] until, at the coming of Jesus Christ, we are brought out of misery, poverty, and need and into God's great kindness. A Christian whose heart does not throb with hope and expectation for the future is a poor wretch, however much he or she boasts about the seriousness of their faith. Unless their heart vibrates over those things that must and will come, they are and will remain impoverished. Therefore, we too want to consider—consider in hope—how much will have to come about before all is accomplished. We will not get very far if better things do not come, if the Lord does not become more tangible and his glory more perceptible. [We remain impoverished] if his wonder-working hand is not with us and with the world around us, and if there is not more resistance to the devil. If we see how crooked, corrupt, and incomplete everything still is, and yet still feel satisfied as if nothing were wrong, then our Christianity is a poor thing, however orthodox it may be. May the Lord help us to remain truly humble and to look forward in hope to his mercy, which will make all things right. For, "hope does not disappoint us!"

All the Earth Shall Be Filled with Glory

Then the LORD said, "I do forgive, just as you have asked; nevertheless —as I live, and as all the earth shall be filled with the glory of the LORD—. . . ."

—NUMBERS 14:20–21 (NRSV)

The first watchword on the Moravian Brothers' calendar, which we read this morning, was this: "Thy testimonies are my heritage forever" (Ps 119:111). This text is one of the testimonies of the Lord, which is passed on from one year to the next. Each year we long that his promises are fulfilled. This promise is no exception and is strengthened with an oath, as if to mean, "However long the delay, however improbable it looks, even if it seems that nothing will ever come of it—I will never give up! Nothing shall revoke the word that is now spoken, 'All the earth shall be filled with the glory of the Lord.'"

This word does not just stay behind with the old year, but is carried over to the new. It is a tremendous word to which we can also hold in the Lord because he swore an oath when he spoke it. More than three thousand years have passed since this promise was given. Must it now fall by the wayside or disappear like smoke? Does it have no further value for us? Do we mean to say, "That is an old saying, no longer valid?" No! My dear friends, we will leave it as it stands. We want it exactly as it is written, hoping that a time will come when we will see "all the earth filled with God's glory." The disciples saw the beginning of this glory when they saw Jesus for the first

Editors' Note: The sermon is dated January 1, 1858.

192

time: "We have beheld his glory, glory as of the only Son from the Father [. . .] full of grace and truth" (John 1:14). There the glory of the Lord was revealed. The glory of God was to be seen in Jesus. In the account of the changing of the water into wine at Cana, we read that the Lord manifested his glory; here the glory of God came into the world (John 2:11).

This glory appeared first in the Lord Jesus and [shone out] through him in the land of Canaan. After his resurrection Christ told his disciples to go into all the world, baptizing all those who believed (Mark 16:15–16). The glory of the Lord would continue to flow, but now over the borders of the promised land and into every nation on earth. And so, fifteen hundred years after the proclamation of the testimony in our text, the redemption began. Now nearly another two thousand years have gone by, but unhappily the earth is not yet filled with the glory of the Lord. Certainly great efforts are being made in all directions, and the Lord acknowledges much of what is undertaken in his name and through his strength—but, how little room there is for the glory of God upon earth!

What then shall we do? On New Year's Day we always look into the future with feelings of joy. What can encourage us? Hardly anything! Today we have virtually nothing to console us except a three-thousand-year-old promise. Nevertheless, the promise still stands, even though we can't see how it can ever become true. All the more we must hold tightly to this oath sworn by the Lord. Don't lose faith in it just because it hasn't been fulfilled yet. Remember, the first witnesses of the gospel, Jesus' disciples, weren't able to fulfill the Lord's directions. Does this mean the Lord hasn't come, that his vision has passed and will never come to fulfillment? Is this what we are supposed to believe? No! We dare not. The Lord swore, "but truly as I live . . . ."

It is tempting to believe that the "thoughts" and "plans" of God have somehow changed, perhaps because of the great unfaithfulness and ingratitude of Christ's followers, who should know better. Maybe God has changed his mind and decided to let only a few come to glory, condemning the rest of us. Even if we wanted to indulge in such thoughts, we could not persist in them. In the first place, it was God who spoke these words, and that means far more than if some man or woman spoke them. Also God pledged his word. Now, you poor human child, will you doubt this and say with a smile, "It is written there, all right, but nothing will happen"? How dare we think this way and then at the same time hear our great God solemnly swear, "But truly, as I live . . . all the earth shall be filled with the glory of the Lord . . ."?

So what are we to do? It's very simple: Believe in what God has spoken! Hope whether you see anything happening or not. For we know this promise cannot fail. A time will come when a giant step forward will come—the acceptable year of the Lord where his glory will break in and be seen among all the people of the earth. "Now it comes in earnest!" It will be a time that is no longer just a potential, consisting of just a flimsy structure. Now a real foundation will be laid, and his movement will go irresistibly forward until all his promises are fulfilled.

Let us therefore give all honor and glory to God and pray that we may be allowed to see him. God's kindness, such as Israel was able to experience through the word "I do forgive," is also part of this glory, as is also the merciful aid against all enemies and obstacles. It belongs to God's glory that on the basis of grace and forgiveness of sins, the sick are helped, those who suffer find relief from their afflictions, and those who mourn cease their lamentations—in short, that all who are in need are given divine help and joy. Among all children of humankind no eye will remain dry throughout this coming year. We will most likely shed many tears because the glory of the Lord has not been revealed. We will most likely continue to experience misery and heartache, yet, let us also joyfully remember the promise, which was once made and solemnly sworn to and which sooner or later will certainly be fulfilled.

What is it that must inwardly grip us and hold us together? Hope alone! Hope for ourselves, for all our brothers, sisters, and children, for the whole of creation. Hope alone will sweeten our lives. Without hope everything is bitter, but with it God's Word becomes powerful. Though there is still tribulation, hope shows us that even this will help to bring about God's future. As heralds, as forerunners of the fulfillment of God's great promises, let us hope. No matter what this year brings, the Lord will keep his promise. God will demonstrate his glory, be it insignificant or mighty, joyous or sad. Everything must work in service toward that which the Lord has promised. That which he has sworn to here was also sworn to even more strongly in Isaiah 45:23–24:

> By myself I have sworn, from my mouth has gone forth in righteousness a word that shall not return: "To me every knee shall bow, every tongue shall swear." Only in the LORD, it shall be said of me, are righteousness and strength.

So, dear friends, stop wishing for minor dreams! Don't let them become your chief interest. No. Consider the oath sworn to us by God that all the earth shall be filled with his glory. Our prayers must be directed toward his word! Prepare yourselves for this by thinking constantly about God's righteousness. Carry this promise of hope deep within you. This promise from God can be fulfilled and would come more quickly if it was our first and last concern, if we would simply believe it wholeheartedly and truly accept it.

May the Lord, our God, be compassionate and teach us to watch for those things that are of most importance, so that we may be faithful to his loving promises. Let us seek above all else the kingdom of God and his righteousness. All other things must pale in comparison to this. How great is our God who looks upon us in our weakness in such a wonderful way! Let us remain within his covenant. He eternally does all things well. Amen.

The Right Hand of the Most High

The right hand of the Most High can change everything.

—PSALM 77:10 (LUTHER'S TRANSLATION)

Every now and then we come across a passage of Scripture whose significance becomes apparent only at certain moments, even though we may have read it many times before. This is true with the above text. Many of us have heard it often enough, but then in a dull frame of mind haven't thought anything much about it. Then we hear it again, perhaps in a time of great distress when we see no way out. Suddenly, a bright light seems to blaze before our eyes. "The right hand of the Most High," it says, "can change everything." Is this really true? How wonderful. What great promises lie within it! Everything—great or small, high or low, visible or invisible, physical or spiritual—the right hand of the Most High can change everything.

By the words, "the right hand," we take this to mean the following: When God stretches out his hand, he begins his work. For a long time he lets everything pass, his hand is at rest and he appears unconcerned. But when he "awakens," arises, and sets to work, how quickly everything is changed. Things happen we never thought possible! Therefore, let us wait patiently, quietly enduring whatever goes on around us. At last he extends his right hand! Then our hearts rejoice, yes, all creation rejoices. Suddenly, everything is transformed into his great glory.

Just prior to this David cries out:

Editors' Note: This sermon is dated 1874.

Will the LORD reject us forever? Will he never show his favor again? Has his unfailing love vanished forever? Has his promise failed for all time? Has God forgotten to be merciful? Has he in anger withheld his compassion? (Ps 77:7–9).

Can we not speak this way in our time? Where is his favor? Where is his promise, his compassion? Is it not as if he has spurned his faithful and will no longer show grace, that his promises have ended, that he has forgotten us, and that he has shut up his compassion toward us? It appears everywhere that the enemy has gained the upper hand. It seems as if everyone has deserted the Lord and brazenly mocks him. Nowhere does the helping God show himself. But have patience—do not lose heart! Say with David, "It is my grief" (Ps 77:10). Let the worst happen! Suddenly, the Lord arises! And in the twinkling of an eye everything changes! Yes, how quickly can his grace, his goodness, his promise, his compassion, begin to shine on us once more! There will come a day when streams of life giving water will gush forth over us, and not only us, but over all the generations of the earth. If we would only believe, surely we shall see the glory of the Lord unfolding in splendor over all flesh. Amen.

The Lord Looks Down from Heaven

The LORD looks down from heaven on humankind to see if there are
any who are wise, who seek after God. They have all gone astray, they
are all alike perverse; there is no one who does good, no, not one.

—PSALM 14:2–3 (NRSV)

This psalm tells us that God looks down upon the earth, and despite
what he sees he still looks. How wonderful this is. It's as if God looks
and says, "I cannot bear to look upon them any longer. I must create
something new among them." For who else could bring about anything
good? Who else could truly be without corruption? All of us lack the vital requirement. In looking down at us, the Lord knows that he himself
must come—our loving, compassionate, God and Lord. He himself has to
intervene, and so the Word came—the Word, the Son of God, who in the
beginning was with God, but who became flesh and dwelt among us so
that something good was in our midst. Now God could look down from
heaven and see that there was at least one person on earth who was good.
Jesus was there, he who always did the Father's will, was pleasing to God.
He offered himself on behalf of others; and now the Father can look down
from heaven with delight and rejoice in all those who are joined with his
Son in faith. Since then, it can no longer be said that, "They have all gone
astray, they are all alike perverse; there is no one who does good, no, not
one." In Jesus Christ, the Beloved One, many have been made incorruptible
and worthy of God's love.

Editors' Note: This sermon is dated 1876.

Yet the Father in heaven still looks upon the world with sadness. So-called believing Christians are plentiful, but there are very few who possess the kind of faith that expresses itself in daily life. Many believe, but only in their own salvation. They believe hardly at all that Jesus will at last reveal himself in glory and bring about the redemption of the world!

We live in a time when we can hardly see ahead, and many feel that the very worst may shortly come about. But are these the wise Christians who actually seek after God? As God looks down, what does he see? Can he find anyone truly asking for the Savior's help, to whom all authority is given in heaven and upon earth? Are they wise, who no longer believe that a miraculous intervention on the part of God is possible, who no longer trust that our beloved God and Savior are able to fulfill the promises to which he swore? Are these the ones that seek God? Ah, that we would become truly wise, that God might see uncorrupted people among us, who really ask about him!

God's Great Compassion

He will again have compassion upon us; he will tread our iniquities under foot. You will cast all our sins into the depths of the sea.

—MICAH 7:19 (NRSV)

What a wonderful watchword for the New Year! All of us want our sins to be forgiven, to be freed from our guilt. Today especially we wish that God may cease to look at the sins of previous years and show us compassion and grace in this New Year. Whoever enters the New Year with childlike humility and a contrite spirit, gazing upward to God, may well have their old guilt covered and left behind. How wonderful it would be if these sins were to be cast into the depths of the sea, that is, into eternal oblivion! To be sure, most of us prefer to enter the New Year with a light heart rather than with a grieving and contrite heart. But let us not forget that it is also important to have an urge to show an interest in each other and in humankind as a whole, that we step out of our customary egotism and concern ourselves with the needs of other people.

Our New Year's text has a lot to say to us in this direction. Throughout his book, Micah brings to light Israel's great sins and how they all had to undergo the most severe judgment, with only a few escaping. Those who survived he called the "remnant of his possession." Looking to God, Micah cries, "Who is a God like you, pardoning iniquity and passing over the transgression of the remnant of your possession? He does not retain his anger forever, because he delights in showing clemency (Mic 7:18)." Micah is thinking of all those who God will turn to with love. The transgressions

Editors' Note: This sermon is dated January 1, 1875.

of earlier generations can no longer burden or destroy them. Micah fore-sees God's great and universal compassion: "He will again have compassion on us; he will tread our iniquities under foot. You will cast all our sins into the depths of the sea." What a tremendous, all-embracing time of grace is promised here, a grace that will come, and we can also believe it will apply for all past generations.

This time of grace began with Christ, but only a few people experienced it at first. It has still not been given in a wider sense, in the way so frequently expressed in the promise. May we not expect that one day the promise in our text will be fulfilled? The prophets indicate many things that can give us hope for the great and universal compassion of God to come over Christendom, and indeed also over the heathen world, as it once did over Israel. [. . .] When the time of the Lord's return comes, a great stream of grace will penetrate the whole world, showing the way to new life. How good it feels to be able to have this hope, and what a heartache it is to not have such hope! The promise, however, gives us the courage to hope.

Therefore, let us pray for this great time of grace and redemption. Pray that our gracious God, the Compassionate One, may have mercy upon everyone, "treading their iniquities under foot." May he also forgive the most evil of the evil ones, the murderers and adulterers, the thieves, swindlers and unjust of all descriptions, the sorcerers and perjures, the gluttons and winebibbers, the unbelievers and blasphemers. In short, may he forgive all of them—whatever monstrous things they have done and however terribly they have lived. May he visit them with kindness and with the mighty power of his Spirit. Through recurring powers of his Holy Spirit, may he urge them to repentance and to a change of heart and make them into different and real men and women, acceptable to him, our gracious God and Savior.

But let us first be given a wide open heart, such as God gave to the prophets and such as Jesus had—a wide open heart that can build upon the words of Paul, "The saying is sure and worthy of full acceptance, that Christ Jesus came into the world to save sinners" (1 Tim 1:15). It is as Micah says that their sins are cast into the depths of the sea. A great and universal compassion, reaching into the farthest expanses—what a tremendous mercy that would be!

O Jesus, dear Savior, thou Lamb sacrificed for the sins of the world—is not this your purpose? Yes, we see into your heart—you will do this, you will bring about such "an acceptable year of the Lord." Amen.

Advent

Hosanna to the Son of David! Blessed is he who comes in the name of the Lord! Hosanna in the highest!

—MATTHEW 21:9 (RSV)

Behold, he comes!" Many people acclaimed the Savior's Advent as he entered Jerusalem. They shouted to the whole city, "Behold, he comes! It is he who was to come, for whom we have waited. He was promised by our prophets! Here he comes! Hosanna! ('May the Lord help us!') He is blessed because he helps!" Our text is a song of praise for the arrival of the Lord. Advent reflects a time of longing—the yearning for redemption. The entire time from Adam until Christ was a time of longing. All the world longed for salvation. On his deathbed Jacob said, "I wait for thy salvation, O LORD" (Gen 49:18). The Lord spoke also of this to his disciples, saying, "For I tell you that many prophets and kings desired to see what you see, and did not see it, and to hear what you hear, and did not hear it" (Luke 10:24). Thus, even before Christ came, there was great longing for a Savior.

This longing has never ceased. We also have this longing, not for the first coming of the Lord, but for his second coming. He will come, not as a small child in the manger, but in his glory. He will restrain the enemy and fulfill everything he paved the way for in his first coming. We all wait for this. As Paul expresses it, "We ourselves, who have the firstfruits of the Spirit, groan inwardly as we wait eagerly for our adoption to sonship, the redemption of our bodies. For in this hope we were saved. But hope that is seen is no hope at all. Who hopes for what they already have? But if we

Editors' Note: This is listed as an Advent sermon. No date is given.

hope for what we do not yet have, we wait for it patiently" (Rom 8:23–25). On his deathbed Jacob prayed, "I wait for thy salvation, O LORD." Paul also said, "We wait for it patiently." Even now we continue in this expectation. We wait for our adoption as sons and daughters, for the redemption of our bodies, and above all, for the revelation of the glory of the children of God. This waiting for the glory of Christ to appear is expressed in the story of Jesus' entry into Jerusalem, where he comes as the King proclaimed by the prophets. In this Gospel his royal power and glory are both recognized; everyone shouts for joy, spreading garments in his path and using branches on the road to honor him.

When Christ comes again in glory there will be a universal awakening. He will be praised everywhere! On all sides there will be a great awakening, and many will confess their reverence for Christ Jesus. Ah! How much must happen before we all acknowledge Jesus as Savior! The beloved Savior certainly had many friends before he entered Jerusalem, but it was only upon entering Jerusalem that he was so powerfully honored. When Jesus entered Jerusalem, songs of praise resounded. But this honor was only accorded to him near the end of his life. It may also be like this when he comes again, when the Lord Jesus will be honored by great numbers, when his name and honor will spread in ever-widening circles through all Christendom and through the whole world. This honoring given to the Lord will be beyond any glory we can imagine.

When Jesus entered Jerusalem, songs of praise resounded. Some of the crowd went before him, and some followed after. We can assume that those who went ahead represent Christendom, and the others the Gentiles who also hasten to honor the Lord Jesus. They all shouted together, "Hosanna to the Son of David! Blessed is he who comes in the name of the Lord! Hosanna in the highest!" [When he comes again, we will all do the same.]

The Branch of the Lord

In that day the branch of the Lord shall be beautiful and glorious,
and the fruit of the land shall be the pride and glory of the survivors
of Israel.

—ISAIAH 4:2 (RSV)

This passage consists of a wonderful promise that will be fulfilled after the many prior judgments described in the first chapters of Isaiah. Although these judgments are concerned with Israel, they have a prophetic meaning for the whole of history—right up to the return of Christ. When the prophets use the expressions "in that day," "at this time," or "in the last time," they are referring not only to the time of Christ's first coming but also to a time after Christ. Then all God's thoughts of redemption, all Christ's promises will finally be realized. Christ stands in the center between the time of proclamation and the final day of redemption. He also begins the time of salvation. As the Risen One, he alone fulfills God's promise.

In our text Christ is called the branch of the Lord and the fruit of the land, pointing to his divine and his human origin. He is the branch of the Lord because he is the Word of God and is himself God who descended from heaven and became flesh. He is the fruit of the land, being physically descended from men who are of the earth, formed of clay. Now our text says, "In that day the branch of the LORD shall be beautiful and glorious." This refers to a time long after Jesus first came, when he was regarded as worthless. Jesus continues to be regarded as worthless and will be so regarded until, in the last days, he appears in beauty and glory! In our time

Editors' Note: This sermon is dated 1874.

too Jesus is not accepted for who he really is. In great or little things he is seldom thought about—even when it seems he receives recognition. He is still not honored. It's as if he had never existed. He cannot make himself known and felt in all his power because we think and talk about him with indifference and coldness of heart.

But in that day—and herein lies the greatness of the promise of our text—when the time of salvation dawns here on earth, the branch of the Lord will suddenly become beautiful and glorious and will reveal the imminent coming of Christ. People will then honor Christ as the true branch of the Lord, the One who is from God, as God's Son. Then we won't see him only as the Son of Man of dubious ancestry, as many do now.

How will this transformation happen? We know that without the help of the Holy Spirit, nobody is able to truly call Jesus, "Lord." We must be born of the Spirit to know who Jesus truly is. Thus, we learn from Isaiah that in the last days there will be a renewed outpouring of the Holy Spirit, an outpouring like that in earlier times. Then the branch of the Lord, Jesus Christ, shall once more be beautiful and glorious.

Don't say to me, "Here you go again!" I do come with this again because it is true! If you don't look deeply enough into the Scriptures you will not recognize that, "the LORD will appear again as the fruit of the land, glorious and beautiful." For this reason he will also be called the fruit of the earth, which will spring forth wonderfully among the people—earthly people. He will come again, revealing to us his many gifts and powers, signs and miracles. Then the Son of Man will be truly recognized as the Savior. All those who sigh—those in misery and sin and who are heavy laden—will look up to him in joyful trust. He will become beautiful and glorious to all those who remain in Israel, who have escaped judgment upon earth and still live, those who belong to true Israel and have become a part of Israel because they have been grafted on to Jesus, the vine, the representative of Israel.

The Lord will be seen as beautiful and glorious. He will soon establish himself in pride and glory. Pray that he will soon draw close to us with the Holy Spirit! A great promise such as this can never fail! Amen.

Praise to the Coming One

"Blessed is he who comes in the name of the LORD."

—PSALM 118:26 (NIV)

These words were sung every year at the festival of the Passover. This psalm expresses a living trust in the Lord, who would one day come with his infinite power and aid. These words express more than the entreaty, "Come, Lord, and help!" It's as if the first signs of his coming can already be seen like the early rays of the rising sun.

This psalm is also prophetic; the Savior of the world is coming, seen by those whose faith has been awakened. When Jesus entered Jerusalem the people sang these words, proclaiming him as the Promised One. Jesus came in the name of the Lord, bringing the power of the Most High. He came to establish salvation and bring peace. Being now at the right hand of the Father, there is still much distress. So we keep longing for his coming and long to see the day when we will all cry out, "Blessed is he who comes in the name of the Lord, in the power and glory of his Father!"

Meanwhile he has ascended to his Father. How much distress is left behind among us, in spite of so much comfort offered through him! And yet, as we await that day he is always near us, especially when we call for him. We yearn steadfastly for his coming and long to see the day when we may cry out, "Blessed be he who comes in the name of the Lord, in the power and glory of his Father!" Still, we know that he is on the way to us the whole time, especially when we call upon him. He told his disciples, "I will not leave you as orphans; I will come to you" (John 14:18). We know he

Editors' Note: This is listed as a Palm Sunday sermon. No date is given.

will come—we must be content with this, for now. We also know he is near whenever we feel the blowing of his Spirit and whenever our hearts burn within us, as the disciples experienced on their way to Emmaus. So even today, whenever we receive unexpected help from him, we cry out, "Blessed is he who comes and brings help from heaven."

Each day we wait for his coming, when he will bring to fulfillment all that our hearts long for. "Come, Lord Jesus." We must cry out; then we shall hear, "He comes, he comes!" Even during a time of great distress when all seems lost, his faithful followers will see him coming from heaven. They will raise their heads and cry out with joy and jubilation, "Blessed is he who comes in the name and the power of the Lord!" Our glorious Savior, Jesus Christ, you are everything to us.

The Glory of the Lord

For darkness shall cover the earth, and thick darkness the peoples;
but the LORD will arise upon you, and his glory will appear over you.

—ISAIAH 60:2 (NRSV)

This is a beautiful word to consider in light of this holy day of Easter. The Savior has risen in order that night and darkness shall eternally cease, so the glory of God may become tangible to suffering and groaning humankind.

It is especially needed today as there doesn't seem to be much light of Easter. Everything looks exceptionally gloomy. We see so much night, so much darkness around us and within us. Relationships, even among friends and acquaintances, are often heavy and depressing. We have forgotten what it is like to be strengthened by the Risen Lord. We must pray for the Easter splendor that blazed so brightly at the first Easter! In a flash this blaze, with great noise and power, destroyed all the powers of Satan. With what treachery and barefaced wickedness people tried to destroy the Savior! The devil's legions incited thousands to cry out, "Crucify him!" The attacks of darkness achieved their aim: They crucified Jesus claiming, "Now we have won." It was as confused as a violent battle. But behold! On the third day the Lord overthrow hell, overpowered Satan, and terrified the enemy. [Unlike the shouting crowds,] all this was done in complete quiet and without commotion. The outcast rose from the grave as if nothing extraordinary had happened.

Editors' Note: This sermon is listed as an Easter sermon. No date is given.

That is how God displays his power. It will be the same at the end of time. Think of the millions upon millions who have died. Amid what struggles, buried beneath how many tears, and in what great sorrow, need, and lamentation each one breathed his last breath! How much gloom there is for those who are dying and for those who are around them. What grief, anxiety, and quaking of hearts—how many sleepless nights! If all this could be brought together it would make a mountain higher than the highest peak, filled with lamentations and misery. But see! Observe how the Risen One brings light into our dark world. Changes take place, all the devil's clamoring is in vain; the dead rise up and all tears are wiped away. We stand and behold with amazement the glory of the Lord. The Coming One makes all things new. We can finally see who God is and who are against him. He who dwells in heaven laughs at them. With a wave of his hand all godlessness comes to an end. All this will spur us on to believe in Christ whatever may happen. We will smile, however rough and stormy life may appear. What are all the efforts of darkness then? Nothing but a gust of wind that blows on by without leaving even a trace. Just think when the dead will rise again to life. There will be no more misery, no more suffering or corruption, no more affliction of any kind. When the Almighty appears in his glory, everything else will fade into nothingness.

If only all who now celebrate this great day might have some conception of how great is the resurrection of Jesus Christ! The heaviest and darkest events can try to overcome us, but Jesus has risen! His life will bring light to the whole world, to everyone. What a miracle it would be if this Easter Christ's radiance would encompass the whole world! It will happen! Just as truly as Jesus is called "the first fruits of those who rise from the dead," he will wrest everything from the power of death and reveal God's glory over the dark world. Praised be his name!

A Wholesome Shaking-Up!

For thus says the LORD of hosts: Once again, in a little while, I will shake the heavens and the earth and the sea and the dry land; and I will shake all the nations, so that the treasure of all nations shall come, and I will fill this house with splendor, says the LORD of hosts.

—HAGGAI 2:6–7 (NRSV)

When something new occurs in the kingdom of God, it will shake us all up. Shock waves will go through nature itself, possibly through all creation. Easter morning was ushered in by "a great earthquake." With one stroke a new time in history began. The night was turned to light, heaven and earth drew near to each other, humankind once more came within reach of God, and the angels of God appeared to people. As if nothing extraordinary had happened, the Savior who was torn away from us, cruelly tortured and executed, became alive again. The followers of the Savior rejoiced; life had sprung from death. Nothing can be more glorious than this!

But all this came about through chaos. Such confusion is always an indication of a new time. We know this from the Old Testament when Mount Sinai quaked and fiery clouds went up from it before Moses received the law. The same can be said of when the Israelites crossed the Red Sea and the Jordan River. In Elijah's time too there were other phenomena and shakings from nature. Then, when the Savior was born, the heavens also trembled, as the angel proclaimed the birth of Christ. This was the beginning of a new era. With an earthquake the Savior died, and with an earthquake he rose

Editors' Note: This sermon is listed as an Easter sermon. No date is given.

again from the kingdom of death. Yet in all this, nothing was destroyed. This is important. The earth moves, but no harm is done. On the first Easter Day no cries of distress were heard; people were shaken up inwardly, but no physical damage was caused. [. . .]

What the Lord Jesus began needs to continue; it cannot die. It might be overshadowed at present, but one day the Risen One will pierce the darkness for good. Before we know it, the whole world might suddenly experience Easter radiance and Easter joy—a time when we will feel as if we were transported from hell into heaven.

Our text today also points toward this time when it refers to the consolation [treasure] of all nations that shall come. For centuries Jesus has hardly been noticed, but a time will come when every person will urgently seek him. Then there will be earthquakes and signs in the heavens and the "dead" world will be awakened. We need not presume that this will bring great harm; rather we may expect that it will again be like the first Easter morning. God Almighty will be compassionate; he will awaken us, but not destroy the world. [. . .]

Praise be to God! Lift up your heads and rejoice that the day of redemption is coming near! Be glad, knowing that the full fruits of God's love will be experienced throughout all creation. Rejoice! Jesus is risen. He lives. He is here! We will go to meet him joyfully with the cry, "Blessed is he who comes in the name of the Lord!"

The Coming, Going, and Return of Jesus

Being asked by the Pharisees when the kingdom of God was coming, he answered them, "The kingdom of God is not coming with signs to be observed; nor will they say, 'Lo here it is!' or 'There!' for behold, the kingdom of God is in the midst of you."

And he said to the disciples, "The days are coming when you will desire to see one of the days of the Son of man, and you will not see it. And they will say to you, 'Lo, there!' or 'Lo, here!' Do not go, do not follow them. For as the lightning flashes and lights up the sky from one side to the other, so will the Son of man be in his day. But first he must suffer many things and be rejected by this generation."

—LUKE 17:20–25 (RSV)

Advent means arrival, and its real meaning has to do with the yearning for the coming and return of the Lord Jesus Christ. The arrival of Christ itself is, of course, celebrated at the holy feast of Christmas. The prophecy in Psalm 118 has already put into the mouth of the church a word pertaining to the arrival of the expected Savior. It describes how people go forth to meet a king, crying, "Hosanna! Blessed is he who enters in the name of the Lord! Hosanna in the highest!" So should our cries rise to greet the Coming One!

There is in the Gospel of Matthew (21:9) a text just for this day. The people greeted the Savior riding into Jerusalem with the words, "Hosanna

Editors' Note: This sermon is dated Advent, 1879.

to the Son of David! Blessed is he who comes in the name of the Lord! Hosanna in the highest!" This is a picture of how it will be in the future. That was the cry then, even though the salvation that Jesus was to bring to the world had only just begun and was not yet fulfilled. To One who is able to restrain all the misery of the world and to raise up the glory of the kingdom of God, it is appropriate to meet him and shout, "Hosanna to the Son of David! Blessed is he who comes in the name of the Lord! Hosanna in the highest!" The same is true with regards to the whole time of expectation for his second coming. The Lord Jesus himself again puts into our mouths these words which he spoke to his opponents: "For I tell you, you will not see me again until you say, 'Blessed is the one who comes in the name of the Lord!'" (Matt 23:39). Now, this saying is also hallowed anew for the Christian church. We stand in great expectancy so that we must truly cry out to heaven, "Hosanna to him who comes, the Son of David! Hosanna to him who comes in the name of the Lord!" We want to place ourselves into this expectation today. Ah, if only the time would come soon!

In faith we hold firmly to this "soon." It will not be long delayed; it will soon be possible for the time to come. Let your longing for his coming grow during this new church year and do not allow it to recede into the background through temptation or difficulty. [...] We often ask, "When will the Savior come?" This is because we personally know him. But the Pharisees did not know Jesus. To them, the idea of a king was strange; they didn't really want one—they wanted a kingdom, but not a king.... Thus, when Jesus said, "The kingdom of God is in the midst of you," they would not have understood what Jesus meant. Jesus was saying, "The king is already here!"

Yes, he was there. All his miracles and actions demonstrated his royal presence. Indeed, he was the very source of the kingdom of God. But then he went away again, with the promise that he would return. In this passage from Luke, all three of these ideas come into focus.

HE WHO BRINGS ABOUT THE KINGDOM OF GOD IS PRESENT

How do we understand this? When we think of a kingdom we immediately think of all kinds of pomp and pageantry and the display of royal splendor. This is not how we should think of the kingdom of God. Instead, our attention should be on the One who rules. His appearance is not that of a worldly king; he displays no royal dignity or splendor. He, as the King and Ruler to whom all things are subjected, imparts calm majesty, quietly bringing salvation to hundreds and thousands in body and soul. He stands there with might and absolute power; even hell lies beneath his feet. Satan stands bound before him, and thus he can strip this "armed man" of his weapons and take away his household goods. However much the powers of darkness rise up against Jesus, they achieve nothing—all this was as nothing to the Savior.

Jesus helped everyone and freed everyone from the oppression of darkness. In this sense, he is the Lord. He is the Ruler, the Stronger One to whom all things are subject. Whatever might happen to come, he is Lord over it. Even when thousands surrounded him, people experienced quiet blessings from him. He brought light. Sickness, agonies, and infirmity—all the powers of death had to yield to him. There is not one time he was unable to conquer evil. How many sinners there were whose hearts he opened! How many sins he forgave, calling to one or the other, "Take heart, my son, my daughter, your sins are forgiven! You shall taste my grace, my kingly grace."

When we reflect deeply on who Jesus was, then indeed we can see he was truly the king of Israel. He never used pomp or outward show. In fact the very opposite: he appeared poor and lowly. And yet, even the forces of nature were overcome when he walked upon the water, multiplied the loaves, and turned water into wine. Everywhere it is he to whom all things are subjected. And what power he demonstrated against the most violent one who ravages the human race—against death! Death had no hold over him; death vanished and must vanish when Jesus comes. Even his disciples would be given power by him to awaken the dead.

Therefore, Christ was right when he pointed out that one could not say of God's kingdom, "Lo, here it is!" or "There it is!" for the kingdom of God is everywhere, "in the midst of you." He thus declared that no matter where one found himself, it is the Lord who rules, not Satan. The question, "When will the kingdom of God come?" is thus superfluous. The kingdom is already here! The King has revealed himself, at least initially, in all of his royal splendor, and no one can overpower him! In Christ Jesus, therefore, the kingdom was present.

HE WHO QUIETLY FURTHERS THE KINGDOM IS ABSENT

Jesus says, "The days are coming when you will desire to see one of the days of the Son of Man, and you will not see it." Jesus stood before the people as God's Son, but he told them that he would have to suffer greatly and be rejected. He would not be able to personally continue his work among the people. His enemies would kill him. And even after rising from the dead, few would understand who he really was. So he left his disciples, and in his place he sent them the Holy Spirit. [. . .]

Today we long to see Jesus. And that is what the Savior announced here. We see and feel very little of Jesus' work today. So much has changed. Satan appears to be master once more. We have allowed ourselves to come under the dominion of darkness, and now—how we long to be with Jesus and experience his powers once again, to see him in his wondrous glory! But this will not happen; he remains far off until the day of his coming.

Unfortunately, people try to create the day of the Lord artificially. False prophets arise claiming that Christ is about to return. The Savior warns us to beware of such people. [. . .] Anyone who tries to tempt us in to believing that the day of the Lord has arrived must be avoided. Even if we are in distress, harassed and tormented, we must have patience. A fight is demanded of us each day. Jesus forewarned us: "How much you will desire to see even one of the days of the coming Son of Man, and you will not see it!" We must persevere patiently and not lose courage. What was given will not be lost. The glory and grace of Christ cannot be extinguished forever. Be patient! He who is seated in heaven is also still here and he is the Lord who allows us every year to celebrate Advent. Certainly we also receive much joy from him. What strength that gives us to press on through all suffering and tribulation! How close he comes to us in the holy Meal of Remembrance, and how the fellowship we experience comforts and restores us! How glad we are to be allowed to come to his table today, when he comes near and offers himself and the fruits of his martyr's death to us for this time of his absence. How much we still have of him!

HE WHO FULFILLS THE KINGDOM WILL COME

However, much distress will remain [. . .] and so we must continue to cry out, "Come, Lord Jesus!" Without our aching and longing for "his day," his return will not come. There must be people who cry out, "Lord, have mercy, take pity on us! Lord, remember your promise to us!" If tribulations were not so painful, all our longing for a Savior would soon vanish from the earth. Let us not feel downcast if just toward the time when the Lord comes, pain and suffering increase to such an extent that we can't even think what to believe. Trouble seems to "cover our heads," nearly drowning us. This happens so we learn to cry out with our whole hearts, "Come, Lord Jesus, come!"

We will be consoled by his compassion because we already see signs of Jesus' approach: dawn breaks into our night. Many sick will be healed, many of the desolate will receive help, and many will be free who seem overpowered by the enemy! How wonderful it is for so many people—the dawn breaks! Come and see—the dawn breaks! And when in your need you faithfully call to the Lord, you will soon see that the dawn breaks. Countless people will recognize that a healing Savior is close by.

And so the third thing will come true: Jesus will return. He will come back in a manner described as lightning flashing in the sky from one side to the other. When that happens, the whole world will see it. But something will precede this. When I say that "the dawn breaks" add that this morning light will grow as bright as the light of the rising sun. Suddenly he will come, the One who relieves all suffering—Jesus from heaven. This expectation is our comfort.

The Lord said, "As the lightning flashes and lights up the sky from one end to the other, so will the Son of Man light up our lives." God's mercy will awaken in us the cry, "Hosanna to the Son of David! Hosanna in the highest! Blessed is he who comes in the name of the Lord! Hosanna in the highest!" This song of praise will echo in us with every sign of glory shown by God. This will continue until he comes to us as truth on the day of his return—the whole truth. "Hosanna, yes! Hosanna to the Son of David! Blessed is he who comes in the name of the Lord! Hosanna in the highest!" Amen.

The Help of God

"For my thoughts are not your thoughts, neither are your ways my
ways," declares the LORD. "As the heavens are higher than the earth,
so are my ways higher than your ways and my thoughts than your
thoughts . . . ."

—ISAIAH 55:8–9 (NIV)

Today many people think that God has completely cut us off from his
grace; that he no longer cares about the world, and is just letting things
drift away. So many only see judgment ahead, as though our beloved God
brought nothing but death and destruction, permitting no grace and kindness from above to be seen any more. When we are tempted to think this
way, remember these words from Isaiah. God comes and brings us this
tremendous comfort, "I'm not going to destroy you, I did not even think of
this. 'My thoughts are higher than that, as high as heaven is from the earth.'
I want to help you, to rescue you from all your sighing and distress. That
is my intention; even when I judge you, I will not destroy everything or go
back on my promise. No! 'My thoughts are higher than your thoughts.'"
Yes, let us comfort each other with these words. God wants only his will to
be done for each of us. Even when distressing events occur and we think
life can't get any worse, the Lord has only good in mind. The Lord Jesus
says about the last, most difficult times, "Raise your heads, because your
redemption is drawing near!" (Luke 21:28).

Accept his assurance of grace and be hopeful. Yes, when everything is
in confusion, the redemption of creation is close at hand. Whoever seeks the
Lord, will find the way through. You who grieve because the grace of God

seems to be so far away, console yourselves with God's exalted thoughts, which are so much greater than ours. And when you draw close to the Lord, don't give up hope that his thoughts are for the world's salvation. They will come as sure as the light of day dawns. They must be fulfilled. In the most difficult times his love for the world will become apparent.

Therefore, even today, take this seriously to heart, earnestly and honestly resolving to do better, to be more faithful, to think more along God's lines, to be freer of the world and of all evil deeds. Hold onto the Lord and be more childlike; always look up to him and allow yourself to be made free from sin through the blood of Jesus Christ, for he forgives much. We will trust him; we will not complain; we will not lose heart and groan, but only wait—wait expectantly. He will comfort us even when all we see is darkness. If only we could see into his thoughts for the world's salvation. Remain courageous, whatever happens! Oh, that his Holy Spirit is poured out over us and that the time comes when "groaning" creation will be comforted forever.

The New Heart

I will give them a heart to know that I am the LORD; and they shall
be my people and I will be their God, for they shall return to me with
their whole heart.

—JEREMIAH 24:7 (RSV)

The Jews had been taken away to Babylon as captives. They were very
unhappy and wanted badly to return to their home. The Lord sought
to comfort the captives, although he also let them know that they must wait
patiently for seventy years. After that the Lord would lead them back into
their own country and bless them as he had done previously.

The promise of our text, however, goes further. [. . .] The prophecy
looks ahead to a time when God will give his people new hearts—new purpose. It is a timeless word and ultimately brings together the future and the
purpose that God has in mind for the very end of the age. The prophecy
overlooks the corrupt times, which do not lead to the final goal, treating
them as though they had never existed. More than five hundred years later
Christ was born, but his people hadn't changed. How far are we still from
having new hearts? That we know all too well! [. . .] But why, why do we
ignore such a wonderful, comforting promise, a promise so glorious—a
new heart that knows him and comes to him as the Lord?

We find many similar sayings in the prophets, yes, also in the law of
Moses, where it says that finally a change will take place among the people
so that they will, in every way, become a people after God's heart. When the
Lord himself speaks so consistently of his promise, is anything too much
to expect from those last days of the fight against darkness, when the Lord

our Savior will come? Yes, Israel will one day turn to the Lord. We read this in the letter to the Romans. It will happen before the Lord comes, but only in the last days, when the "full number of the Gentiles has come in" (Rom 11:25). This may seem impossible to us, but only because we do not take into account sufficiently that God intends to do this. Is anything impossible for God? Does not the promise itself contain the possibility—yes, the reality, that the promise will at last come?

Isn't there something that we Christians—baptized in the name of Christ and thereby part of the seed of Abraham, some even who are his actual descendants—should understand and learn from such hopeful words? If this is so, then we can look forward to a time of universal conversion. We hardly dare to talk about this. But God is merciful. He sent his Son to become Savior of the world. Let's look ahead bravely. God's eternal decree must be fulfilled; his promise will come true.

The Outpouring of the Spirit

I will pour out my spirit on all flesh; your sons and your daughters shall prophecy, your old men shall dream dreams, and your young men shall see visions.

—JOEL 2:28 (RSV)

Peter proclaimed that this prophecy was being fulfilled at the time of Pentecost and that it would spread gradually over the whole world: on all flesh, upon all nations! [. . .] Here we are reminded of the saying of the Lord, "What is born of the flesh is flesh, and what is born of the Spirit is spirit" (John 3:6). The word "flesh" denotes all that is separated from God, all that exists for itself, without God. That's how it was and is among all nations. But the promise is that we all will be united once again with God. His Spirit will breathe upon us all. And all who long for God shall return to him.

"I will pour out my Spirit," Joel records. A pure and godly attitude shall be aroused in all who will accept it, so that they will forget all that is temporal and sensual and turn to the eternal and heavenly. This already comes about through the Gospels and abroad through mission, which since its beginning has given to many, many people a different, higher direction, bringing them closer to God. However, there is something more behind the saying, "I will pour out my Spirit." It brings to expression the peak of humanity's union with God, when that which is godly will flow in torrents over humankind, just as it was at the first Pentecost. Then the whole outward appearance of humanity changed, at least when they were filled with the Spirit of God. When the Holy Spirit descended upon the early Christians it was quite apparent that a drastic change had taken place (Acts 8:17; 10:45). We are promised that we too will change completely when we are filled with the Spirit of God.

What Peter said at the first Pentecost concerning the promise in Joel was something that had only just begun. This is obvious the moment we look at ourselves; we are a long way from the grace that was promised then. The Holy Spirit is not only lacking in the world, but in us. Even if we accept, as we must, that the Spirit of God works in us, there is still so much that is unclear, untrue, unholy, and self-willed in our natures, so much that is not under the discipline of the Spirit of God. So much so that it is hard to discern anything of God within us. Thus, we are accustomed to confuse what we call "spirit" in a person, with all their human gifts, with what is actually an unmistakable gift of God from on high.

Clearly, there is still something more to be fulfilled on earth, for the Spirit shall "come upon all flesh." But when—as is certain—all flesh is called to partake in the kingdom of God, then we may hope that the time will come when the Lord will carry further what was started at the first Pentecost, so that God's purposes may be finally accomplished.

SECTION 2
THE EXPECTANT CHURCH

The Wise Men's Star

Now when Jesus was born in Bethlehem of Judea in the days of Herod the king, behold, wise men from the East came to Jerusalem, saying, "Where is he who has been born king of the Jews? For we have seen his star in the East, and have come to worship him." When Herod the king heard this, he was troubled, and all Jerusalem with him; and assembling all the chief priests and scribes of the people, he inquired of them where the Christ was to be born. They told him, "In Bethlehem of Judea; for so it is written by the prophet:

'And you, O Bethlehem, in the land of Judah, are by no means least among the rulers of Judah; for from you shall come a ruler who will govern my people Israel.'"

Then Herod summoned the wise men secretly and ascertained from them what time the star appeared; and he sent them to Bethlehem, saying, "Go and search diligently for the child, and when you have found him bring me word, that I too may come and worship him." When they had heard the king they went their way; and lo, the star which they had seen in the East went before them, till it came to rest over the place where the child was. When they saw the star, they rejoiced exceedingly with great joy; and going into the house they saw the child with Mary his mother, and they fell down and worshipped him. Then, opening their treasures, they offered him gifts, gold and frankincense and myrrh. And being warned in a dream not to return to Herod, they departed to their own country by another way.

—MATTHEW 2:1–12 (RSV)

Editors' Note: This sermon is dated Epiphany, 1880.

It was not just to the Jews that the Savior appeared as light and salvation, but also to the Gentiles, for he came upon earth to be Savior of the whole world. Therefore, when he came, he had at least in some way to be announced to both Jews and Gentiles. The announcement to the Jews had already taken place and was easy to make because there were still sufficient seeking, expectant souls filled with longing, and it was not even necessary to go far from Bethlehem to find people to whom the newborn Savior could be proclaimed. Close to the town of Bethlehem, perhaps a quarter of an hour away, keeping watch in the fields, were the shepherds to whom the angel of the Lord appeared in glory. The shepherds understood the significance of what was proclaimed to them concerning the Christ child. So they hurried toward the place where the little child lay. Finding him, they rejoiced, and upon their return they shared their joy and the news with those who were eagerly awaiting the deliverance of Israel. Even as a small child, there was a large circle of friends among whom the Savior could quietly grow up knowing, "These are my people whom I must help."

But the Gentiles! Where would the angels find Gentiles to tell them about this birth? Yes, there were many Gentiles nearby, even in the promised land, but who would understand? Who would rejoice? The angel of the Lord must have looked near and far to announce the message that Jesus Christ, the Savior of the world, was born. Nobody could be found in the vicinity who was even the least bit interested in this message. That's how great the darkness was. There were so few to be found in the promised land who would receive the news, and even fewer in the Gentile world. The angels had to travel farther and farther away until they finally found people in the distant East to whom they could tell their message. The angel of the Lord could appear only to souls who eagerly awaited God's message: The Savior of the world is born!

Today, the news of the Savior has spread throughout the world. But how would it be if the angel of the Lord went around seeking for people of hope now, people who truly long to see the promised revelation of the Jesus Christ? Would he find people who firmly believe that the world will be put right and that the great redemption will be given to all the generations of the earth? I doubt it. The angel of the Lord would be at a loss. For most of us believe the news of his coming only up to a certain point. The moment our "belief" costs us something, we pull back, shrink away.

This is true even among those who seem to really care, who dedicate themselves to truth and who work out helpful theological systems. But, when it comes to total commitment, well, that's a different story. There is, therefore, a difference among people of hope; many talk and prattle about the coming of Christ, but as soon as anyone becomes serious they shake their heads—they believe only with the head, not with the heart. They do not respond with joy in the thought that the Lord's day is approaching. No. They withdraw!

There is a peculiar enmity toward the light—subtle, very subtle and strange. Today, the darkness knows how to present itself as light, and yet it is darkness. It is unbelievable how remarkable our day and age is. We have the light, but then twist it so much that we end up in darkness; it is twisted so much that we no longer have a happy and courageous heart for the future. It is a special trick of the evil one to hang a dark mask over the light itself, which goes unnoticed. Ah, dear friends, we have a tremendous fight on our hands. We must do everything we can to take care that the light, which appeared in Christ, is freed from its dark mask. Pray and beg the Savior that he will shine again as the true light that breaks into this world.

But back to our text. The angel of the Lord had to travel far until he finally encountered a small circle of people who were looking up to the God of Israel in a spirit of genuine hope. In their longing they were at last permitted to see the coming of the "King of the Jews." We know nothing about this circle—how they conducted themselves, how they were bound together in love, or how they studied the Word of God. No one even knows how pure, genuine, or simple they were. We know nothing about them, only that such a circle really existed among the Gentiles. Who knows? Perhaps there are small, hidden circles that exist like them in our own times as well.

We desperately need people of hope who search together, who look forward to the coming of the Lord. It is such a travesty that there are so few people that hope. Instead, we preoccupy ourselves with fearful pictures of the future: terrifying and fearful events of terrible abominations, committed by an Antichrist and painted in the most fantastic, livid colors. Just about all that remains in people's minds of the coming of Christ is the appearance of the Antichrist, dangerous and horrifying. No one turns to God with hope. That is also a very special trick of the evil one in which he brings us to the point when we do not wait expectantly, when we put off the hope of Jesus' coming to the far distant future, making it irrelevant to our day. And then we lose sight of the fact that when the Lord comes again, he will come with new grace. It is of the highest importance for circles of people to come into being here and there who will talk over in fellowship the future as shown in the Scriptures, according to which the Lord will come with new grace and reveal himself in majestic victory. That will be a time when he will cast down the bulwarks of darkness and not permit them to be raised again, and he will convert people and not destroy them.

The hope in Scripture, according to which new hearts shall be given to the corrupted world and hearts of stone will be taken away from us—this hope must above all be given again, must come alive again. We must regain hope that the millions who now, unconcernedly, go against God and his Word are not lost! Sadly, the majority today are alarmed when people speak together about the hope of a coming Savior, "the King of the Jews," which the Holy Scriptures (particularly by the prophets and the sayings of the Lord) put before us abundantly. It is taken as something artificial when such Christian circles are formed and then make it their task to look in the Word of God for everything that is lovely and friendly, bringing a message of comfort and help and redemption promised for the last day. I want this to be known, and whoever understands let it speak to him, for when such circles arise, it helps greatly to hasten on what is to come.

The Lord looked kindly upon the wise men from the East, but in the promised land there was terror. Among the Gentiles there was joy. In the promised land, however, when the Messiah's arrival was proclaimed there was terror! One can see how emphatically this is the case with us. Christians are shocked nowadays when one speaks of Christ's coming. Back then all Israel, even the king, thought, "When the Messiah comes there will be confusion as never before and nobody will be able to find the way through." Everyone was terrified, the whole of Jerusalem was terrified. Instead of saying: "What did you say? But that is wonderful! Our promised king is coming! How great a time that will be!" Instead of this, they were shocked as soon as they heard it.

It is like this today. When we think of God's future today we tremble with fear and foreboding. But if only our hearts were trembling with joy, ready to be changed, then this would be marvelous! A shock like this may come, in which all will collapse; not, however, to sink into corruption, but to be saved—for salvation is to come from he who is, and was, and who will be. That must be the keynote of our hope. Salvation, salvation, salvation! This is what the coming of Jesus brings to us.

If only I could make this one thing clear to everyone. Jesus is coming to bring salvation, not disaster; to announce joy and peace, not terror and destruction. If only we would look forward with trembling joy. The

Savior said, "Now when these things begin to take place, rejoice, because your redemption is drawing near!" (Luke 21:28). But now, instead of hearing this, people are afraid and shake and tremble. Instead of rejoicing that redemption is drawing near, they quake. But salvation, salvation, salvation, shall come through the promised Savior. He will drive away the darkness. He will break through the night, bringing light, truth, and joy, not sorrow. He will turn the yearning of creation toward himself. He will break through everything, creating a new world, a new heaven and a new earth. All pain and misery will yield to him, and our tears will be wiped from our eyes. Yes, we should be eager for the day of salvation, because the coming Savior, Jesus Christ, declares only salvation.

We know that there were also people to be found in the East who looked for salvation and whom the angel of the Lord approached. Two thousand years ago, these people beheld a "star." That was no ordinary star in the sky, otherwise everyone would have noticed it. The Jews in Palestine would have seen it and asked about it. No. That star could only be seen by people of hope. The star was no less than the angel of the Lord. That star was God's message to the world: "The King of the Jews is born. Go and inquire after him!" The wise men understood this. They had seen the star of the newborn King of the Jews. Without this understanding, they would not have undertaken the long journey. "We have seen his star in the East and have come to worship him." How else, apart from revelation, would the wise men be able to talk like this? A small child would naturally think, "They talked with an angel, who looked like a star, who was sent to us by the Lord." They had been shown a miracle, and so they made the long journey, asking as they went along, "Where is he? Where is your king?" Yes, but what kind of king? No one knows. No one knows anything about a king. What a shock this must have been to the wise men!

But you see, the Lord makes himself known to people of hope, wherever they are, even now. Anyone who comes eagerly, following the Scriptures honestly, simply, and with purity of heart will be led by the Spirit. The light will dawn in them and it will be as if an angel walked before them. But we must seek. If we fail to search in the Scriptures, if we fail to look out for the star, we will not notice it. The Lord's star is not seen by everyone. You cannot see it if you are inwardly asleep. We have to have an upright, simple, sincere heart that really yearns for Christ's coming. Whoever is not filled with such longing and is only concerned with themselves, only wanting his or her own salvation, with no heart for the sighing creation—that one will not see a star, even when it is there; they will not see the glory of the Lord.

When you feel the need of creation, however, and sigh over the misery that fills the whole earth, having compassion with the unbelief of those led astray, and your soul is filled with all these things and sighs: "God and Lord, come to us! Don't abandon your promises. Help us to hope." If you stand like this before our Lord, his star will appear. Yes, we will receive his star in our hearts. I have it, and many others have it. This star of hope can never be extinguished. It will never fade—the star of hope born in the heart from the Word of God, so that one must say that the time is near when the Lord of all lords and the King of all kings will reveal himself and his holy ones to the whole world.

Beloved ones, the time is coming when the Lord will reveal himself to his people through many signs. He must show himself to them: he must and will help them, especially when they stand all alone. The star has still to appear, but it will come only when our hearts seek it, where there is passion for it—a sighing, striving, and aching for great mercy, which is promised to the world and must come. Yes, the star will return, and then it will shine not just for a few, but it will quickly spread its brilliance over the whole world. Yes, it is of Jesus Christ, who once appeared, that we must think today. The beginning was small, but great, boundlessly great, is the salvation and deliverance brought by our exalted Savior, Jesus Christ. He comes! He comes into the world for the salvation of all—he, who is and was, will come. He comes for the salvation of sighing creation, to complete and fulfill all that was promised through the prophets.

The Presentation in the Temple

When the time came for their purification according to the law of Moses, they brought him up to Jerusalem to present him to the Lord (as it is written in the law of the Lord, "Every firstborn male shall be designated as holy to the Lord"), and they offered a sacrifice according to what is stated in the law of the Lord, "a pair of turtledoves or two young pigeons."

Now there was a man in Jerusalem whose name was Simeon; this man was righteous and devout, looking forward to the consolation of Israel, and the Holy Spirit rested on him. It had been revealed to him by the Holy Spirit that he would not see death before he had seen the Lord's Messiah. Guided by the Spirit, Simeon came into the temple; and when the parents brought in the child Jesus, to do for him what was customary under the law, Simeon took him in his arms and praised God, saying, "Master, now you are dismissing your servant in peace, according to your word; for my eyes have seen your salvation, which you have prepared in the presence of all peoples, a light for revelation to the Gentiles and for glory to your people Israel."

And the child's father and mother were amazed at what was being said about him. Then Simeon blessed them and said to his mother Mary, "This child is destined for the falling and the rising of many in Israel, and to be a sign that will be opposed so that the inner thoughts of many will be revealed—and a sword will pierce your own soul too."

Editors' Note: This sermon is dated 1857.

There was also a prophet, Anna the daughter of Phanuel, of the tribe of Asher. She was of a great age, having lived with her husband seven years after her marriage, then as a widow to the age of eighty-four. She never left the temple but worshiped there with fasting and prayer night and day. At that moment she came, and began to praise God and to speak about the child to all who were looking for the redemption of Jerusalem.

When they had finished everything required by the law of the Lord, they returned to Galilee, to their own town of Nazareth. The child grew and became strong, filled with wisdom; and the favor of God was upon him.

—LUKE 2:22–40 (NRSV)

Jesus was presented at the temple forty days after his birth, in accordance with the law. The mother of the firstborn son was to go to the temple soon after the birth—just as soon as she was able—and offer sacrifices to the Lord and give thanks for the grace and help that she had been given. She came offering her son to the Lord, "This child that you have given me, is yours; he shall belong to the people of God. Please accept him as a blessed member of your people." The baby would then be brought and blessed, and from then on was always regarded as a subject of God, the supreme King, having part in all the blessings and promises of God.

It would do us well to remember how appropriate it is for us to present our children to the Lord and through holy baptism testify that our children should also be looked upon as members of the body of Jesus. Those who reason against infant baptism should reconsider God's precepts and be much more cautious. Has God changed between the old and the new covenant? Does he say in the old covenant, "Your children are also mine," but in the new, "I want to know nothing of your children until they have grown up and have decided for themselves?" But a Jewish infant was not asked, "Do you want to?" If their father was a Jew, they would be given to the Lord. If, when a child had grown up, they said, "No, I do not want to be part of this," they could leave if they thought this was better.

Therefore, we must not belittle the claim that God has upon a child whose parents belong to him. With baptism it is also a matter of the Savior's claim. He has a claim upon our children because we belong to him and we must, therefore, bring them to him. If later they should wish to withdraw from the rulership of the Savior, they are, of course, free to do so. However, it will not be accounted to their good; they will bitterly regret it. But we mustn't ignore the danger of not bringing our children to the Savior, for they could later accuse us of keeping them from the Savior.

But this is not the main point of this passage in Luke. What should draw our attention is the fact that an old man and an old woman, Simeon and Anna, "looked for the consolation of Israel." This is expressly said of Simeon, but not of Anna in so many words, though we can assume it from the way she spoke of the Savior to those who were looking for the redemption of Jerusalem. This is a special quality these two people had. But they were not alone in this, for Anna spoke about him to all who were looking for redemption. It is said of Anna that she did not depart from the temple. And it was there that she must have encountered expectant people. We can assume that there must have been a small group of seeking people, quietly present, who thought of the future of the Lord with great earnestness. They were in the temple, praying for God's promise to be fulfilled. They were not highly placed Jews, not leaders, not scholars; they were very quiet people who carried this longing in their hearts. They spoke with one another about it, repeatedly. They were precious souls, the most precious in the whole of Israel.

When it is said that Anna never departed from the temple, worshiping with fasting and prayer night and day, you have to picture a grieving widow, one who fasted and longed out of a great expectation. In her old age she does what earlier the prophet Daniel had done. When Daniel saw that the seventy years of exile had been completed, he began to pray and fast. For fourteen days he prayed that God would fulfill his promise to deliver his people from the Babylonian exile. Maybe he worried that it wouldn't happen, for the nation was unworthy and had even forgotten about returning to the promised land. Perhaps the Israelites would rather remain settled where they were, forgetting about Jerusalem altogether. As the people had forgotten Jerusalem, Daniel could believe that perhaps the Lord would also forget his people, saying "If you do not want this, then I will withdraw my promise"—because God himself often said that he would only give his promise on condition that the people showed themselves worthy to see the fulfillment. But Daniel dared to step into the breach and came before the Lord with such deep and passionate ardor that in the same instant God commanded that a remnant of his people return.

Similarly, there was also a prophecy, concerning the same Daniel, with the well-known "seventy weeks" (Dan 9:24). Although these seventy weeks were, it would appear from studying our text, almost past, the whole of Israel seemed to be indifferent; there was nowhere a real, lively desire forand nowhere an upright faith in the fulfillment of the prophecy; and only a few took it upon themselves to struggle and strive with the Lord that he would not go back on his word and that he would fulfill his promise.

At the time of Christ's birth, there was also a small group of people who together made up a "Daniel"—a small band of men and women. The group could well have been afraid that God had forgotten his promise, especially because his people were so corrupted and too distant from him to care about his promise. Perhaps they felt the position dangerous and thought, we had better come together and plead with God so that he will not withdraw his promises and cast out Israel forever. And so they prayed and struggled. Through the prayers of these faithful ones, the Lord remained firm to his promise. At the appointed time he sent his Son Jesus into the world.

The Lord rejoiced when he saw this expectation and longing for the Messiah. He not only gave Simeon an answer, but it was said of Simeon, "The Holy Spirit was upon him." The Holy Spirit only comes where there is longing for the kingdom of God. The Holy Spirit is given in order that, through the Spirit's powers, creation itself will be led back to God. There were many other devout and God-fearing souls at that time; but since they did not look for the "consolation of Israel," they didn't have the Holy Spirit upon them. There were scribes and theologians learned in Scripture, but not those who allowed themselves to be led, filled, and moved by the Spirit. Their piety had no power, no inner strength. They wanted only knowledge about divine matters, not a true inner life. The Pharisees ignored the central promise of God—the coming of the Son of Man who would redeem the world. [. . .] They were consumed with selfish worry and had become dry and offensive, envious and slanderous. If only they had longed for a Savior! But Simeon, who unlike them was really determined that God's promise must be fulfilled, was filled with the Holy Spirit. Being a faithful fighter for the Lord, he received the gift the Holy Spirit, even before the Lord's victory on the cross.

Simeon longed to see God's promise, the Savior himself, before he died. This is quite a contrast from those who only want to die. Although quite old, he did not want to die before the Savior came. There is a reason for this. He saw how the expectation of the Savior had become less and less. Perhaps he had not found anyone in the large circle of his friends who took it as seriously as he did. He must have thought, "When I die, all the hope of the people of God will be carried to the grave; there will be nobody left to take up the cause." If Simeon had only known fighters like himself, people who took the promise as earnestly as he did, he might have been content to die in peace. He could have said to his fellow seekers, "I beg you to accept this command: strive, struggle, pray, and never give up." [. . .] Maybe Simeon knew that when he died, people would stop looking for the Messiah, and then the Lord would change his mind.

This Simeon makes us think of Daniel, who didn't stand up until the angel of the Lord said, "Daniel, your prayer has been heard" (Dan 9:21–23). Like Daniel, Simeon struggled with God, contending with God not to let him die, fighting for his life so that he could pray, cry, struggle and fast. The great earnestness with which he took up this fight was heard—he received an answer. Here it says, "by the Holy Spirit," but it could have been through an angel who called to him, "Simeon, you shall not die until you have seen Christ the Lord."

Simple stories like these are more significant than we think, and it may come to light how much the whole world is indebted to Simeon for his fasting, prayer, and struggle. In the same way, we are indebted to Anna, already eighty-four years old, who also prayed. She and others must have supported Simeon; they must have kept helping him up and strengthening him while he did the same for them. [. . .] They must have known how he felt about not dying before the promise was fulfilled, and because the Spirit of God was with him, he must have inspired them and others, strengthening them to continue on.

It must have been difficult for them all to remain firm in the midst of all the indifference and all the pious snobbery of the Pharisees. They needed much strength of purpose, especially as they became weaker with age. It must have taken tremendous effort for such an old man as Simeon to keep up his spirit, to keep looking only to God's promise, while the rest of the world had already forgotten it. Simeon had seen many generations pass. Nevertheless, his heart and head held no other thought than that God's promise be fulfilled.

Dear friends, these are important accounts and also significant for our times. We have, doubtless, still many pious and God-fearing people with us; but all of us are charged by the Lord to wait—"Be like the servants who are waiting for their master to come home" (Luke 12:36). With this, he wishes that we act in such a way that it can be seen that we are waiting from hour to hour, until that which is promised occurs. The Lord Jesus told his disciples that he would return again, "in the glory of his Father" (Matt 16:27). He thus holds forth the hope that everything must still be subjected under his feet; that the whole world must still become his; that sin must still be destroyed upon earth; that the rulership of the evil one must still be overthrown, in order that the Lord alone shall be almighty.

This is promised to all who believe if they but wait. But where are those who watch? Who today recognizes that the world lies deeply in evil? Who still thinks, "I will strive and struggle until at last the Lord shall stretch out his omnipotent hand"? Instead, we turn a blind eye to sin. The power of Satan runs rampant and we are content to sleep. The pious and God-fearing too have only used their earnestness and zeal to ensure their own salvation; they couldn't care less about creation and its need to be torn out of bondage. Where are the people who are waiting diligently, like Simeon and Anna? True, there are a small number of people who eagerly wait, crying out, "O dear Savior, don't let me die until your victory is seen." But what about the rest of us? The piety and fear of God in so many people is a poor, weak, powerless thing. It has a great deal of outward show—like at that time in Israel—but little content. For the most important thing left to us by the Savior is overlooked. Only the teaching remains. It is talked about, but few have it burning in their heart and soul. And so, many pious and God-fearing Christians are afraid when it is announced, "The time has come!" They are afraid that it will be with them as it was with Herod and the city of Jerusalem, when upon hearing the message of the wise men from the East, the whole city was troubled. They think, "Oh dear, what will befall us? How awful it will be! Now the persecution of the Antichrist will be upon us. If only I could die beforehand!" And out of pure fear the main issue is disregarded and people think: "If only I and my children do not have to face this!"

Let us not shrink back or cower. Let us not lose sight of the message because we are afraid. Keep in mind the example of all those who over the generations have waited for the redemption of Jerusalem. [. . .] Our Gospel [reading] today stirs such thoughts in us. Whether there are ears to hear, I do not know. But whoever has ears to hear, let them hear! Reflect upon this and see to it that you listen quietly, like Simeon, Anna, and the others, who in those times looked for the consolation and redemption of Israel. Amen.

The Holy People

The kingship and dominion and the greatness of the kingdoms
under the whole heaven shall be given to the people of the holy ones
of the Most High; their kingdom shall be an everlasting kingdom,
and all dominions shall serve and obey them.

—DANIEL 7:27 (NRSV)

This holy kingdom described in Daniel will be given to the people of
the Most High. The Most High is our Commander, but even he cannot
gain anything without a holy people. They must fight for it. A small band,
fighting under Christ's leadership will succeed. The Savior says, "Fear not,
little flock, for it is your Father's good pleasure to give you the kingdom"
(Luke 12:32).

God's kingdom, with its dominion and power, will be given to this
little flock, through their Commander-in-Chief, Jesus Christ. They will
overcome all things. The holy people will secure the kingdom, will fight
for its dominion and power everywhere on earth, and when this is accomplished Christ will have won. All creation will serve and obey him.
Everything, everything must come under his sovereignty, and in the end
he will free all creation from its chains. We must plead with him to help us.
He will overcome all hostility because all power has been given to him—in
heaven and on earth.

Lord Jesus, we praise you. You conquer death and hell with your all-
powerful strength, and through you we also will conquer evil. We ask you
to stand with us in all our struggles and remain with us until your promises

Editors' Note: This sermon is dated 1880.

have been fulfilled. The time will finally come when you will deliver all creation from bondage. Amen.

The Salvation

I wait for your salvation, O LORD.

—GENESIS 49:18 (NRSV)

The whole world groans, and our good friend Jacob felt this too. Upon his deathbed Jacob blessed his children, one after another, and in the midst of this he paused for breath with the words, "I wait for your salvation, O LORD." He was already waiting for the same thing we are waiting for—the fulfillment of God's promises of salvation. These are blessed words that Jacob spoke, words that have helped countless people, living and dying, so that they too have learned to cry out, "I wait for your salvation, O LORD." We should be like this—people waiting for God's salvation and for our Lord who will bring it. For when we wait we are part of a long expectation, which began two thousand years before Christ and has continued right up to today. We are only links in a long chain of expectant people that stretches over the millennia. It is wonderful, actually it is a joy, to wait and to feel this close bond with all those who have waited expectantly for God's kingdom. This expectancy will endure until that which is awaited comes to pass, and then we will rejoice with one another because, "The hope of the righteous ends in gladness" (Prov 10:28).

O Lord our Savior! You are faithful and true and your promise will be fulfilled. Even though your servants have waited long, your salvation will come at last. Yes, it must come, and we patiently look forward to it. Even though your salvation has not fully come yet, you are present with us as our friendly and loving Savior. We all wait for you and long for you. Amen.

Editors' Note: This sermon is dated 1880.

Hold Firmly to Expectation

Be like those who are waiting for their master . . . .

—LUKE 12:36 (NRSV)

To wait for one's master] means first of all to believe in a coming Lord, and then, if I have to wait for him, to believe that he will come soon. If he was not coming back for 100,000 years, I couldn't wait for him. Yet, I do wait for him, even though I am not exactly sure how long it will be before he returns. The Lord tells us that we should expect him any and every moment. Don't ever think, "I am sure that he will not come back in my lifetime." This would not be holding firmly to expectation. People have told me that they believe everything I say, except for the word "soon." But this is the very heart of the matter—we must really believe in the Coming One. To believe this demands that we accept him as the One who is coming soon. To believe this means that we ourselves expect to experience the start of his coming. That is the faith that believes the impossible is possible. Christ will come when nobody expects him or considers it possible. One day the Lord will indeed reveal himself to us. Then, it will be plain that he is coming soon.

Lord, our Savior, Jesus Christ. Be merciful to us this day and let us be commended to you. O Lord, let the time of your coming, for which we are waiting, break in upon us soon. Increase the number of your expectant ones. Lord, you are faithful. Turn toward us, your waiting children, and deliver us from all evil. O Lord, hear our prayer, and grant it! Amen.

Editors' Note: This sermon is dated 1880.

Those Who Seek God

Do not let those who hope in you be put to shame because of me,
O Lord GOD of hosts; do not let those who seek you be dishonored
because of me, O God of Israel.

—Psalm 69:6 (NRSV)

We must ask the Lord to protect his servants—that they are not disgraced or put to shame. There is still a small company that can be characterized by the words: "Who hope in you, Lord GOD of hosts, who seek you, O God of Israel." And they seem always to be exposed to the attacks of the evil one and always find their hopes, longings, and seeking confronted by difficult situations. But the Lord God of hosts promises to help them all. And he does! In this way the world recognizes that, "No one who hopes in you will ever be ashamed" (Ps 25:3).

This is a remarkable verse, for it speaks of those who expect from the Lord much that is not yet given. Those who truly honor Jesus Christ must always be hoping and waiting. Our witness, our faith will have gone very wrong if we can't be recognized as those who hope and wait—those who long for the Savior, looking for him even when he seems to be far away.

"Who hope in you, who seek you," is quite a different expression from, "Those who believe in you, those who love you." [. . .] The difference is quite significant. Those who hope and wait are people who expect the kingdom of God to break in. They wait for the fulfillment of the promises that God has made and look for the unfolding of God's glory that will one day descend on the whole earth and to all people. They are not satisfied, but truly hope and seek for this. The others are satisfied with what they have already.

Certainly, those who truly wait possess an advance portion of God's promise, but they are not satisfied with it, for they know that God wants to give much more. And yet, this makes them hope and long all the more.

Expect the Impossible

Is anything impossible for the LORD?

—GENESIS 18:14 (NET)

Let us consider how this scripture applies to the renewed outpouring of the Spirit of Pentecost, for which we wait. For the Lord promised to send us the Spirit again as he did at Pentecost. Although the Spirit appears to have retreated since then, this does not mean that it's not possible for God to pour out his Spirit again. Consider the pillar of cloud and fire, which in Israel was called, "The glory of God." That was a pillar as high as heaven and it shone by day and by night. It shone in the wilderness for forty years and was even seen in the promised land. Finally it disappeared completely and nothing more was known of this great glory. Then David came, and the Spirit of God was upon him. Solomon succeeded him, and when the temple was completed, behold, the pillar of fire fell from heaven and was again present (1 Kings 8:10–11). Later it disappeared once more, but then at Pentecost it reappeared again, this time in a more complete way. The glory of God showed forth like never before. What about today? God's glory will come again, just as did the glory of the pillar of cloud and of fire, just as did the Spirit at Pentecost. The pillar of fire was the symbol of the Holy Spirit, and it must come again. And so, we must wait and hope for it to come. How astonishing it would be if this sign of the pillar of cloud and fire became visible today! Then God's people would hurry toward it. We must pray for it until we have it anew. We believe that nothing is impossible for the Lord. The outpouring of the Spirit is promised to us and to our children. It must come! How else can the world ever change unless this seeming impossibility becomes possible again?

Come, Lord Jesus!

"See, I am coming soon; my reward is with me, to repay according to everyone's work. I am the Alpha and the Omega, the first and the last, the beginning and the end."

Blessed are those who wash their robes, so that they will have the right to the tree of life and may enter the city by the gates. . . .

"It is I, Jesus, who sent my angel to you with this testimony for the churches. I am the root and the descendant of David, the bright morning star." The Spirit and the bride say, "Come." And let everyone who hears say, "Come." And let everyone who is thirsty come. Let anyone who wishes take the water of life as a gift. . . .

The one who testifies to these things says, "Surely I am coming soon."

Amen. Come, Lord Jesus!

The grace of the Lord Jesus be with all the saints. Amen.

—REVELATION 22:12–14, 16–17, 20–21 (NRSV)

At the beginning of each New Year we should think of that year, proclaimed by the prophet Isaiah and called by him, described as "the acceptable year of the LORD." This year is one where all those bound and imprisoned shall be freed, and all those in fetters shall be set at liberty. In freedom, they can enjoy the pleasures of grace. This "acceptable year of the LORD" began at the time our Savior was born. He himself pointed always to his return—to the time when all we need shall be fulfilled, and

Editors' Note: This sermon is dated New Year's Day, 1880.

when we shall be set free from all our sufferings. It will be a time of eternal blessedness.

Today the text begins, "See, I am coming soon; my reward is with me." At the end we hear Jesus say again, "Surely I am coming soon. Amen." We have waited two thousand years and this has yet to happen. But Christ says "soon," and does so twice in our text. This is significant. No matter how much time elapses, his coming is still "soon." "Soon" means unexpected; that is, "all of a sudden." It can come anytime—right now, just as it did in the time of the apostles. Each generation is therefore justified in thinking, "Soon he will come." Who knows, maybe we will even experience it! Every generation must have this hope.

With this word "soon," we are given a responsibility. The time of Christ's coming does not only depend on the Lord. Had it rested solely with him, it could have come to pass in any generation and year, as it could happen even in this year of 1880. It is not his will that it has not yet come. We must hold to this with all certainty—that it is not the fault of the Lord. It is because there is something missing in those of us who call ourselves his. The Lord said, "Blessed are those who keep my commandments." Have we failed the Lord by not following his commandments? If we have, then things have to come to a standstill. But when his commandments are kept, then the wheel of his plan turns again and his purpose moves forward.

Jesus said, "Seek first the kingdom of God and his righteousness, and all these things shall be yours as well" (Matt 6:33). As long as we live for material things, as long as we think it is enough to follow certain religious forms, his coming kingdom is thwarted from advancing. We must seek his kingdom above all else, so that he becomes our Master, Ruler, and King right here on earth. It has sometimes happened, as we well know, that we have sought to make human beings lords in the kingdom of God. But that is not the work of the Lord, but of us humans who want to take over everything in our own way—who do not ask if this is pleasing to the Lord or not. We do not keep God's commandments and do not consider that he should become King in the hearts of all people and prevail throughout the whole world. We stand in his way and say, "The kingdom and the rulership shall belong to us, not to Jesus!" We do not say it quite in this way, but the meaning is the same. In every age, from the very beginning on, the Lord Jesus has not been accorded the honor properly due him. He has often been left standing outside, and human beings have behaved as if they were the kings. The Lord Jesus could weep over the folly that has swept through all of Christendom and humanity. It did not occur to people to help him fight against the powers of darkness, but rather, in order to gain something, they gave themselves to the powers of darkness. The desire for the powers of the Spirit to be given them, in order that Jesus might become Lord, occupied a very small part of their time and effort.

It is no surprise, then, the "soon" has been delayed. God takes no pleasure in coming to people who don't wait or look for him, whose coming makes no difference to them. [. . .] That's why we see so little promise of his coming soon—of "the acceptable year of the Lord." But this could all change. His coming could happen, and soon!

How? The Lord gets his people ready in secret, just as he quietly prepared Simeon and others who waited for God's kingdom. Of these the authorities knew nothing. In the quiet of their simple dwellings they turned to their God to ask that at long last he would send the Savior of the world. So it may well be that today there are also small groups of people seeking for a deeper commitment to the Lord. They want to find something more fulfilling for their lives than just a peaceful death. They could, and will, meet hostility. But what these small bands determine in quiet with the Lord, against the powers of darkness, will eventually be revealed. The future actually lies with them.

Our real hope is to work quietly, in harmony with the Lord. In the world around us a different atmosphere rules. There are all kinds of movements and happenings, so much happens that it is easy to go from one exciting thing to another. But that is all nothing—it has no value. What is of God, things we don't readily hear or see, happens quietly, faithfully in secret. From here, from small circles, the word goes out, "He comes! He is coming!"

John writes, "Surely he is coming soon." We read, "The Spirit and the Bride say, 'Come!' And let him who hears say, 'Come!'" All who want to belong to Christ must learn to say, "Come!" Whoever does not have this word on their lips and in their hearts and in their lives is doing nothing toward Jesus' coming. The Spirit always says, "Come, Lord Jesus!" I would almost say that the Spirit never speaks without impelling us to say, "Come!" Otherwise, only human thoughts, human feelings, human endeavors are expressed—nothing divine. The Holy Spirit does not speak without the little word "Come!" being laid upon everyone's lips, whatever kind of Christian belief we follow. The Spirit is always ready to say to each one, "Think of the coming Savior." Anyone who does not perceive and accept the witness of the Spirit in their innermost being, anyone who is not truly able to call out, "Come!"—then I just have to say this—they are not filled with the Holy Spirit, however devout their words sound and whatever good influence they appear to have.

Therefore, cry out for his coming! When the need is burning in our hearts, "The Bride says, 'Come!'" Those who cry out for this can truly be called his "Bride people." They yearn together for the marriage with the Bridegroom and to exclaim, "Come!" They stake their very lives upon his coming, even if they are very few. The Spirit puts "Come!" into the hearts of his "Bride people."

Will he then today put it into the hearts of many people to look up longingly and call, "Come!"? Oh! There is reason enough, for everything is so disturbed and corrupted that we can see no way by which help could be given. It appears to be a lost cause whichever way we look. When we look at our world today, who is there to help us? Only the Savior. For when he comes, everything will be changed. In the meantime, there are forerunners and deeds of grace that precede him. Rays from the coming splendor do shine upon languishing humankind, and they point us to the coming Savior. They show how close he is, how active he is. If we would but listen, we could hear his voice. There is a rustling sound in the air, and everything is moving. It is a sign that he is on the way. But what a change that will bring! The whole of humankind will heave a deep sigh if only once they are able to perceive something of their Savior's return. But before we even realize all this, it will be told to the Bride: "Say, 'Come!'"

Today the very first words out of our mouths should be, "Jesus, come!" How wonderful to imagine a great echo, with the words "Come! Lord Jesus" resounding in the hearts of all who confess him as Lord. May it be that such a resounding can be heard, even by the angels. "Angels, come down to us!" (Ah! that I might dare to speak like this.) "Look for whoever longs to exclaim: 'Come, Lord Jesus' Look for them!" I know for sure that the little ones say it. It is on their lips, "Come, Lord Jesus!" But how many of us adults cry out? If the angels examined our hearts, would they hear the words, "Come, come!" or would they sadly look away, saying, "We can do nothing here." We can never really know what the angels might find. But believe me, we become different people the moment we cry out: "Come, come soon!"

Jesus said, "Let him who is thirsty, come, let him who desires, take the priceless water of life." This is a promise to anyone who says, "Come!" Our thirst will be quenched with the water of life that is priceless. When you say "Come!" then at once you go to the spring and take the water of life without price. It is worth it! Believe me the longing for his coming pleases the Savior so much that he gives us a strange sense of well-being. He gives us a special contentment. It is like being touched by the Savior or an angel of God [. . .]; his promise of complete redemption abides deep within us.

Now the eternal word of the Lord will always be before us: "Surely, I am coming soon." And when many hearts cry out, "Come!" then the wheel will turn faster and faster, so fast that very quickly everything will be fulfilled. Every cry of "Come!" brings the wheel into greater momentum. When the Lord sees a longing for him upon earth, when he sees a deep thirst for him, much grieving for him, then he will rise up and quench our thirst. And when he says once more, "Surely, I am coming soon. Amen"—then we will call again, "Yes, come, Lord Jesus!"

The passage ends with the greeting, which also applies to the whole New Year: "The grace of the Lord Jesus be with you all. Amen."

Watch! The Lord Will Come Soon!

Take heed, watch; for you do not know when the time will come. It is like a man going on a journey, when he leaves home and puts his servants in charge, each with his work, and commands the doorkeeper to be on the watch. Watch therefore—for you do not know when the master of the house will come, in the evening, or at midnight, or at cockcrow, or in the morning—lest he come suddenly and find you asleep. And what I say to you I say to all: Watch!

—MARK 13:33–37 (RSV)

We stand at the end of the church year and cannot conclude it unmoved, because thinking back on it we see the many blessings and mercies of our God. Undisturbed, we have had the blessing of his Word and have rejoiced abundantly in this. We have also had ample proof that the Lord was among us, when we spoke of him and remembered his promises. For outward things too we must give thanks, because we have seen and felt God's blessing in all kinds of ways—spiritual and temporal blessings are closely connected. When life is too heavy and cares are too much, this detracts from spiritual blessing, and it is difficult to keep an open ear for the Word of life which brings about our eternal salvation. Accordingly we need to offer up our thanks for both spiritual and temporal blessings to our God, for by means of both he seeks to win our hearts. But when we see how we have conducted ourselves under such blessings, then we must humbly say, "The Lord does all things well, but we do not know how to act rightly. We incline, always wrongly, toward the one side or the other and are in great

Editors' Note: This sermon is dated 1876.

need of more stability. May our merciful God give us this also through our present meditations, so that we may take a new mind and will with us into the coming church year, rejoicing in new and even greater blessings from the Lord."

Our Gospel text helps us to take up the right attitude so as to not be brought to shame on his great day. The Lord cries out, "Watch!" In this parable Christ compares himself to a man going on a journey, who when he leaves home puts his servants in charge, each with his work. But notice: The Lord is going away, but is also coming back. It is not as if he is finished with everything and now it is left up to the servants of the household. As it says, "He commands the doorkeeper to be on watch." The doorkeeper is to keep watch, for Jesus will return. When and how depends on how the servants whom he has left behind have conducted themselves; whether they have been watchful, be it in the evening, at midnight, at cockcrow, or in the morning, or whether he finds them asleep.

You can imagine what great news this must have been to the disciples. We have never heard of someone leaving the world and then returning after a number of years. Granted, the prophet Elijah ascended into heaven, and he and Moses appeared again with Christ on the Mount of Transfiguration. This may have made it a bit easier for them to believe that they would see him again. [. . .] But Jesus is not interested in his disciples just seeing him again. When he returns, he will come as "master of the house." He will demand an account and inquire whether his servants have done what they were instructed to do. It will be a serious matter when he returns, for he will come in judgment. Hence, he tells his disciples, "Take heed, watch and pray, for you do not know when the time will come."

Who is the Savior speaking to? Who is he referring to? Obviously to his immediate disciples. If the Lord Jesus had returned quickly, he would have surely been referring to these disciples only. But over 1800 years have now passed. To whom then is he speaking? Who are the servants? Now, in addition to the apostles there are other servants of Jesus Christ, servants of the gospel, who are the apostles' successors. They are ones who have taken their cause upon themselves. Such servants take special care not to be concerned only with themselves, but for all; they have a heart for everyone. They strive to help everyone to stand rightly upon that great day when the Lord comes again. Now at the end of the parable the Lord adds: "And what I say to you," (that is to his disciples) "I say to all: Watch!" This warning to "watch" applies to everyone who has accepted the gospel—those who have been baptized, who confess Jesus and believe in him. This parable applies to every Christian, to us.

Sadly, most Christians today think no further than their own salvation and eternal blessedness. They look no further than saving themselves. Consequently, very few really care about the Lord's return. People today do not need his coming again, they live their own Christianity, believing they will die blessed and that everything is as it should be with them. Most people behave like this, and so the words of today's Gospel reading hardly fit into their Christianity. If these words had not been said to us by the Lord, it would certainly not occur to us to be on the watch, looking out for the return of our Redeemer. But, it is clearly written, "Watch, for you do not know when the master will come—lest he come suddenly and find you asleep!" Christians seem astonished by this. Although everybody hears Christ's word, most have no real understanding. Oh, how few people think it important that Christ Jesus is to be expected! In fact, many even find it downright irksome to talk about the coming of the Lord and how he will demand an accounting of all those who have heard of him.

Oh, how much would be gained if only this one thought lived in our hearts: "Jesus will come again! Jesus will come again soon!" Especially in our time, how much would already be won if, today, all churchgoers, in all parts of Christendom, would grasp this one thought: "Jesus will come again! Jesus will come again soon!" But we remain indifferent and skeptical. "Oh, maybe this is something we should believe, but who of us can know when this might ever occur? Beside, we've been waiting for thousands of years. Who knows how many more thousands of years we'll have to wait? It's a waste of time to even think about it." This is the way we talk about such questions of faith—nothing is ever allowed to deeply touch our hearts. [. . .] If the Savior visited us today, would he find anyone who seriously thinks about his coming? If an angel came right now, writing on a piece of paper the names of those who live for Christ's return, his list would surely be quite short. [. . .] Seriously, where are the people who expect the coming of the Lord, who are faithfully serving and watching for his return?

Jesus said, "Watch, for you do not know when the Lord will come— lest he come suddenly and find you asleep." Yes, beloved ones, it could make us tremble to think, "Christ can come at any moment, he will come quickly, he will come soon!" It would have no purpose to be always watchful of what this or the other signifies, noting the signs of his coming—if, in spite of this, something is not kindled in us. Something must be lacking when no spark of hope is kindled in us. It's as if we need to be shocked and jolted before this really takes root in hearts. Preaching doesn't work. The more one talks about faith, the sleepier people get. It does not grip them, nor do they approach it in all seriousness. I therefore implore the Savior every day, "Oh, let something happen—a sign, a sound, a trumpet blast, or some other indication from the heavens—so that we might seriously seize upon the fact that you will return soon!" [. . .] Oh, if only there were a brilliant sign in the heavens, a great light, that might shock us out of our stupor: "Things are serious. He is coming! He is coming!"

I once came to an inn, while I was an assistant pastor journeying to the mission house in Basel, to work as a teacher of missionaries. The inn-keeper's wife sat down with me, and we talked about what I was planning to teach. Suddenly she exclaimed: "But, sir, if what you say is true, the Lord must be coming soon. We must get ourselves ready!" I thought to myself, "Here is a woman who truly understands." Though she was not learned, she grasped the idea that when the gospel begins to spread throughout the whole world, the Lord will soon return. And indeed, the whole world will soon have heard the gospel. But even this sign counts for nothing among people, along with so many other things that point to the end. People still don't take seriously the coming of the Lord. Oh, that we may not be caught off guard and suddenly hear, "The Lord comes," and he finds us asleep. "And all tribes of the earth will wail" (Rev 1:7).

You dear ones, examine yourselves. Do you secretly think, "The Lord must have been exaggerating; the apostles had to wait and were disappointed, so we mustn't take Christ's words too literally . . ." and so on? Test yourselves thoroughly, [. . .] or you will be asleep when he comes. Oh, if I could only stress that he really will come soon! But when I say, "soon!" then disbelief and the spirit of doubt begin to appear again. People think to themselves, "Oh, here he comes again with his 'soon' and nothing happens." If only I could help you believe in the return of the Lord. But I can't. It has to come from within you. Only then will you say over and over again, "Soon— yes, soon—he will come again. Let's be ready. Who knows how quickly he will be here?" But today I am not welcome to say this! It is looked on as an exaggeration. Anybody can talk or explain it away as exaggerated or laugh-able—that is not difficult. But to stand fast in a serious matter, to ward off the enemy and not relax—that is really difficult and not everybody can do this! But whoever does exclaim it, that person will experience many things and will see that the Lord's coming cannot long be delayed. What I would give to be able to awaken this thought in everyone I meet. The Lord is near! He can all of a sudden come. But I will say this, that even if we do not know when the last things will break in, the time is near when the signs will be seen; the time of the signs of which Luke speaks: "There will be terrors and great signs from heaven" (Luke 21:11). Yes, this time of the signs is surely closer than most of us believe.

Beloved, listen to the repeated cry of the Redeemer, "Watch!" He knocks wherever people keep watch. Wherever he enters he asks, "Where are the people who watch?" When the Lord knocks and hears from us, "Come in!" he enters bestowing blessings. Great things are experienced when there is fellowship with the Savior. Yes, when we watch and wait for our Lord, he brings joy to people. Christ cares deeply that we watch. For, when we stop watching he stops coming toward us, perhaps for thousands of years still: "Sometime he will come! Yes, one day he will come, one day—one day!" But the Redeemer says: "Behold, I come soon, bringing my recompense," and "Blessed are those servants who are found awake when the Lord comes."

Oh, let this speak to you today! For why should you not want his Word to prevail? Why should you think it stupid when he says: "Watch, for you do not know when the Lord will come!"? Whatever you do, learn to watch, learn to hope, learn to wait, and to surrender yourselves completely to the great hope of Christ's imminent return. He comes for us. He comes for the world. Oh, Savior, we long for you to come soon! Yes, come soon! Amen.

When Will the Kingdom of God Come?

He was once asked by the Pharisees when the kingdom of God would come, and he answered, "The kingdom of God is not coming visibly, and people will not say, 'Look, here it is!' or 'There it is!' for the kingdom of God is within you."

And he said to his disciples, "The time will come when you will long to see one of the days of the Son of Man, and you will not be able to do so. Men will say to you, 'Look! There he is!' or 'Look! Here he is!' Do not go off in pursuit of him, for just as when the lightning flashes, it shines from one end of the sky to the other, that will be the way with the Son of Man. But first he must go through much suffering, and be refused by this age."

—LUKE 17:20–25 (GOODSPEED TRANSLATION)

Beloved friends in Christ Jesus, there are two concepts in our text today that we should consider so that we may get a feeling of Advent and its significance. These words are: "the kingdom of God" and "the day of the Lord."

They are the two great words, which the loving Savior brought to the world and which embrace everything we can possibly expect and wish for. The kingdom of God has come and will come. And the day of the Lord Jesus Christ will also come. Whoever can understand and assimilate these two things knows what Advent is all about. For Advent means—Arrival!

Editors' Note: This sermon is dated Advent, 1853.

Thus we speak of the advent or the arrival of the kingdom of God and the day of the Lord.

O Lord, give us grace that we may understand rightly and take into our hearts what we are most in need of, so that we may share in your kingdom and have joy in your approaching day. Help us, Lord. Give us new nourishment for our souls from your Word, so that, comforted, we can continue our pilgrimage until all that you have promised has come to pass. Amen.

I. THE KINGDOM OF GOD

Now, to return to our text. The Pharisees asked the beloved Savior: "When will the kingdom of God come?" The Lord answered, "Repent and believe in my Word, for the kingdom of heaven is at hand." It is perhaps to this word that the Pharisees refer when they say, "When will the kingdom of God come, of which you preach?" Instead of answering the question "when," the Savior tells the Pharisees what kind of kingdom will come, giving them a whole new understanding of the "kingdom of God." The Pharisees were thinking of an earthly kingdom in which Jerusalem would become a renowned city of God under a triumphant king. The people of Israel would appear in splendor and all the people of the earth would tremble before them, exclaiming, "There is no other kingdom on earth like Israel." It would be a kingdom to which everyone would have to pay homage and bring their gifts. This is what the Pharisees understood by the kingdom of God. They yearned for such a kingdom because they were under the oppression of the Romans, living, as they felt, in heathen servitude. The Lord tried to set right this misunderstanding. He said, "It will not be as you think; the kingdom will not be visible; people won't be able to say, 'Lo, here it is,' or 'There!'" When God's kingdom comes there will be no great general or powerful king, with his court in Jerusalem, dispatching messengers to all parts of the country, celebrating brilliant triumphs, ruling all with his scepter, bringing all peoples together under his mighty rod. No. The kingdom of God will not come like this. None of these things will happen when God reigns. There will be no earthly liberation and worldly splendor. The Savior is clear: "Do not seek for the kingdom of God in visible signs, for this kingdom is within you. The kingdom of God is already here, or at least it can be here in you and in everyone who hears me and who repents and believes." When the kingdom of God is in your midst, there is no need to ask "When?" It does not come as you think it will, even if you waited many millions of years for it.

How then does the kingdom of God come? What is it really? The kingdom of God, God's rulership, dwells within us. In other words, the Lord takes possession of our heart. When the Lord gains possession of someone and has power over them, then the kingdom of God is established. When a person repents and believes in the gospel, then the Lord rules and reigns in them. Accordingly, at any moment and in any person the kingdom of God can break in. So, at this Advent time we must ask the following: 1) Is the kingdom of God within me? 2) Is it within you? 3) Is the kingdom of God within many hearts?

Is the kingdom of God within me?

The kingdom of God, dear friends, shall come within us; we shall belong to the Lord. When this happens, everything that we are and have will belong to our God. Then he is the Lord, his kingdom is within us, and our hearts are the palace of the King and the temple of the Holy Spirit. Then we can ask ourselves: "Have we already celebrated Advent? Has the Lord entered our lives already? Do we belong to the Lord?" Before the Savior came, Satan ruled in the hearts of people; Satan's kingdom was established there. But now Satan's kingdom can be replaced by the kingdom of God residing in our hearts. We no longer have to serve evil and perverse things. Instead, we can depend on God's goodness. Him, our only helper in need, shall we honor. Ah, dear friends, how many thousands refuse to surrender their hearts to God and instead serve some false god? How many thousands do not allow a place in their hearts for God, but remain servants of Satan, allowing sin to run rampant within them, not letting themselves be rescued from their corruption? They do not want to be freed from the powers of darkness. They remain bound in slavery, corrupted and, therefore, lost, because the rulership of God through Jesus Christ is not yet established within them. Ah, how wonderful, if today were to be an Advent day—a day of the coming of the kingdom of God into many hearts! So ask yourself whether the kingdom of God is within you!

Can God's kingdom really come to us? Just follow the Savior without asking too many questions. Repent and believe in the gospel, then the kingdom of God will enter into you. You will belong to the Lord. Give yourself to God and say, "I dedicate myself to you, forgive my sins. I will faithfully live by the grace you offer." Place yourself under the mild yoke of Christ and you will discover true salvation. You will be assured that his kingdom will grow; it will take possession of the whole earth and penetrate into the hearts of all people.

When will the kingdom of God come? Would to God that in answer to this question everyone could say, "Praise God, I have already experienced Advent!" But because there are so many who are unable to say this, perhaps also not many of you, we must all again and again, as often as we celebrate Advent, look to the future, to a time in which the kingdom of God becomes reality. Each one of us must pray, "Oh, that in my heart the living God alone may rule, that the Savior would live in my heart. Only his will shall rule and my desire is only for God and my Savior. Oh, that all perversity, evil, and godlessness were cast from me, that I might become a pure, single-hearted temple of God—certain that he is my God and I am his child throughout eternity." I wish for each of you an Advent like this. But because we are not changed all at once, may each day be Advent for us. May the King of all kings ever anew and more completely enter and conquer our hearts, until all that is unfit is banished and uprooted from his holy presence, so that with his whole glory he may dwell within us.

Is the kingdom of God within you?

But we mustn't stop there. We need to pray that God's kingdom is found among everyone we meet, in all those we live and work with. We must ask God to help us help our neighbor to receive his kingdom. It is not right for anyone to be concerned with himself alone. A person will not go forward if at the same time they do not take thought of their neighbor that by the grace of God the heavenly kingdom may also be established in them. [. . .] Our hearts have to long and pray for them—to speak kindly, warn earnestly, give comfort, even at times to admonish, to prayer together, and so on. We will not stay close to Jesus if we don't think of our neighbor and their need to experience God's rulership in their lives.

Is the kingdom of God within all hearts?

Now the third thing we must sigh for is that God's kingdom may be revealed in all hearts. [. . .] At no other time has the rulership of the prince of darkness been so extensive as in our time. A pious effort here and there to foster a better spirit or to help alleviate some need is not the kingdom of God! Moreover, preaching does very little. In fact, the more one preaches, the colder, lazier, more obstinate—often more impudent and more godless—people become. It is quite clearly to be felt that the kingdom of God is not within them, but that Satan's kingdom is still firmly grounded in many millions of hearts. When will God's kingdom come? This is the question on our lips. When will things really change? When will all people receive, at last, a deep impression of our true Ruler and King? When will the time come in which every knee shall bow and every tongue confess that Jesus Christ is the Lord? Or even just those whose hearts are receptive to the Lord—when will they be subject to the one Ruler and King, who longs to conquer and save all hearts?

This is the manner in which the kingdom of God will come into the world: not through kings and emperors bearing Christendom along with outward pomp (as if pomp made any difference), but within the heart of each person, and when each person will seek nothing other than to do the will of God through the Savior and unto death. Oh, if such an Advent as this should come! And it will come! Such an Advent must be awaited and hoped for by many millions of hearts. It must come to all the peoples of the earth; otherwise all flesh will go the way of destruction, as in the time of Noah. When the Lord sent forth his twelve disciples unto the ends of the earth, to gather to themselves children of the kingdom, it was quite different from today. At that time thousands amazingly submitted their lives to the King of all kings. Since then, however, our Ruler, the Savior who was raised to the right hand of God, has apparently lost most of his majestic rights, along with the respect that his subjects ought to show him. There is hardly a person now who wants to serve the Ruler. Everybody now says: "Is he supposed to be our Lord?" Most people simply talk about what kind of life they want lead and do not inquire of him who should be everything to them. Right to this present day there is no one more despised than our most high and glorified Savior, who has rights over every heart.

One could well ask, wistfully, at this Advent: "When, oh when, will things be different? When will this heavenly kingdom arise in our hearts? When will all peoples of the earth turn and subject themselves to Jesus, their Ruler? When will they hasten to him, cry out to him, pay heed to his will, and allow him to make them just and blessed? When will it be?" Every time we celebrate Advent, sadness must steal over us because things look so miserable in so many places. Year after year the same, always the same picture of wretchedness, the same desertion from God, the same contempt for God. Oh, that we might all unite in begging and praying that the kingdom of God be hastened and that the time of victory comes near.

II. THE DAY OF THE LORD

We have a second word to consider, which affirms our first one: "The day of the Lord." The phrase, "The kingdom of God is not coming visibly," has been taken by many people to mean that the Ruler will not visibly return and take up his kingdom. In other words, God's kingdom should be understood spiritually; it is therefore not necessary for us to await the return of the Savior, who has been raised to the right hand of God. But they overlook that in the same speech the Savior speaks of "his day." We must therefore differentiate between the kingdom of God and the day of the Lord.

The day of the Lord will come, and it will be like "lighting that flashes and shines from one end of the sky to the other." The Savior clearly indicates why he uses the word lightning. The lightning flashes, that is to say, it happens with extraordinary speed. He will come down from heaven and light up the sky from one side to the other. In the same way as the lightning can be seen everywhere in the sky from the furthest distance, so suddenly shall we see the sign of the Son of Man. This is how he will return. This is somewhat different from what he says of the kingdom of God. It is for this reason we also say a word about the day of the Lord. The day of the Lord is at one and the same time the climax and pinnacle of the kingdom of God. When all hearts are subject to him; when, as the book of Revelation expresses it, the Bride, or the church of the Lord, is clothed in the fine linen of righteous deeds; when the people are made ready to serve the Lord—then the Lord will come suddenly and he will free his people from the tension that they feel. Then they will more faithfully and fully desire to serve the Ruler.

But before this all happens there will have to be much tribulation. The more complete the kingdom of God becomes in our hearts, the more active Satan resists. Be on your guard toward the end, for when the Lord sends his Spirit to win hearts and many people respond to his love, the fury of the old dragon will awaken and his rage will dramatically increase. Anyone who has the kingdom of God within them will come into deep need and extreme danger; their lives will be made miserable. Then under such pressure those who serve God's kingdom will have to groan, pray, and beg for help, and at long last the Lord will quickly come like lightning. He will save his chosen ones, and they will reign with him for all eternity. That will be the day of the Lord, the Lord's victory.

Until that day comes, the kingdom of God will be established among all those who follow him. For, remember, he cannot come unless there are people who allow him to call them his subjects. The evil one won't be judged as long as he holds people in bondage—as long as we pay homage to him. The Lord cannot come, for if he did he would have to judge everybody. Humanity must pass through deliverance, redemption, and the restoration of what is lost. Thus Advent paves the way for the kingdom of God in the hearts of humankind and prepares the day of the Lord. The more that we serve the one true Lord, the nearer is the day of the Lord—a day of redemption for the children of the kingdom. When will this day come? The answer is simple: When the kingdom of God has won many, many hearts—when God's will is rooted in hearts so deeply that no power of darkness can suffocate it. Then the day of the Lord will come. Therefore, all of us who yearn for deliverance must above all else pray that God overpowers the hearts of people with his abounding mercy. He wants us to become subjects to him wholeheartedly. The great time of deliverance will come when Christ is Lord within us.

This word, "the day of the Lord," also has a very serious side. There will still be many who won't accept warning; nothing seems to move them. They refuse to let the Holy Spirit work within them. They remain lazy, inert, and indifferent, and won't let the Lord be their supreme good. They want only to court Satan and his ways. There will always be a world of serpents, the seed of the serpent, a world that will absolutely refuse to submit itself to the kindly voice of the Lord.

For those whose hearts are iron-fisted, the day of the Lord will be a day of terror, for on that day they will be overpowered and shattered. For them the time of judgment draws near, when they must atone for their rebelliousness and stubbornness, for their lack of attention and diligence. For we each know what is in our hearts. So we must consider. Who of us are serious about submitting to the Savior as Lord? Who among us still love darkness more than the light? Who among us are more like stones— whatever we do has no real or lasting effect? Consider if you might not be among these. Woe, then! For upon such the day of the Lord will strike like lightning. The Lord will speak in wrath, even though for years and years he has shown patience. He will come to judge, and he will do so even if the process of judgment lasts a long time, in an attempt to win you over. But when neither love nor blows avail, the day will come at last in which the godless, those who refuse to belong to the Lord, who refuse to bow to his rule and reign, will perish.

Whoever has ears let him hear! Let us make way in our hearts for the Lord, so that he as king and ruler can reign and we may rejoice in his day. [. . .] Pray without ceasing that the Spirit of God will come to you and to many, many others. Let your worries go so that ultimately the name of the Lord Jesus is firmly established in your hearts. A time of grace must come when the expectation of his children is one of full and complete joy! Amen.

Jesus Before the Door

Behold I stand at the door and knock; if any one hears my voice and opens the door, I will come in to him and eat with him, and he with me.

—REVELATION 3:20 (RSV)

The Lord speaks the above words in the last letter to the churches in Revelation, concerning his return. We can very well apply this to the coming of the Lord into every heart. These words are especially directed to the believers, whom he wishes to use to prepare the way of his coming return and for battles to be won on earth. Those who do this are the real conquerors; they surrender themselves to him and sacrifice everything for him and his kingdom, so that the kingdom at last becomes a reality. The Lord continues: "He who conquers, I will grant him to sit with me on my throne, as I myself conquered and sat down with my Father on his throne" (verse 21).

More than 1800 years ago the Lord "stood before the door and knocked," announcing that he was ready to come if the church would but open the door to him and let him enter. Gladly he gives us counsel as how to hasten his coming. We open the door to him whenever, despite the powers of darkness, we sincerely long and wait for him. The door is opened when we witness to his coming and receive only insults and opposition, a price that nowadays people do not want to pay. Since people throughout history have not wanted to hear this message, Christians have cowered and done so little to advance the Lord's return. He remains outside the door.

So today we don't even hear the Savior's knocking! Too many more important things fill our hearts and minds. Even if we wanted to be eager servants of the Lord, we spend our time rushing madly around completely absorbed in our own concerns. We neither understand nor notice signs from above. We simply don't have an ear to hear his gentle knock. The evil one sees to it that there is always plenty of "noise in the house." He is constantly interposing situations of apparently "great importance," but does so with the sole intent of causing bickering; the knocking is not heard. We lose so much time arguing; just think how much energy is lost every day! When will we stop being consumed with worldly affairs? There is so much confusion everywhere—in governments, and even churches. We argue and argue and argue. All the while, the Savior has to "screen" out the clamor so he can be heard. He does this again and again, but still we do not listen. When will we sober up and stop our drunkenness with worldly affairs? Only then will we understand Jesus and take deeply to heart how much his return means to him and how very much we stand in his way.

Thankfully, there are individuals who do hear Christ's knocking and do open the door of their hearts. The Lord will enter straightaway and make use of whoever opens the door for him and responds with his heart to the signs of his coming. He will enter into those hearts of all those who do not, with a shake of their head mock and let this understanding pass them by, but rather, listen and are inspired to patiently hope. Whoever arms and prepares themselves in faith and in prayerful fellowship with Jesus awaits his return. What is the first thing the Lord does when he enters? He eats with us, sitting down at the table with us to be served. Joyfully the Lord accepts our love, earnestness, and devotion, refreshing himself in this. Remember how Jesus made himself known to his followers by the breaking of bread (Luke 24:30–31)? They felt his closeness as they partook in the Lord's Supper. They received gifts and powers, patience and faith, and joyfully accepted all that Christ offered them. They understood what the Lord was asking them to do, and so they were ready to prepare the path for his Spirit. Believe me, nothing brings so much spiritual blessing as when one earnestly and fervently partakes of the great refreshment and redemption that Jesus brings from heaven.

"He who opens the door will also eat with him." This points to what the Lord promises us concerning the great feast in the kingdom of God, which he will share with his people after he has come again in his glory (Luke 14:15). "Truly, I say to you, he (the Lord) will gird himself and have them sit at table, and he will come and serve them" (Luke 12:37). What a gift it will be for all the faithful ones at his table, after all the many hard battles they successfully overcame. There will be continual joy as the Lord offers them "the hidden manna" (Rev 2:17). From "the tree of life" (Rev 22:2), he will share with them tranquility and eternal peace. Open the door to him, please! You will not regret it! Amen.

The Lord Comes

Blessed are those servants whom the master finds awake
when he comes.

—LUKE 12:37 (RSV)

The Lord wants to come. He came to earth, went away again, and will return—return visibly. Judgment is linked to his return. And when he appears all of us—both the living and the dead—will be seriously dealt with. Those of us who are alive should be especially watchful, because we will be judged and dealt with first.

Suppose the time were near. [Jesus would have to return] to a world that is almost completely asleep. For, with few exceptions, hardly anyone thinks seriously of Jesus' coming. His return is almost entirely forgotten, although it is an article of faith. This already makes it evident that we lie in a deep sleep. It is remarkable how greatly the attitude of Christians is influenced by whether they do or do not believe in the future coming of Christ. For to truly contemplate this future and to visualize it strengthens the wakefulness of the inner man more than anything. When one really thinks of this future, it brings a deep stirring into the heart, unlike anything else. I know this from my own experience, to speak a little of myself. From childhood on I had the opportunity to hear much about this—and I still feel the impression that it made upon my whole being. I have often noticed that when people are concerned with the future of Christ—as it was in the time of my youth—their Christian faith was much fresher and more vigorous than it is now, when almost everywhere there is silence.

A "gospel" that is not related to the coming of the Lord has no power, no significant effect. The apostles always pointed toward the coming of the Lord. Right from the start at the first Pentecost, and every opportunity thereafter, they pointed people to Christ's return as the fulfillment of God's revelation to humankind. Who would care about a Messiah that remained as distant from humankind as God himself? How would this be good news? It wouldn't! A gospel in which sin and its consequences remained was surely not good news. It certainly wouldn't satisfy the sighing and longing of creation. No! The gospel is the joyful news that the time is near when all sin will cease and all things corrupted by sin will be completely renewed. This time has begun!

Therefore, we must watch for Christ's coming. We must remember him and put everything right within ourselves and with everyone else. We cannot carelessly live for carnal pleasures or keep on indulging in sin. We must not keep living a boring life of cheap thrills full of worldly influences. Our hearts have to be filled with divine purpose. We must be consumed with what wants to break in from above. O Lord, help us!

The Promise of the Spirit

He has been raised to the right side of God, his Father, and has received from him the Holy Spirit, as he had promised. What you now see and hear is his gift that he has poured out on us.

—Acts 2:33 (GNT)

Peter spoke these words at Pentecost to the multitude gathered by the house where the Holy Spirit had descended upon Jesus' disciples. Everyone was amazed; they saw what looked like tongues of fire, which spread out and touched each person there. With loud voices the disciples praised the works of God, which he accomplished through Jesus Christ. Some bystanders mocked the disciples as drunkards, but Peter stood up and explained what was happening. He spoke of "the pouring out of the Holy Spirit," which Joel the prophet had prophesied would come to pass in the last days (Acts 2:16–17).

Peter then reminded his listeners of Jesus and of his crucifixion and death and how he arose from the dead on the third day. This was still fresh in everybody's mind, to which they could testify. He told them that Jesus was appointed to sit at the right hand of God, glorified in the other world, having received the promised Spirit from his Father. "This is what you see and hear now happening amongst us. From now on Jesus will pour out and impart this Spirit to all his disciples."

The Holy Spirit? Yes. The Holy Spirit, who was quite extraordinary, springing from the bosom of the Father. Jesus now sat at the right hand of God and was given power over everything in heaven and earth. That

Editors' Note: This sermon is dated 1876.

power had now descended on his followers. Jesus, the Son of Man, through his obedience was raised to the highest glory to be at the side of God. His innocent suffering and death, which he did not evade because he knew God had chosen him to become the Redeemer of the world, changed God's whole relationship to humankind.

Now we again can draw close to the beloved Father through Jesus Christ his Son, who intercedes on our behalf and who offers powers from above in fulfillment of God's promises to us. This happened through the outpouring of the Holy Spirit. This outpouring was granted to those who were loyal to Jesus. They were the firstborn to enter into living fellowship with God, as the Father himself promised to his Son. Out of Jesus' suffering he was raised to the right hand of God. And because of this, anyone who now believes in Jesus is united with God through the power and presence of the Holy Spirit. An intimate relationship between God and those who truly believe has been assured.

This complete unity of the Holy Spirit with God is beyond our comprehension, even though the power of his Spirit is upon all those who are actively close to Jesus. Just why this power has diminished since the time of the apostles we don't understand, but we must pray that it will be renewed through his Holy Spirit. God will again bring us into an intimate relationship with him, just as he did at Pentecost.

All the more we need to fervently ask for a renewed outpouring of the Holy Spirit. Such a prayer won't fail us, especially because increasing numbers are praying for it. Before we know it, the great day when Christ returns will be here. Therefore, prepare for the future of the Lord. God's mercy and faithfulness is great. What he began he will accomplish! Amen.

Thy Kingdom Come!

Thy kingdom come.

—MATTHEW 6:10 (RSV)

The kingdom for whose coming we pray is a kingdom that includes not only the earth but also all the heavens. It does not represent an earthly kingdom only. This kingdom is only fully established when "God will be all in all"—throughout creation and when everyone acknowledges and hallows the name of God. This is the kingdom of God.

God's kingdom began when Jesus was born. Until then the prince of this world, who was in opposition to God, aspired to rule everywhere; he had so much footing in the world that he already claimed this earth as his own (Matt 4:8–9). The prince of this age worked unceasingly, drawing the created order away from the rightful Father and into "the nets of darkness" under his authority. But Jesus, Son of Man, attacked by this prince remained faithful and obedient to his Father, until he died on the cross. Jesus' obedience opened the way for the kingdom of God to break into this dark world. He preached that the kingdom of God was at hand, although to begin with just the new king was there, and his subjects were very few. Before his death he said, "The Holy Spirit will convict the world of its sin, because the prince of this world now stands condemned" (John 16:11). Even though this prince of this world was judged, he is still not disposed of. [His final judgment is yet to come.] The faith of the disciples makes it possible for us to wait until that time comes. Time is still required before all earthly kingdoms are conquered, before all governments and authorities that oppose God are overthrown and removed.

Now this should be our central concern as we pray. We need to pray that all the kingdoms of this world, both visible and invisible, are conquered and that this would proceed rapidly. This is what it means to pray, "Thy kingdom come." Unfortunately, there are few people who pray seriously enough for this to happen. They just live carefree, without doing anything toward the coming of the kingdom of God. What we need is to feel the pain of the Father in heaven. So many of his children are far from him—so far away that he is not yet able to stretch out his fatherly hand to gather them into his kingdom. We need to feel his pain. We need to let it weigh on us. His pain should be our pain. He is Lord over everything, but if we don't recognize this, we will not truly be at peace—not even in the beyond. Yet, God's kingdom is on the march; it is growing as people turn to faith in Jesus and are born into the light from out of darkness. A great deal is expected of us. Apart from prayer, our foremost charge is to spread the gospel as much as we can, because it is said—not to angels but to us: "Go into all the world and preach the gospel to the whole creation" (Mark 16:15).

Lastly, the coming of the kingdom for which we pray lies in the revelation of the glory of the sons and daughters of God, for which creation itself waits with eager longing (Rom 8:19). As we pray, we must cry out, day and night, with a burning heart: "Thy kingdom come!" The Savior hears us, and in response he will succeed in fulfilling his will. A day will come when we shall rejoice, for on that day we shall receive testimony that we have worked with heart and soul, with zeal and self-sacrifice, so that at last, with the coming of the kingdom of God, the longing of creation is realized.

The Changed Body

But our citizenship is in heaven, and it is from there that we are
expecting a Savior, the Lord Jesus Christ. He will transform the body
of our humiliation that it may be conformed to the body of his glory,
by the power that also enables him to make all things subject to
himself.

—PHILIPPIANS 3:20–21 (NRSV)

Our citizenship is in heaven, yet we believe God will reveal his glory
on earth. This is the great Christian hope and the chief goal of the
Christian life. This is why it is vital that our whole life testifies to our belief
that Christ will return to establish his kingdom. Those who don't show in
their lives the longing and expectancy for the coming Savior have no citizenship in heaven. But people whose heart and soul are with Christ yearn
for him to come down to earth and take up his rightful reign. They pray,
"Thy will be done on earth as it is in heaven."

In the time of the apostles, Christians constantly sighed, "Oh, may the
Savior come soon!" In doing so, they gained strength from above for their
daily life. If our life is bound to heaven, in expectation of the coming Savior,
we will experience a foretaste of the powers of God through the Holy Spirit.
We will personally experience the rulership of Christ through his heavenly
gifts—gifts that will be given to all the world when he comes in the glory
of his Father.

We wait for the Savior all the more eagerly because we know that when
he comes, he will change our lowly body to be like his glorious body. With
all creation, we still groan under this mortal body, longing for freedom. So

271

we reach out toward the future of Christ, knowing that as we do we will no longer be weary—we will receive a completely different body. The dead will rise and the living will be transformed; everyone will be changed, just as the Savior was. This is what we wait for when we acknowledge that our citizenship is in heaven. There will always be scoffers, those who scorn such faith and hope. But we must not shrink back. It is only hostility toward the cross of Christ if we try to shelve the coming of Christ because we are ashamed to proclaim him to the unbelieving world.

Paul wants to assure us and make it clear, when he says, "This change of our body is by that power of his which makes him the master of everything that is." In Christ there lies the great creative and majestic power of God, which makes him Lord of creation, so that death too must cease and so life will penetrate everything. This will be and it is well with those who believe this. It is well with all those who, with the Savior, have their citizenship in heaven, and who already have powers of eternal life by which they are assured of the future change!

The Fight for the Kingdom

For thine is the kingdom, and the power, and the glory, for ever.
Amen.

—MATTHEW 6:13 (KJV)

The end of the Lord's Prayer points to the ultimate purpose and victory of God's kingdom on earth. It reminds us of the struggle with the evil one, from whom come all temptations. The Lord's whole prayer ends in words that express our trust and certainty in the Father in heaven and that provide the basis and assurance of victory. This firm belief in God's final victory is the only justification for bringing any prior petitions to God and for living in them (Matt 6:9–13). A person who wishes to make the prayer of the kingdom his own, must experience the kingdom, the power, and the glory of the Father. The disciples accepted and lived by what they saw and recognized in the Lord Jesus. In its most perfect sense, only the Savior can pray like this.

The petitions in the Lord's Prayer actually express the sighs of the Savior, who, while on earth, placed himself among sinners, separated from God, sighing with them in their misery. Any true disciple of Jesus prays and sighs as he does. In fact, the more you long for the Savior the more you are part of the sighing for the kingdom of God. We separate ourselves from the Savior if we no longer want to pray the Lord's Prayer anymore—which is what some already feel, thinking of ourselves as perfect Christians who are beyond this. But the more perfect you are, the more you sigh for the kingdom of God; for your struggle is against the kingdoms of the world. Without the coming of God, things will never be different on the earth.

Therefore, the faith assuring word, "Thine is the kingdom," embraces the yearning and the expectancy of the coming of God and his kingdom. Only then the will of God will be done completely on earth, as it is in heaven. Only then will domineering and self-willed behavior end and all people will yield to the will of the Father, who rules over everything with fatherly love. Thus it will be, for "Thine is the kingdom, dear Father in heaven. Oh, hear our pleading, which we bring before thee as the Savior's plea and prayer!"

The prayer continues: "And thine is the power." We do not pray in vain, for we know that for our heavenly Father all things are possible. If as people of the kingdom, people who serve the Savior, we ask in the right spirit, he can accomplish everything we ask for. He has the power to establish his kingdom and to care for our daily needs before we have need of them; he cares as much for bread as for forgiveness of our trespasses, protection from temptation, and finally deliverance from evil.

"Thine is the glory." This we pray at the end and can surely say this. Glory, praise, and honor belong to God the Father. All creatures on earth will proclaim this glory, even if in the world of sinners many refuse to acknowledge or bow down to him. This will not remain forever. No! That would be intolerable. "Thine, dear Father, is the glory in all that lives. In Thee we live, move, and have our being, with all creation." We know this to be true. And so the word, "Thine is the glory," is spoken out of the knowledge that in the end the revelation of the glory of the Father will encompass the whole of creation. We have a glimpse of God's glory, a glory that brings peace to the soul of all who pray and who are still engaged in so many hard struggles. All the more so, these very ones can now know that this is forever!

With an inner calm we can say, "Amen." As Luther put it, "Yes, yes it will happen like this." Yes, to those who with burning hearts faithfully bring before God this prayer, it will happen, to the greater glory of the Father. In the midst of all our sighing, everyone, including all groaning creation to whom it will also be revealed, will jubilantly draw near to the future glory which God will unfold.

The Peoples' Feast and Its Effect

On this mountain the LORD of hosts will make for all peoples a
feast of rich food, a feast of well-aged wines, of rich food filled with
marrow, of well-aged wines strained clear. And he will destroy on
this mountain the shroud that is cast over all peoples, the sheet that
is spread over all nations; he will swallow up death forever. Then the
Lord GOD will wipe away the tears from all faces, and the disgrace
of his people he will take away from all the earth, for the LORD has
spoken.

It will be said on that day, Lo, this is our God; we have waited
for him, so that he might save us. This is the LORD for whom we have
waited; let us be glad and rejoice in his salvation.

—ISAIAH 25:6–9 (NRSV)

The prophet Isaiah gives a description of the future fulfillment of God's
kingdom here on earth. [. . .] It comes from Isaiah's pleading heart.
"O Lord, you are my God; I will honor you; I will praise your name; you
have done amazing things." [. . .] Isaiah's heart is overflowing with what he
has to proclaim! His heart overflows with songs of praise and thanksgiving
because the Lord has promised his people a banquet for all nations of the
world. Isaiah speaks here as a teacher and instructor, not as one bearing the
word of God on his lips or using the expression: "Thus spoke the LORD."
[. . .] We know from many other passages how the prophets were profound-
ly affected by divine matters, which were put into their mouths directly by

Editors' Note: This sermon is dated 1879.

275

God. Our text, although not put directly into the mouth of Isaiah by the Lord was, nevertheless, laid upon his heart. They are not the words of a calculating person, but words from a man filled with the Spirit of God. The prophet speaks perfect truth and in such a way that we get the impression that the Lord himself is speaking. Hence, "The LORD himself has spoken."

It is evident that this word is not yet fulfilled; it is awaiting fulfillment. To make it clear and to bring it quite close to the souls living in his time and in the ensuing centuries, the prophet must use what was then Mount Zion as a basis for his hopeful and prophetic words. However, it is not necessary to assume that all his prophesies must come to pass upon this particular mountain in Palestine. For now the country is devastated. Even Mount Zion is almost levelled, and the people are dispersed outside the promised land. But now the promise is being fulfilled, wherever there is lively talk of the God of Israel and wherever his people are. Through the suffering and death of Jesus Christ in Jerusalem, an essential part of the promise has, of course, been fulfilled, that is to say the actual preparation of the great good that awaits all nations. Seen spiritually, all nations must seek salvation in Zion and Jerusalem, because from there it came and has been wrought for us all. But now salvation can be experienced wherever the gospel is proclaimed in all clearness and purity; for the Savior will be with his own "until the end of the world," that is "until the end of the earth," and where he is there is salvation, there is Zion, there is Jerusalem.

What then is promised?

I.

"Here on Mount Zion the LORD Almighty will prepare a banquet for all the nations of the world—a banquet of richest food and finest wine." This picture depicts the spiritual food that will be offered by the God of Israel to all the peoples of the earth. It will be pure, hearty food, marrow, which is known as the most nourishing food, and the purest wine without the cloudy yeast. This was fulfilled through the Savior. He prepared this meal while he was alive; he gave the bread, that is, himself, and he gave his flesh—his very self. The true wine is his blood. He said, "I am the true bread which comes down from heaven, and he who eats of me will live forever" (John 6:32–51). "He who eats my flesh and drinks my blood has eternal life" (John 6:51–57). The feast that strengthens and refreshes everyone has been prepared by him for all people. But this has yet to be given to all peoples.

However, it is prepared for all and in the course of time everybody will receive it. When this happens, the whole earth shall become a paradise, a holy land. It will consist of the same spiritual food as was provided in the promised land. This spiritual food shall be spread over all the earth until everybody receives of it; throughout the whole world the table is spread, so to speak, for all peoples.

Because this feast has not yet been proclaimed everywhere, and not everyone can participate in it, we still wait for the prophecy to be fulfilled. But a great awakening is promised to all nations and will be experienced wherever the gospel is preached. There is a special power of God that belongs to the gospel—the Holy Spirit. It is through the Holy Spirit that the gospel will come to rich fruition; it will renew every heart—everyone and everywhere—and the world will be refreshed and happy, because through this humankind will have received a new life from God. Therefore, Isaiah's picture of a great feast for the people is described elsewhere in Joel: "I will pour out my spirit on all flesh" (Joel 2:28). This is the great purpose of the Lord. The Father in heaven has conceived this in his heart and he will bring it to fruition in his time.

II.

When this occurs, something else will happen: "He will destroy on this mountain the shroud that is cast over all peoples, the sheet that is spread over all nations." It is self-evident that the terrestrial Mount Zion is not where all the people are, and all people are not where the terrestrial Mount Zion is. But the destruction of the covering and the veil begins on the mountain; it has begun through Jesus Christ. It was lifted, but not from all the world; the veil must be cleared away throughout the world and from all nations. Isaiah speaks of the dark veil that is cast over all people. There still exists this veil almost everywhere. We can all sense how we don't live in a godly and pure air. Evil spirits still rule in the atmosphere, and they continue to surround the children of God who fight against them. Yes, all of us are befogged by a dark cloud; the great power of darkness still smothers us. How powerless we often feel, how dull our spirit, how unfree we still are! How much anguish of soul we have to endure! How often our thoughts are clouded, and we cannot grasp even the simplest truth! There are people who cannot be reached—they are so closed, so torn, so veiled, and so "covered" by satanic coverings, even within Christendom.

At the beginning of the church it was not like this, but eventually the veil fell on believing Christians too. Hence, what is noble in our day has become clouded; no one has strength enough to overcome sin and evil. We hardly realize how much unclarity is in us and surrounds us, how much we must discard in order to fully experience the grace of Jesus! The gospel of Christ's atonement is no longer understood. And even when we do understand it, we don't grasp or enjoy the meaning of it. [. . .]

But now, look what is promised: "All demonic covering is to be taken away." The trumpet blast of grace will sound forth so mightily that all devils will flee, and all of us will be free! Just as the sick and those possessed were freed at the time of Jesus, so we will all be freed from this demonic covering and veil. We cannot understand how this will happen, but it will happen. But consider the fact itself, that is to say, what a grace it will be throughout the whole world when humanity is freed from demonic influences. Oh, what inner nourishment we have from Jesus—all that we learn from him! What a tremendous joy it will be when this vast evil covering is entirely destroyed, when the full value of his "food" will be tasted and accepted!

III.

Along with the removal of the cloud of sorrow from over the nations, another thing will happen: "The Sovereign Lord will destroy death forever!" All that oppresses us are offshoots of the death in us. They make us dead and insensitive to everything divine. Once these veils disappear, then death will be overcome. In the end death will be swallowed up. This will be for all eternity; what has once been swallowed up is no longer there. It is gone, destroyed forever!

When this will happen, now or after a long time, I do not know. Life without death may actually still be given by God to us soon. We naturally think that death is a process of nature, but we must show that death does not belong here! Isaiah makes it clear that everything, including the removal of death, is to happen in these times—or at least a beginning will be made in these times. Death is no more once we depart from this earth, but death is also removed when a new life of genuine peace affects real life around us.

IV.

When death is gone, then so is pain, and with it all the many afflictions and diseases that plague us. And when all pain, all grief and agony of death are removed, then all tears will be wiped away! "The Sovereign Lord will destroy death forever! He will wipe away tears from everyone's eyes and take away the disgrace his people have suffered throughout the ages. The Lord himself has spoken. It will be said on that day, 'Lo, this is our God; we have waited for him, that he might save us. This is the Lord. We have waited for him; let us be glad and rejoice in his salvation.'" In the end, there will be a tremendous and joyful deliverance, and everyone will gladly exclaim, "Lo, this is our God! [. . .]" All people will be glad and rejoice in his salvation.

For those who know the Lord Jesus some of this joy can be experienced now. Still, there remains a great deal of sorrow. But a day is coming when we will all have joy without sorrow. Oh, what a time that will be! Yes, the Lord has spoken, and the Lord will also do this for us. Amen.

Johann Christoph Blumhardt's Last Devotional Meeting, Held on February 21, 1880

When I thought, "My foot is slipping," your steadfast love, O Lord, held me up.

—Psalm 94:18 (NRSV)

We might fall when we move too quickly and self-confidently. But, when we "get up" and turn to the Lord, he helps us. How often we fail in our life, and how often our beloved God must correct our clumsy attempts! The path before us seems smooth so we become overconfident and then stumble and fall when our way becomes unreliable.

> I tell you, I will never again drink of this fruit of the vine until that day when I drink it anew with you in my Father's kingdom (Matt 26:29).

Meanwhile, we drink this fruit of the vine at the holy meal of remembrance—the Lord's Supper. We drink this "in the Father's kingdom." It is a great comfort that we are able to drink a little drop of the kingdom of God, a "kingdom-drop." This represents the blood of Christ. This is his gift to us; he no longer drinks it here on earth. We drink the wine and eat the bread, remembering Jesus. In his kingdom of glory we will receive it in full measure. May the Savior hear and answer our prayers and be close to us. Without him our life has no meaning.

> He who eats of my sacrificed flesh,
> And he who drinks of my blood

That flowed out in death and was shed
For the good of all mankind—
He will receive eternal life
Though dead and laid in earth,
For on that day when judgment dawns
I will awaken and draw him to me.

Lord Jesus Christ, we entrust ourselves to your loving care and await your help. Bless all who are here, young and old, also those who are absent and those for whom we intercede. O Savior, let all those who seek you find you! Amen.

General Index

Scripture Index

Isaiah *(continued)*

Jeremiah

Daniel

Joel

Micah

Habakkuk

Haggai

Malachi

NEW TESTAMENT

Matthew

Mark

Luke

The Blumhardt Source Series

Johann Christoph Blumhardt
A Biography
Friedrich Zündel

The Gospel of God's Reign
Living for the Kingdom of God
Christoph Friedrich Blumhardt

Gospel Sermons
On Faith, the Holy Spirit, and the Coming Kingdom
Johann Christoph Blumhardt

Make Way for the Spirit
My Father's Battle and Mine
Christoph Friedrich Blumhardt

CPSIA information can be obtained
at www.ICGtesting.com
Printed in the USA
BVHW030831110919
558066BV00021B/42/P

9 780874 862454